Using Residential Appraisal Report Forms

Second Edition

Readers of this text may be interested in the following publications from the Appraisal Institute:

- *The Appraisal of Real Estate,* 13th edition
- *Appraising Residential Properties,* 4th edition
- *The Dictionary of Real Estate Appraisal,* 4th edition
- *The Student Handbook to* THE APPRAISAL OF REAL ESTATE, 13TH EDITION
- *Study Guide to* APPRAISING RESIDENTIAL PROPERTIES
- *Valuation by Comparison: Residential Analysis and Logic*

Using Residential Appraisal Report Forms

Second Edition

URAR, Form 2055, and the Market Conditions Form

By Mark R. Rattermann, MAI, SRA

Appraisal Institute • 550 W. Van Buren • Chicago, IL 60607 • www.appraisalinstitute.org

The Appraisal Institute advances global standards, methodologies, and practices through the professional development of property economics worldwide.

Reviewers: Kathy Coon, SRA
Larry Disney, SRA
Karen Mann, SRA

Chief Executive Officer: Frederick H. Grubbe
Director of Marketing and Member Resources: Hope Atuel
Senior Manager, Publications: Stephanie Shea-Joyce
Technical Book Editor: Emily Ruzich
Manager, Book Design and Production: Michael Landis

For Educational Purposes Only

The materials presented in this text represent the opinions and views of the author. Although these materials may have been reviewed by members of the Appraisal Institute, the views and opinions expressed herein are not endorsed or approved by the Appraisal Institute as policy unless adopted by the Board of Directors pursuant to the Bylaws of the Appraisal Institute. While substantial care has been taken to provide accurate and current data and information, the Appraisal Institute does not warrant the accuracy or timeliness of the data and information contained herein. Further, any principles and conclusions presented in this publication are subject to court decisions and to local, state and federal laws and regulations and any revisions of such laws and regulations.

This book is sold for educational and informational purposes only with the understanding that the Appraisal Institute is not engaged in rendering legal, accounting or other professional advice or services. Nothing in these materials is to be construed as the offering of such advice or services. If expert advice or services are required, readers are responsible for obtaining such advice or services from appropriate professionals.

Nondiscrimination Policy

The Appraisal Institute advocates equal opportunity and nondiscrimination in the appraisal profession and conducts its activities in accordance with applicable federal, state, and local laws.

Library of Congress Cataloging-in-Publication Data

Rattermann, Mark, 1951-
Using residential appraisal report forms: URAR, Form 2055, and the market conditions form/by Mark R. Rattermann.–2nd ed.
p. cm.
ISBN 978-1-935328-06-3
1. Real property–Valuation–Handbooks, manuals, etc. 2. Real property–Valuation–Forms. I. Title.
HD1387.R353 2005
333.33'2--dc22
2009032039

Table of Contents

Foreword vii

Introduction 1

About the Author 3

Page 1 of the URAR and Form 2055
Purpose, Subject, Contract, Neighborhood, Site, and Improvements 5

- Purpose Section 5
- Subject Section 5
- Contract Section 18
- Neighborhood Section 22
- Site Section 33
- Improvements Section of the URAR 44
- Improvements Section of Form 2055 63

Page 2 of the URAR and Form 2055
Sales Comparison Approach and Reconciliation 67

- Sales Comparison Approach Section: Supply and Demand Analysis 67
- Sales Comparison Process, Logic, and Purpose 68
- Sales Comparison Approach Section: Sales Comparison Grid Identification Data 75
- Sales Comparison Approach Section: Sales Comparison Grid Elements of Comparison 80
- Sales Comparison Approach Section: Additional Information 110
- Reconciliation Section of the URAR 117
- Reconciliation Section of Form 2055 119

Page 3 of the URAR and Form 2055
Additional Comments, Cost Approach, Income Capitalization Approach, and PUD Information 121
Additional Comments Section 121
Cost Approach Section 121
Income Section 131
PUD Information Section 132
Page 4 of the URAR and Form 2055
Scope of Work, Intended Use and User, Market Value, and Statement of Assumptions and Limiting Conditions 139
Scope of Work 139
Intended Use and User 140
Definition of Market Value 140
Statement of Assumptions and Limiting Conditions for the URAR 143
Statement of Assumptions and Limiting Conditions for Form 2055 145
Page 5 of the URAR and Form 2055
Appraiser's Certification 147
Appraiser's Certification 147
Page 6 of the URAR and Form 2055
Appraiser's Certification (continued), Supervisory Appraiser's Certification, and Signature Block 153
Appraiser's Certification (continued) 153
Supervisory Appraiser's Certification 154
Signature Block for the URAR 154
Signature Block for Form 2055 155
The Market Conditions Form (Fannie Mae Form 1004MC/Freddie Mac Form 71) 157
Introduction 157
Market Research & Analysis Section: Preamble, Address, and Instructions 158
Market Research & Analysis Section: Inventory Analysis 159
Market Research & Analysis Section: Median Sale & List Price, DOM, Sale/List % 162
Market Research & Analysis Section: Overall Trend 165
Market Research & Analysis Section: Additional Information 167
Condo/Co-Op Projects Section 169
Appraiser Section (Signature Block) 171
Other Methods of Measuring Change in a Market 171
Summary and Conclusion 179

Foreword

Using Residential Appraisal Report Forms provides up-to-date, relevant instructions for completing Fannie Mae and Freddie Mac's Uniform Residential Appraisal Report and Exterior-Only Inspection Residential Appraisal Report. This second edition has also been updated to address the new Market Conditions Addendum to the Appraisal Report, which is now required by Fannie Mae and Freddie Mac for all mortgage origination appraisals. Designed for individual or classroom use, this new guide can be used as a reference by experienced appraisers and as a training manual for novices.

In this easy-to-use book, the URAR and Form 2055 are discussed page by page, section by section, and line by line. Similarities and differences between the forms are addressed as the discussion progresses. "Case in Point" examples are provided to illustrate common issues and scenarios that arise in the course of appraisal practice. These examples focus on strategies for achieving best practice and overcoming common mistakes made in the field, providing practitioners with the tools needed to perform residential appraisal assignments with confidence and competence. The scenarios are based on the author's actual experience as a residential appraiser for more than 30 years as well as many years of teaching and answering questions from practicing appraisers.

The Appraisal Institute has played a significant role in promoting research and providing educational materials for real estate appraisers. This second edition of *Using Residential Appraisal Report Forms* is another effort toward providing residential appraisers with contemporary and relevant instruction for performing single-unit residential appraisals.

Jim Amorin, MAI, SRA
2009 President
Appraisal Institute

Introduction

This book is intended for use in classroom discussion and as a reference guide for appraisers, loan underwriters, and institutional policymakers. It provides detailed guidance for using the two Fannie Mae and Freddie Mac single-unit residential appraisal report forms: the Uniform Residential Appraisal Report (Fannie Mae Form 1004/Freddie Mac Form 70), which will be referred to as the URAR, and the Exterior-Only Inspection Residential Appraisal Report (Fannie Mae/Freddie Mac Form 2055), which will be referred to as Form 2055. The Market Conditions Addendum to the Appraisal Report–Fannie Mae Form 1004MC/Freddie Mac Form 71 or the Market Conditions Form for short–that is now required by Fannie Mae and Freddie Mac for appraisals of one- to four-unit properties dated after April 1, 2009, is also discussed in detail. The appraisal of condominiums, cooperative units, small (two- to four-unit) residential income properties, and manufactured homes will not be discussed.

The URAR and Form 2055 are discussed page by page, section by section. Sections that are the same on both of the forms will be addressed as one, and sections that differ between the two forms will be explained as needed.

Throughout this book, a graphic at the top of even-numbered pages indicates the page of the URAR currently being discussed; the applicable section of the page is highlighted.

This book is intended to apply to appraisal practice in most areas of the United States, but it is recognized that there will be many situations for which the discussion, examples, or issues may not apply to practices in a particular state, county, or city. Despite this, users of this book will find a wealth of information, practical advice, and tips for completing these forms that are at the heart of residential appraisal practice.

Keep in mind that as with all professional work, the responsibility for completing the forms as well as appraisal assignments correctly lies in the hands of the practitioner. This book discusses current issues and suggests responses to many common appraisal situations that may arise, but ultimately the appraiser will have to decide on the correct response for each situation. The "Case in Point" examples used throughout this book illustrate common scenarios in the field of real estate appraisal and may apply to many situations, but they do not apply to all situations. The individual appraiser will have to decide if the discussion is applicable to his or her unique situation on a case-by-case basis.

The Uniform Standards of Appraisal Practice (USPAP), established by The Appraisal Foundation and accessible at *www.appraisalfoundation.org*, are cited throughout this book. These standards are germane to the discussion at hand because most appraisers follow them in nearly all of their work. The standards change on a regular basis, so some citations that were in effect at the time this book was written may no longer be current. As time passes, updating these citations may be important to any discussion of these forms.

Fannie Mae and Freddie Mac rules, regulations, and guidance regarding completing the forms are also referenced throughout the book and instructions for accessing this information online are provided. In the last section of the book, instructions for completing the Market Conditions Addendum are provided and methods for measuring market change beyond the parameters of the form are discussed.

Many lenders, investors, and bankers use appraisal forms originated by Fannie Mae and Freddie Mac. As a result, this book will focus on these organizations' intents, regulations, and interpretations while acknowledging, when necessary, other users of the forms. Because these forms apply to general appraisal practice, they need not be aligned with any particular lender or investor. Appraisers wishing to familiarize themselves with Fannie Mae's current rules and guidelines need only go to *www.efanniemae.com* and click on "Appraisers" under the "Industry Specialists" heading. Similarly, guidance from Freddie Mac can be found at *www.freddiemac.org* by clicking on "Single-Family" under the "Doing Business with Freddie Mac" heading.

About the Author

Mark R. Rattermann, MAI, SRA, has been a multidisciplinary real estate appraiser and broker in the metropolitan Indianapolis, Indiana, area since 1978. He was born in Louisville, Kentucky, and has lived in Evansville and Jeffersonville, Indiana, and Cincinnati, Ohio. He currently resides in a suburb of Indianapolis. Mr. Rattermann is a 1977 graduate of Indiana University and has a bachelor of science degree in business. He received the Appraisal Institute's SRA designation in 1982, the SRPA designation in 1989, and the MAI designation in 1990.

Mr. Rattermann is the author of many books, including *The Student Handbook to The Appraisal of Real Estate, 13th Edition*, *Valuation by Comparison: Residential Analysis and Logic*, *Using the Small Residential Income Property Appraisal Report*, *Using the Individual Condominium Unit Appraisal Report Forms*, and the first edition of *Using Residential Appraisal Report Forms*.

Mr. Rattermann has been published in *The Appraisal Journal* numerous times and was the 1994 recipient of the Sanders A. Kahn Award as well as the 2005 recipient of the Swango Award for outstanding articles. Currently, he writes a biannual residential column for the *Journal*.

The courses and seminars Mr. Rattermann has developed include *The New Residential Market Conditions Form*, *Using Spreadsheet Programs in Real Estate Appraisals–The Basics*, *Appraisal Challenges: Declining Markets and Sales Concessions*, and *Residential Sales Comparison and Income Approaches*. He was the 2007 recipient of the William N. Kinnard Award for professionalism in appraisal education.

Mr. Rattermann is currently a senior partner with REsource, LLC, a real estate appraisal firm located in Indianapolis, and owner and manager of Education REsource, LLC, a real estate education company.

Uniform Residential Appraisal Report

File #

The purpose of this summary appraisal report is to provide the lender/client with an accurate, and adequately supported, opinion of the market value of the subject property.

SUBJECT

Property Address | City | State | Zip Code

Borrower | Owner of Public Record | County

Legal Description

Assessor's Parcel # | Tax Year | R.E. Taxes $

Neighborhood Name | Map Reference | Census Tract

Occupant ☐ Owner ☐ Tenant ☐ Vacant | Special Assessments $ | ☐ PUD | HOA $ | ☐ per year ☐ per month

Property Rights Appraised ☐ Fee Simple ☐ Leasehold ☐ Other (describe)

Assignment Type ☐ Purchase Transaction ☐ Refinance Transaction ☐ Other (describe)

Lender/Client | Address

Is the subject property currently offered for sale or has it been offered for sale in the twelve months prior to the effective date of this appraisal? ☐ Yes ☐ No

Report data source(s) used, offering price(s), and date(s).

CONTRACT

I ☐ did ☐ did not analyze the contract for sale for the subject purchase transaction. Explain the results of the analysis of the contract for sale or why the analysis was not performed.

Contract Price $ | Date of Contract | Is the property seller the owner of public record? ☐ Yes ☐ No | Data Source(s)

Is there any financial assistance (loan charges, sale concessions, gift or downpayment assistance, etc.) to be paid by any party on behalf of the borrower? ☐ Yes ☐ No

If Yes, report the total dollar amount and describe the items to be paid.

NEIGHBORHOOD

Note: Race and the racial composition of the neighborhood are not appraisal factors.

Neighborhood Characteristics				One-Unit Housing Trends				One-Unit Housing		Present Land Use %	
Location	☐ Urban	☐ Suburban	☐ Rural	Property Values	☐ Increasing	☐ Stable	☐ Declining	PRICE	AGE	One-Unit	%
Built-Up	☐ Over 75%	☐ 25–75%	☐ Under 25%	Demand/Supply	☐ Shortage	☐ In Balance	☐ Over Supply	$ (000)	(yrs)	2-4 Unit	%
Growth	☐ Rapid	☐ Stable	☐ Slow	Marketing Time	☐ Under 3 mths	☐ 3–6 mths	☐ Over 6 mths	Low		Multi-Family	%
Neighborhood Boundaries								High		Commercial	%
								Pred.		Other	%

Neighborhood Description

Market Conditions (including support for the above conclusions)

SITE

Dimensions | Area | Shape | View

Specific Zoning Classification | Zoning Description

Zoning Compliance ☐ Legal ☐ Legal Nonconforming (Grandfathered Use) ☐ No Zoning ☐ Illegal (describe)

Is the highest and best use of the subject property as improved (or as proposed per plans and specifications) the present use? ☐ Yes ☐ No If No, describe

Utilities	Public	Other (describe)		Public	Other (describe)	Off-site Improvements—Type	Public	Private
Electricity	☐	☐	Water	☐	☐	Street	☐	☐
Gas	☐	☐	Sanitary Sewer	☐	☐	Alley	☐	☐

FEMA Special Flood Hazard Area ☐ Yes ☐ No | FEMA Flood Zone | FEMA Map # | FEMA Map Date

Are the utilities and off-site improvements typical for the market area? ☐ Yes ☐ No If No, describe

Are there any adverse site conditions or external factors (easements, encroachments, environmental conditions, land uses, etc.)? ☐ Yes ☐ No If Yes, describe

IMPROVEMENTS

General Description		Foundation		Exterior Description	materials/condition	Interior	materials/condition
Units ☐ One ☐ One with Accessory Unit		☐ Concrete Slab	☐ Crawl Space	Foundation Walls		Floors	
# of Stories		☐ Full Basement	☐ Partial Basement	Exterior Walls		Walls	
Type ☐ Det. ☐ Att. ☐ S-Det/End Unit		Basement Area	sq. ft.	Roof Surface		Trim/Finish	
☐ Existing ☐ Proposed ☐ Under Const.		Basement Finish	%	Gutters & Downspouts		Bath Floor	
Design (Style)		☐ Outside Entry/Exit	☐ Sump Pump	Window Type		Bath Wainscot	
Year Built		Evidence of	☐ Infestation	Storm Sash/Insulated		Car Storage	☐ None
Effective Age (Yrs)		☐ Dampness	☐ Settlement	Screens		☐ Driveway	# of Cars
Attic	☐ None	Heating ☐ FWA ☐ HWBB	☐ Radiant	Amenities	☐ Woodstove(s) #	Driveway Surface	
☐ Drop Stair	☐ Stairs	☐ Other	Fuel	☐ Fireplace(s) #	☐ Fence	☐ Garage	# of Cars
☐ Floor	☐ Scuttle	Cooling	☐ Central Air Conditioning	☐ Patio/Deck	☐ Porch	☐ Carport	# of Cars
☐ Finished	☐ Heated	☐ Individual	☐ Other	☐ Pool	☐ Other	☐ Att. ☐ Det.	☐ Built-in

Appliances ☐ Refrigerator ☐ Range/Oven ☐ Dishwasher ☐ Disposal ☐ Microwave ☐ Washer/Dryer ☐ Other (describe)

Finished area **above** grade contains: | Rooms | Bedrooms | Bath(s) | Square Feet of Gross Living Area Above Grade

Additional features (special energy efficient items, etc.)

Describe the condition of the property (including needed repairs, deterioration, renovations, remodeling, etc.).

Are there any physical deficiencies or adverse conditions that affect the livability, soundness, or structural integrity of the property? ☐ Yes ☐ No If Yes, describe

Does the property generally conform to the neighborhood (functional utility, style, condition, use, construction, etc.)? ☐ Yes ☐ No If No, describe

Freddie Mac Form 70 March 2005 | Page 1 of 6 | Fannie Mae Form 1004 March 2005

Purpose, Subject, Contract, Neighborhood, Site, and Improvements

Purpose Section

The purpose of this summary appraisal report is to provide the lender/client with an accurate, and adequately supported, opinion of the market value of the subject property.

The purpose sections of the URAR and Form 2055 are identical. This section states the goal of the appraisal report. The former Uniform Standards of Professional Appraisal Practice (USPAP) requirement to list the agreed-upon "purpose" of the appraisal has been removed, so this section states the purpose in a general sense.

Subject Section

SUBJECT				
Property Address		City	State	Zip Code
Borrower	Owner of Public Record		County	
Legal Description				
Assessor's Parcel #		Tax Year	R.E. Taxes $	
Neighborhood Name		Map Reference	Census Tract	
Occupant ☐ Owner ☐ Tenant ☐ Vacant	Special Assessments $	☐ PUD	HOA $	☐ per year ☐ per month
Property Rights Appraised ☐ Fee Simple ☐ Leasehold ☐ Other (describe)				
Assignment Type ☐ Purchase Transaction ☐ Refinance Transaction ☐ Other (describe)				
Lender/Client	Address			
Is the subject property currently offered for sale or has it been offered for sale in the twelve months prior to the effective date of this appraisal? ☐ Yes ☐ No				
Report data source(s) used, offering price(s), and date(s).				

The subject sections for both forms are also the same.

Property Address, City, State, Zip Code

The first line of the subject section identifies the location of the property. The street address, city, and zip code are typically assigned by the U.S. Postal Service or the local planning and zoning agency based on the proximity of the property to the nearest postal facility. Typically, the physical address is not used in legal documents because the three elements that make up the address may change. Also, it is not unusual for the address to indicate one city (i.e., where the mail comes from) and the property to actually be physically located outside the city limits.

Although many people think that the address defines the property, it actually does not. Essentially, the address only provides directions for the postal carrier. In some areas of the United States, the rural route system can still be found. This system is based on the mail carrier's route, with each box assigned a different number or letter, such as "Rural Route 4, Box 321a." The system does not define the properties and makes it difficult to even know on which street the box is located. In some small towns, citizens must pick up their mail at the post office because no mail is delivered to individual houses.

In completing this section of the appraisal report, keep in mind that P.O. boxes and other non-property addresses are unacceptable

Page 1 of 6

Uniform

The purpose of this summary appraisal report is to provide the

SUBJECT
Property Address
Borrower
Legal Description
Assessor's Parcel #
Neighborhood Name
Occupant ☐ Owner ☐ Tenant ☐ Vacant
Property Rights Appraised ☐ Fee Simple ☐ Leasehold
Assignment Type ☐ Purchase Transaction ☐ Refinance
Lender/Client
Is the subject property currently offered for sale or has it been
Report data source(s) used, offering price(s), and date(s).

CONTRACT
I ☐ did ☐ did not analyze the contract for sale for the subject
performed.
Contract Price $ Date of Contract

to some lenders. A property that has been assigned a post office box should be identified further by some other description, such as "the residence on the northwest corner of Wayne Street and South Street."

Appraisers confronted with conflicting information about the property address may have to determine which agency ultimately is responsible for assigning addresses in the subject area. While it is important to verify the correct information, the appraisal is not necessarily invalid if no address is listed.

Borrower

Identifying the borrower is of no value to the appraisal process itself, but it is important to the lending process. Not only is the borrower's name used for filing purposes, it also confirms the name on the purchase agreement that the lender gives to the appraiser. With the current problems of real estate fraud confronting many lenders, disclosing the buyer's name essentially indicates to the underwriter which purchase agreement was given to the appraiser.

Owner of Public Record

The name of the public record owner also does not usually affect value. In recent years, fraudulent property "flips" have involved buying and selling the same property within a couple of days or even on the same day. To combat this problem, lenders insist on appraisers identifying the owner of record. In fact, many lenders will not invest in properties that have not been in the owner's name for a certain period of time, such as 6 or 12 months; this means that the appraiser must take the information from the names listed on the public records rather than the purchase agreement. The previous appraisal report forms did not require the appraiser to research the owner of public record. In some areas of the country where updating of county records is chronically slow, this requirement may cause consternation and additional work for the appraiser; however, the time is well spent because it can prevent the appraiser from reporting an incorrect owner of record or from being accused of participating in illegal land fraud.

County

The county in which the property is located is usually obvious and completed correctly, unless the appraiser has taken information from another report and failed to change it to correspond to the new property.

Legal Description

The legal description is a very important section of any appraisal report. It defines the real estate included in the real property that is the subject of the appraisal. Usually, unless the subject property is a condominium or cooperative, the legal description describes the "space on the face of the earth" where the subject's real property interest exists. It should never be abbreviated because appraisers must know exactly what parcel they are appraising. If a complete legal description is not available, the appraiser should describe the real estate, which can include only an outline of the subject on an aerial or plat map. In some locations, the appraiser can draw a map of the subject in relation to other landmarks. The objective is to show the reader the location and boundaries of the real estate included in the appraisal. In some cases, this can be the hardest part of the assignment. Appraisers should not leave it up to the reader to guess at what real estate is included in the property. Making the appraisal "subject to survey" implies that the appraiser does not know what is being appraised. While this may be necessary in some situations, it should be avoided. If it cannot be avoided, the appraiser must show what is being appraised by other means.

Appraisers must know exactly what they are appraising both physically and legally. If the client defines the subject as less than what the owner currently owns, it could create an illegal parcel. If an owner has a legal or even a legal nonconforming use and then splits the parcel, it could create one or more illegal parcels under the zoning regulations in that area. Some secondary market lenders consider it misleading to appraise only a portion of a site. Fannie Mae's *Announcement 08-30* states the following:

> **Appraising the Entire Site of a Property**
> The property site should be of a size, shape, and topography that is generally conforming and acceptable in the market area. It also must have comparable utilities, street improvements, adequate vehicular access, and other amenities. Fannie Mae is clarifying that the appraisal must include the actual size of the site and not a hypothetical portion of the site. For example, the appraiser may not appraise only five acres of an unsubdivided 40-acre parcel. The appraised value must reflect the entire 40-acre parcel.[1]

If the loan is to be sold to Fannie Mae, et al., the practice of only including part of a larger parcel is not permitted. Fannie Mae buys loans for properties in rural areas and even buys loans for properties with large acreage but not properties on working farms. As a result, when an appraiser includes only part of the parcel in the report, the possibility of Fannie Mae buying a loan for a property that is actually on a working farm exists. If the subject parcel is large, it may be wise to include comments on whether or not it is farmed. If the loan is not to be sold to Fannie Mae, the rule regarding partial sites does not apply.

Regardless of who the client for the appraisal is, zoning regulations for the area in question apply. USPAP Standards Rule 1-2 requires that the appraiser know what the subject property is, both physically and legally. In most cases, appraisers cannot know what they are appraising if they cannot outline it on a map or aerial photo. It is important to know–and not guess–what exactly is being appraised.

Assessor's Parcel

Indicating the assessor's parcel number helps to ensure that the property appraised is the property mortgaged. In many markets,

1. Fannie Mae, *Announcement 08-30* (November 14, 2008), 6-7. Available at *www.efanniemae.com*. Direct link: *www.efanniemae.com/sf/guides/ssg/annltrs/pdf/2008/0830.pdf*.

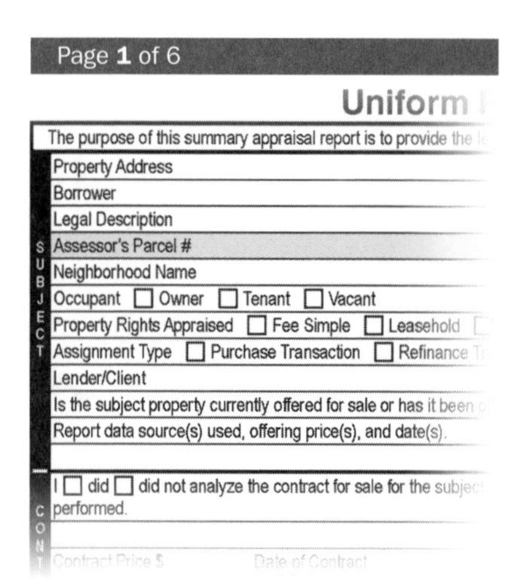
Page 1 of 6

Uniform

The purpose of this summary appraisal report is to provide the

SUBJECT

Property Address

Borrower

Legal Description

Assessor's Parcel #

Neighborhood Name

Occupant ☐ Owner ☐ Tenant ☐ Vacant

Property Rights Appraised ☐ Fee Simple ☐ Leasehold

Assignment Type ☐ Purchase Transaction ☐ Refinance

Lender/Client

Is the subject property currently offered for sale or has it been

Report data source(s) used, offering price(s), and date(s).

CONT

I ☐ did ☐ did not analyze the contract for sale for the subject

performed.

Contract Price $ Date of Contract

declaration pages of title insurance policies list the parcel number, which enables loan closers to match the appraisal with the property encumbered. The parcel number can be used to define the subject when the legal description is weak or when only an abbreviated legal description is available. In some markets, the parcel number is an excellent way for the appraiser to identify and describe the property when a complete legal description is unavailable or so lengthy that it is difficult to include in the report. Some county assessor's records may only list 10% of the legal description; this is not definitive, whereas the assessor's parcel number usually is. However, not all markets use these parcel or identification numbers.

Tax Year/R. E. Taxes $

The real estate tax section allows the appraiser to analyze and report the tax encumbrance on the property. In appraisal reports with reconstructed operating income statements (used for residential properties that are rented), this number should be the same as that reported on the form. The tax levy may vary from year to year, so indicating the specific year for which the indicated tax amount is applicable is necessary.

In many areas, taxes are assessed in one year but are payable in the next. In other areas, the taxes are assessed and payable in the same year, but the assessed values are based on the previous year. The appraiser should be familiar with the taxing system in the subject market and be aware of the impact on value of the tax amounts and sometimes of the taxing system. Some markets' tax systems may be skewed against income properties in favor of owner-occupied residences, which may mean that some sales are comparable and others are not because of the tax burden.

For some property appraisals, the analyst may find that the taxes are higher or lower than the market would expect. For instance, if the appraiser finds that taxes are 10% higher than the market, will it affect value? Will taxes that are 25% higher affect value? Appraisers are obligated to research, report, and adjust for real estate taxes if they are a factor in the market. Underwriters use the principle, interest, taxes, and insurance (PITI) cost when determining if the applicant can afford the payments. If the taxes are too high, some applicants may not qualify for a specific property.

How can appraisers adjust for undertaxed or overtaxed properties? If the taxes are excessively high, an appraiser can choose to adjust for the difference in the cost of owning one property with high taxes versus the cost of owning other properties in the same market with lower taxes that might have been purchased instead. A logical and common method for doing this is to capitalize the extra cost of ownership by applying an appropriate capitalization rate and dividing the difference in the tax amounts by it. Such an adjustment is not required if comparable sales from the same community are available. If they are not available, however, appraisers may be required to adjust for differences in tax rates as shown in Exhibit 1.

Exhibit 1. Perpetual Differences in Tax Rates for Four Comparables

	Subject's Annual Taxes	Comparable's Annual Taxes	Difference	Capitalization Rate		Adjustment
Comparable 1	$4,500	$3,500	$1,000	/0.09	=	$11,111
Comparable 2	$4,500	$3,300	$1,200	/0.09	=	$13,333
Comparable 3	$4,500	$3,321	$1,179	/0.09	=	$13,100
Comparable 4	$4,500	$3,164	$1,336	/0.09	=	$14,844

Based on this example, the adjustment for the perpetual difference in the subject's taxes and taxes on comparable sales from another community appears to reconcile near $13,000. This is logical if all other things are equal because the difference in the taxes is current and will probably continue into the near future. One community may have a perpetual difference in tax rates compared to another nearby community. In some cases, one big employer has a continuous effect on the tax rates and, thus, the cost of property ownership. If one area is home to a big, heavily taxed commercial enterprise and another area has a large non-taxed college or government entity, the services required could be identical but the tax burdens may be much different.

If the difference in taxes was only temporary, the previously described analysis would be invalid. An analysis of a property that has excessive taxes because of an assessment error would not be valid either. To analyze an assessment error, an adjustment could be made to represent the present value of the incremental amount of the higher taxes for the amount of time it takes to correct the problem. For example, consider a property whose taxes are $5,500 per year when all the comparables are assessed at $4,500 per year. The extra taxes resulted because the owner did not file for an exemption available to all owner-occupied properties. The owner can file to get the exemption, but it would not take effect for two years. This amount occurs over time, so it would be logical to use the functions on an HP-12C financial calculator to estimate the adjustment. However, this would probably not resemble market behavior. Assuming that the typical buyer does not always carry an HP-12C, it would be prudent to simply sum the extra expense for the number of years it would take to remedy the problem and use that for the adjustment.

Another reason for higher taxes could be that the community has a higher level of service as evidenced by the following:

- One area has a volunteer fire department, while the other has full-time paid fire personnel.
- One community may have one police officer per 1,000 properties, and another may have two officers per 1,000 parcels.
- One community has a high-cost, high-benefit parks and recreation department, while another community has none.

In some instances, higher taxes can affect property values positively (assuming a higher level of service) but in others, they can have a negative effect.

Page 1 of 6

Uniform

The purpose of this summary appraisal report is to provide the

Property Address

Borrower

Legal Description

Assessor's Parcel #

Neighborhood Name

Occupant ☐ Owner ☐ Tenant ☐ Vacant

Property Rights Appraised ☐ Fee Simple ☐ Leasehold

Assignment Type ☐ Purchase Transaction ☐ Refinance

Lender/Client

Is the subject property currently offered for sale or has it been

Report data source(s) used, offering price(s), and date(s).

I ☐ did ☐ did not analyze the contract for sale for the subject

performed.

Contract Price $ Date of Contract

When an appraiser finds comparables at the same tax levels, real estate taxes need not be adjusted for. When a loan application is processed, PITI are considered. The higher the annual real estate taxes, the less the applicant will qualify to borrow, which affects the number of buyers that can qualify for that property and possibly the market value.

Neighborhood Name

The neighborhood name reports the property's location. If the subject property's legal description is definitive, the entry is redundant. If the legal description is not definitive, this designation identifies the subject area. In the case of properties located in prestigious areas, the neighborhood name can affect value significantly. For a large Planned Unit Development (PUD), it can be used to show the particular phase of the development.

Map Reference

The map reference also reports the location. Depending on the location, this reference could be a page number with cross-references or a county record with a page number and reference. The map reference is sometimes used to describe the subject's location. In some appraisals, the map reference may refer to the county mapping system with plat or page numbers. This information may not be necessary or applicable for all appraisal reports.

Census Tract

The census tract is needed to enable compliance officers to detect violations of lending laws. It has no real purpose for the valuation process. Census tracts are assigned by the U.S. Census Bureau and are used to identify demographics on a map. Because this data is not relevant to a residential appraisal used for lending purposes, the appraiser only needs to report the census tract number rather than the statistics behind each tract.

> Census tract numbers are available on the U.S. Census Bureau's Web site at *www.census.gov*. To find census tract numbers, click on "American Fact Finder," "Maps," and then "Reference Maps."

Occupant ☐ Owner ☐ Tenant ☐ Vacant

The correct box for owner, tenant, or vacant must be checked to indicate the status of the person living in the unit being appraised. This status may impact value slightly. The information tells the lender whether the subject property is owner-occupied or tenant-occupied. Appraisers have been known to cause problems for themselves by not reporting the occupancy correctly.

Case in Point

For a specific loan program, an investor/lender has a policy of not making loans on tenant-occupied properties. The subject of the appraisal assignment is a tenant-occupied, single-unit home. The real estate broker asks the appraiser to indicate that the property is owner-occupied when it is not and to estimate a prescribed value higher than the actual amount. The appraiser agrees to the misrepresentation, and the loan quickly goes into default. The investor/lender sues the appraiser for $40,000, which is the amount of money that he lost.

The lender's attorney argues that if the appraiser had not misled the lender about the occupancy status, the lender would not have made the loan and would not have suffered the loss. To compensate the lender, the appraiser was forced to buy the house at the appraised price. The crux of the problem was the amount of the value opinion on the appraisal report, but the lawsuit focused on the minor issue of occupancy because it was easier to prove in court.

Special Assessments $

The special assessments section of the URAR and Form 2055 requires the appraiser to research any special assessments due and payable, announced, or even rumored to be forthcoming. Special assessments have a dollar-for-dollar impact on value unless they are paid off at closing. Examples of special assessments include

- Water and sewer assessments (usually for installation in existing neighborhoods)
- Roof shingles, exterior siding, parking lot maintenance, and other big-ticket items for projects with common maintenance

In some instances, the developers set up a special assessment district to fund the infrastructure of the project. These assessments are ongoing and can be significant. Researching special assessments may be difficult for an appraiser when the property owner is not available for questioning. In some cases, the appraiser is the only person who asks the tough questions about assessments because the buyers and brokers do not.

Special assessments are commonly levied by homeowners associations for unforeseen expenses. This type of assessment also affects value. The sale price of a subject property is affected if the seller must pay the costs or if the buyer inherits them. The appraiser must know when the sale price is affected by a special assessment. Researching who paid what expenses when closing a comparable sale can reveal significant variances in price that explain why some sales are adjusted more than others. In most appraisals with special assessments, the appraiser must assume that one of the parties is paying the fee. In the case of appraisals performed for mortgage lenders, the decision is typically made by the underwriter, who usually decides to make the loan without the additional liability.

Page 1 of 6

esidential Appraisal Report

ler/client with an accurate, and adequately supported, opinion of th

City

Owner of Public Record

Tax Year

Map Reference

Special Assessments $ ☐ PUD HO

)ther (describe)

saction ☐ Other (describe)

Address

red for sale in the twelve months prior to the effective date of this a

rchase transaction. Explain the results of the analysis of the contr

property seller the owner of public record? ☐Yes ☐No Dat

Case in Point

The subject property is the fee simple interest in a one-acre site in Smallburg improved with a 33-year-old, single-unit home. This property is located in a platted neighborhood built with private septic systems. The homes were also built with private wells, but municipal water lines were brought into the area a few years ago.

Like many homes of the subject's age in Smallburg, the septic systems are failing. The owners in the subject neighborhood petitioned the city utility department to install sewer lines in the platted addition. The cost per lot to each owner for connection and permits was estimated at $21,000. The year before, the property owners voted 67% to 33% to install the new sewer utility lines in the subject platted neighborhood at that estimated cost. Some paid the $21,000 in cash at the time of installation, but most property owners took advantage of the city's financing package of a 10-year payoff at 4% interest. A lien was filed against the owners who financed their installations.

All four comparable sales are residences in the same neighborhood as the subject. The subject is connected to the sewer line, and a $19,256.90 lien (12 months paid down) against the property is in place for this expense. The data in Exhibit 2 was obtained from research.

Exhibit 2. Sewer Adjustments for Four Homes in Smallburg

	Subject	Comparable 1	Comparable 2	Comparable 3	Comparable 4
Sale price		$181,000	$163,000	$163,000	$165,000
Date of sale		2 months ago	4 months ago	3 months ago	7 months ago
Site size	1 acre	1 acre	1 acre	1 acre	1 acre
Utilities	Water/sewer	Water/sewer	Water/septic	Water/sewer*	Water/septic
Improvement age	33	34	32	32	33
Gross living area	1,200 sq. ft.	1,200 sq. ft.	1,250 sq. ft.	1,200 sq. ft.	1,200 sq. ft.
Basement	None	None	None	None	None
Garage	2-car/att.	2-car/att.	2-car/att.	2-car/att.	2-car/att.
Porches & patios	Porch/deck	Porch/deck	Porch/deck	Porch/deck	Porch/deck

* Buyer assumed the sewer lien

The market in Smallburg is a bit oversupplied, but the prices are stable. The extracted adjustment (paired data analysis) for sewers is:

1 and 2 = $18,000
1 and 3 = $18,000
1 and 4 = $16,000

Because the buyer assumed the lien on Comparable 3, the property was still on the septic system for all practical purposes. If the subject was appraised as if it were free and clear of this special assessment, the value opinion would be around $180,000. If it were appraised with the buyer assuming the liability (assessment), the market value would be $163,000.

☐ PUD HOA $ ☐ per year ☐ per month

The next section of the form is for the homeowners association dues in planned unit development (PUD) projects. The owner-mortgagor pays this mandatory fee, and nonpayment can result in a lien against the property. The amount of the fee may require research, or it may be obtained from the property owner. In any case, it is an important piece of information– especially if the appraisal is for mortgage financing purposes. The appraiser can ascertain any impact on price from high or low fees by selecting comparable sales from the same project, and this impact should be reflected in the sales prices. This information is important because it tells the loan underwriter how much an applicant will have to pay each month or year. If the fee is high, the buyer may not qualify for the mortgage loan requested.

The term *condominium* originated from *co-dominion*, which refers to properties owned by more than one person. Many appraisers, brokers, and property owners confuse *condominiums* and *PUDs* because both terms are used to describe homes that are usually attached. State law defines a condominium. In some states, the phrase *horizontal property regime* must be contained in the legal description of a condominium. In others, the word *condominium* itself is required. In still others, different keywords are required. These terms describe rights in realty for real estate that are generally defined both vertically and horizontally, meaning that a condominium property is usually limited from side to side as well as from top and bottom. Condominiums can be attached or detached units. They can even be located underground. In most states, condominium owners as "tenants in common" own interest in the land and rights to use the common area (including the land), in addition to having exclusive ownership of their specific units. Keep in mind that the ownership structure of a property is not based on its design or appearance.

A reliable source for the definition of a condominium in an area is an attorney for the title insurance company, who is generally knowledgeable about rights in realty issues. Since this is a phone call that need only be made once in each state, it is not onerous. Appraisers who are also active brokers can usually call the title insurance company with whom they do business to help them determine the condominium law in that state.

Fannie Mae generally defines a planned unit development (PUD) as any project with a mandatory nonseverable homeowners association. These units can be attached or detached but generally cannot have units above or below them since they are only defined vertically. A PUD can be a simple detached dwelling unit with a small monthly association charge, an attached townhouse unit, or an attached unit in a four-unit building. State law, and not attachment, determines whether a property is a condominium or a PUD unit.

Fannie Mae makes it very clear that zoning is not a determinant for this classification. Some markets' planning and zoning departments use a PUD label for projects that comply with a specific zoning classification. Recently, it has been popular for cities and developers to have a zoning ordinance that allows a developer to acquire a piece of land and then request rezoning of the land into a PUD project. These projects were first conceived with "step-down zoning," in which a developer would put the most offensive uses near the center of the project or away from any owner-occupied,

Page 1 of 6

Uniform

The purpose of this summary appraisal report is to provide the
Property Address
Borrower
Legal Description
Assessor's Parcel #
Neighborhood Name
Occupant ☐ Owner ☐ Tenant ☐ Vacant
Property Rights Appraised ☐ Fee Simple ☐ Leasehold
Assignment Type ☐ Purchase Transaction ☐ Refinance
Lender/Client
Is the subject property currently offered for sale or has it been
Report data source(s) used, offering price(s), and date(s).
I ☐ did ☐ did not analyze the contract for sale for the subject
performed.

residential uses, and then place the least offensive uses closer to the existing homes. This tactic allowed a developer to generate fewer protests against the proposed project and at the same time enabled it to obtain some commercial uses included in areas where such uses might have been more controversial. This PUD zoning classification has no correlation to PUD project classification by Fannie Mae, and the two should not be confused. This subject will be expanded upon later in the discussion of zoning.

It is common for brokers and builders to go to great lengths to name their projects creatively. However, the resulting names are only a marketing strategy designed to present their vision; they may have little to do with actual legal rights.

Case in Point

The Evergreen Development Company recently developed a small project of attached homes containing 64 dwelling units in Smallville. The subject of the appraisal is a unit in the project. The units are designed in large, square, four-unit buildings and are attached on two sides according to the following diagram:

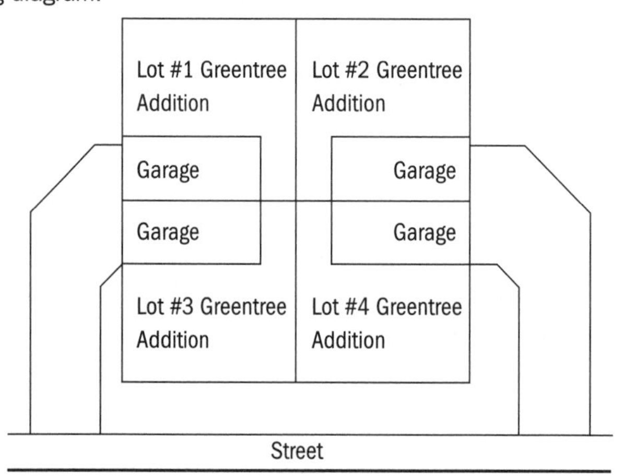

The developer told the buyers that the units were not exactly condominiums, but were better. He referred to them as "quadominiums." When the appraiser asked for the condominium documents, the developer said that there were not any because the development is not a condominium project. When asked for details, the developer explained that each owner owns the land under the unit and the homeowners association owns the rest, including the streets, clubhouse, tennis courts, and park. The monthly homeowner's fee is $22.00.

The appraiser was perplexed because he had never heard of such a property. He called an attorney at the title insurance company for clarification. The attorney replied that each building in the development is divided up into fourths, each dwelling is an ordinary attached home on a foundation, and the site size is the same as the size of each unit, which is about one-fourth the size of the building. The common area includes most of the land that is not located under the buildings and, as is the case for most PUD projects, was deeded to the homeowners association. If a property is not a condominium, it will have some land associated with it.

It is possible for states to have other defined terms for real estate. If so, the title insurance company should be able to identify, define, and discuss the pros and cons of the properties.

Property Rights Appraised ☐ Fee Simple ☐ Leasehold ☐ Other (describe)

Fee simple indicates that all of the typical rights in realty are included. The valuation of a leasehold interest usually applies to residences built on leased land. For these properties, the ownership interest held by the party that owned a vacant lot would be the leased fee interest. The interest held by the person that built the building on the leased land is legally the leasehold interest. Special consideration must be given when appraising a property held in a leasehold interest. Each market treats this analysis differently because of local brokers and their understanding of the market. If a person owns the leased fee interest, he or she receives the monthly (or annual) rent and then regains control of the property at the end of the lease. If the improvements are still in place, the leased fee owner takes control of the improvement as well.

It may be difficult to find residential properties on leased land in some markets. If only a few such properties exist, appraisers may not think to ask about the rights, which can result in a very mistaken value opinion.

Assignment Type ☐ Purchase Transaction ☐ Refinance Transaction ☐ Other (describe)

Next, the appraiser is asked to indicate whether the intended use of the appraisal is for a mortgage loan that involves a transfer of the rights from one buyer to another (standard sale of real estate) or for refinancing an existing mortgage without a transfer of title. If the appraisal is for a purchase money transaction, there will be more questions to answer. For mortgage refinancing, the applicant and the owner of record should be one and the same. Any unusual circumstances should be explained in the section of the form reserved for additional comments. In the past, appraisers were not concerned about the nature of the transaction and the identity of the buyer or seller because the value did not depend on who was buying or refinancing. However, with real estate fraud being a factor today, appraisers must be cautious so as not to get involved in an assignment that could lead to litigation. Appraisers involved in unusual transactions must be prepared to disclose the facts as they know them if it becomes necessary. With all the electronic data compilation that is now possible, some lenders can track the types of loans that are creating problems. This section would allow them to segregate the loans into purchases and refinances.

Lender/Client ______ Address

The appraiser identifies the client, usually the party with whom the appraiser has contracted to perform the assignment, and the client's address. The client's name and other important data are also listed in the signature block located on the last page of both forms.

Page 1 of 6

Uniform

The purpose of this summary appraisal report is to provide the

S U B J E C T

Property Address
Borrower
Legal Description
Assessor's Parcel #
Neighborhood Name
Occupant ☐ Owner ☐ Tenant ☐ Vacant
Property Rights Appraised ☐ Fee Simple ☐ Leasehold
Assignment Type ☐ Purchase Transaction ☐ Refinance
Lender/Client
Is the subject property currently offered for sale or has it been
Report data source(s) used, offering price(s), and date(s).

C O N T

I ☐ did ☐ did not analyze the contract for sale for the subject
performed.
Contract Price $ Date of Contract

Is the subject property currently offered for sale or has it been offered for sale in the twelve months prior to the effective date of this appraisal? ☐ Yes ☐ No

Report data source(s) used, offering price(s), and date(s).

In the past, appraisers were only required by USPAP to analyze current listings of the subject property. Appraisers are now required by Fannie Mae and Freddie Mac to research any listings of the subject property 12 months prior to the effective date of the appraisal.

Case in Point

The subject real estate is a one-acre site improved with a one-story, 1,800-sq.-ft. residence over a full basement with a two-car attached garage. It was originally listed for 30 days at a price of $285,000. The price was lowered to $280,000 for 30 days and lowered again to $274,900 for 60 days. The listing expired 46 days ago when the property was priced at $274,900. The appraiser is given an order to appraise the property today based on "the owner's estimate of value" at $290,000.

Based on the expired listings, the appraiser believes that the property will not sell for more than $274,900. Since the market rejected the property at the previously listed prices, it is illogical to assume that the market would bear more than these prices. Armed with this data, it is hard to convince anyone that the value of the property is higher than the last list price at which it failed to sell. An opinion of market value implies that the appraiser thinks a property will sell for $X, so the previous information clearly limits the value opinion that can be supported. It is possible for a property to have a value higher than the list price, but that usually involves some unusual circumstances and long explanations.

Notice that this part of the form does not require an open-ended answer. Instead, a box must be checked indicating yes or no, so the appraiser cannot ignore the question as easily as before. Underwriters are reluctant to approve or buy loans for which this information is lacking. Fannie Mae further explains this requirement in *Announcement 08-30.* They reiterate that this information is required on all listings in the past year, not just the most recent list price.

> **Research and Reporting of the Current and Prior Listings of the Subject Property**
> Fannie Mae's appraisal report forms require the appraiser to research and comment on whether the subject property is currently for sale or if it has been listed for sale within 12 months prior to the effective date of the appraisal. To clarify, the appraiser must report on *each* occurrence or listing and provide the data source(s), offering prices, and date(s). For example, if the subject property is currently listed for sale and was previously listed eight months ago, the appraiser must report on both offerings. [2]

2. Fannie Mae, *Announcement 08-30*, 6.

Fannie Mae discusses the subject section of the appraisal report in depth in their 2009 single-family *Selling Guide*, which is available on their Web site at *www.efanniemae.com*. Section B4-1.4 on appraisal report assessment discusses issues pertinent to this topic.

To access the guide, type "Selling Guide" in the search box that appears in the top right corner of the home page. The *Selling Guide* can also be accessed by first clicking on "Appraisers" under the "Industry Specialists" heading. Next, click on "Single-Family Guides for free online" under the heading "AllRegs Online." A list of documents will then appear. If pop-ups are blocked, click on "View Support Tips and AllRegs Contact Info" under the "AllRegs Online" heading to access directions for changing the browser settings to allow pop-ups.

Contract Section

CONTRACT

I ☐ did ☐ did not analyze the contract for sale for the subject purchase transaction. Explain the results of the analysis of the contract for sale or why the analysis was not performed.

Contract Price $ Date of Contract Is the property seller the owner of public record? ☐Yes ☐No Data Source(s)

Is there any financial assistance (loan charges, sale concessions, gift or downpayment assistance, etc.) to be paid by any party on behalf of the borrower? ☐ Yes ☐ No
If Yes, report the total dollar amount and describe the items to be paid.

The contract section is the same in both the URAR and Form 2055. This section pertains to appraisal situations in which the property is selling from one owner to a new owner; it does not apply to refinances or foreclosures.

I ☐ did ☐ did not analyze the contract for sale for the subject purchase transaction. Explain the results of the analysis of the contract for sale or why the analysis was not performed.

The first part of the contract section requires the appraiser to indicate if the purchase agreement has been seen and analyzed. The appraiser is responsible for knowing the important details of the purchase agreement. It is commonly known that any sale price can be offset by positive or negative terms. Often, the sale price is greatly affected by the terms of the transaction as expressed in the old real estate axiom: "You name the price, and I will name the terms and buy any real estate you own." This means that any price can be offset by favorable terms associated with it.

Case in Point

A residential homebuilder has buyers—a young couple—who lack a down payment and the money for closing costs but have good jobs. The builder structures a deal tailored to their needs. The home that the couple desires would normally sell for $285,000 (building and lot included), but in this case the price has been raised to $300,000, with the builder agreeing to pay all the closing costs ($10,000) and allow the buyers $10,000 in "sweat equity." The "sweat equity" allowance is supposed to be for work that buyers do on a new home, but in this case is actually a gift from the builder to cover the buyers' down payment. The builder raises the price to compensate for this loss, and the appraiser is expected to deliver a value opinion equal to the sale price.

The question that the appraiser needs to ask in this case is: Did the seller-paid concession affect the price? It would appear so, but it is also possible that the builder did not have to pay a broker's commission, the savings of which were used to cover the extra costs associated with the sale. This situation highlights the impact of the value of concessions and seller-paid financial help for a buyer.

It is important for appraisers to know if financing concessions have been included in a sale price of a comparable so that they can deduct them from the reported sale price. Conversely, if the *subject* includes the concessions, no adjustment is needed. For an assignment to value a property with a reported sale price of $300,000 that includes $20,000 in concessions, the appraiser must be aware that the reported sale price is not really an open market, arm's-length sale of the subject that conforms to the definition of value attached to the report. The appraiser should just assume that the assignment is comparable to a refinance appraisal assignment and should not take into account the reported sale price.

Keep in mind that appraisers do not use the sale price of the subject to establish its value; rather, they should use comparable sales. If the subject has concessions, it is likely to have sold for more than it should have. However, this does not mean that the value is the price less concessions. One sale, even the sale of the subject, does not provide absolute evidence of value.

Contract Price $

The contract price line requires the appraiser to list the reported sale price of any pending transaction. It is not meant for recording historical sales of the subject. Fannie Mae, Freddie Mac, the U.S. Department of Veterans Affairs (VA), the Federal Housing Administration (FHA), and most other agencies require appraisers to be aware of any pending sales, the proposed sale prices, and the terms for such sales. It is imperative that the appraiser have access to the sale price and the terms. Appraisers often give support to the proposed sale price but do not know the terms. Without the terms, the sale price data is useless and should not be given any consideration. A purchase agreement that is not signed by both buyers and sellers does not constitute a purchase agreement.

Case in Point

An appraiser has been assigned to offer an opinion of value on a single-unit home in Bigville for a large national lender. The lender gave the appraiser the order and a copy of the purchase agreement. The buyer signed the agreement but the seller did not. In this transaction, the buyer was also the selling broker. The buyer indicated that he had an agreed-upon sale price, but he had not received the return copy of the purchase agreement from the listing agent.

The sale price was shown as $289,000 on the purchase agreement, but the list price was only $264,900. In this case, the appraiser thought it prudent to call the agent to determine why the property would sell for more than the list price. The listing agent was out, and the agent on duty asked the appraiser to look on line 59, which indicated that a $30,000 decorating allowance was part of the deal. When the appraiser looked at his copy of the purchase agreement, there was no indication that such an allowance had been agreed to. There were two purchase agreements floating around—one with the decorating allowance and one without it. The agreement without the allowance was not signed by both the buyer and seller, while the agreement with the allowance was signed by both parties. The title-closing company was given the fully executed purchase agreement, while the lender was given the unsigned purchase agreement.

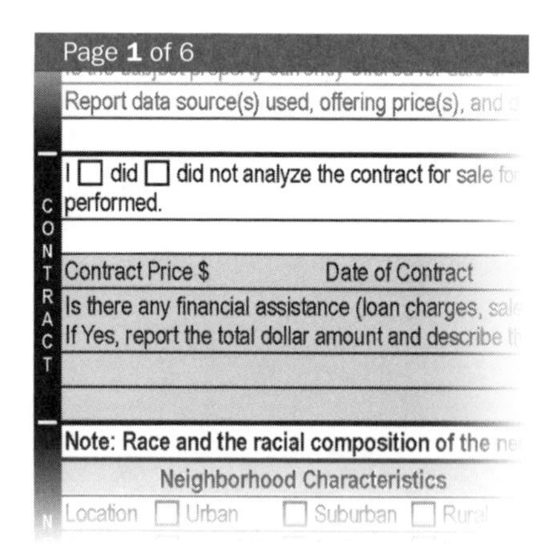

Page 1 of 6

Report data source(s) used, offering price(s), and

CONTRACT

I ☐ did ☐ did not analyze the contract for sale fo
performed.

Contract Price $ Date of Contract

Is there any financial assistance (loan charges, sal
If Yes, report the total dollar amount and describe t

Note: Race and the racial composition of the ne

Neighborhood Characteristics

Location ☐ Urban ☐ Suburban ☐ Rural

Date of Contract

The contract date allows the appraiser to record the date that the sale was structured or the purchase agreement was written. This information is easy to obtain because most appraisers have the purchase agreement in hand when completing the appraisal assignment. The date of sale listed is usually the date pending as listed on the purchase agreement.

Is the property seller the owner of public record? ☐ Yes ☐ No Data Source(s)

The next part of the form requires the appraiser to research the owner of record rather than simply list the person named on the purchase agreement. This information is intended to prevent fraudulent land flips. Appraisers must be wary of situations in which the owner of record is not the person listed on the purchase agreement as the seller. If this situation arises, the appraiser should perform research to find out why and at the very least report all known and relevant data. If the seller, lender, broker, or anyone associated with the sale offers a reason for this discrepancy, that party should be quoted in the appraisal report. While it is not the appraiser's job to second-guess the ownership, it is the appraiser's job to perform basic research.

Is there any financial assistance (loan charges, sale concessions, gift or downpayment assistance, etc.) to be paid by any party on behalf of the borrower? ☐ Yes ☐ No If Yes, report the total dollar amount and describe the items to be paid.

The last part of the contract is now a check box that allows the appraiser to answer "yes" or "no." When sending this report electronically for electronic underwriting, this allows the lenders to set a different standard for underwriting loans with concessions if they want to.

Buyers, sellers, and/or brokers may arrange for undisclosed side deals, so it would be prudent to answer "no" and then state that no concessions were noted on the purchase agreement. An appraiser does not want to say that no concessions exist, just that none are listed in the purchase agreement. A *sale concession* is an amount of money that a seller or persons associated with a sale agree to give a buyer to enable him or her to pay less than what would normally be paid on a net basis or for the purpose of financing expenses (points), the down payment, or closing costs that normally would be paid by the buyer. Concessions are generally used to help the buyers produce a down payment or pay the up-front costs of sale.

The appraiser should be given a copy of any purchase agreement (see Fannie Mae Announcement 08-30). If the seller is paying financing costs for the buyer or providing a rebate, decorating allowance, or other kickbacks, these facts must be listed on the form.

Paying these costs tends to inflate the sale price because the sellers still want to net the same amount of money.

When concessions are reported in the sale price of the subject, it does not require adjustments to the comparable sales. However, when concessions are reported in the sales prices of the comparables, adjustments are usually required. The appraiser is obligated to list concessions for the subject but not adjust for them. When valuing real property, the appraiser's job is to appraise the rights in realty for the specified real estate, not to appraise the deal itself. If the sale price is increased beyond the comparables sale's indications of value because of sales concessions, the appraisal will fall short of that price. The seller concessions included in the subject's sale price are not a reason for an adjustment and, in some cases, will not result in the appraisal opinion being lower than the sale price.

Case in Point

A young married couple is buying a house from the wife's parents. The sale price is $323,000, and the sellers are paying all the closing costs and prepaid expenses. The total paid by the seller on behalf of the buyer amounts to $20,000. The buyers' down payment is $32,300. What is the value of the property? The answer is unknown.

The seller might be inflating the price to account for the concessions. If this is true, the value may be as low as $303,000. It is also possible that love and affection could influence the deal, and value of the real estate is actually more than $323,000 despite the sale price and the large concession. The comparable sales should give support to the appraiser's value conclusion, not the sale price of the subject. The appraiser should not misinterpret this to mean that most property sales based on concessions have market values equal to what the properties are selling for with the concessions. In fact, nearly all sellers want to net out the same amount, so they just add the additional costs to the sale price to compensate for the difference. This usually results in appraisals that are less than the sale price.

After this sale is closed, does it constitute a comparable sale? For 99% of appraisals requested, it does not. The sale suffers from unusual conditions of sale, but it also has seller concessions that may or may not be quantifiable.

Neighborhood Section

NEIGHBORHOOD	Note: Race and the racial composition of the neighborhood are not appraisal factors.			
	Neighborhood Characteristics	One-Unit Housing Trends	One-Unit Housing	Present Land Use %
	Location ☐ Urban ☐ Suburban ☐ Rural	Property Values ☐ Increasing ☐ Stable ☐ Declining	PRICE AGE	One-Unit %
	Built-Up ☐ Over 75% ☐ 25–75% ☐ Under 25%	Demand/Supply ☐ Shortage ☐ In Balance ☐ Over Supply	$ (000) (yrs)	2-4 Unit %
	Growth ☐ Rapid ☐ Stable ☐ Slow	Marketing Time ☐ Under 3 mths ☐ 3–6 mths ☐ Over 6 mths	Low	Multi-Family %
	Neighborhood Boundaries		High	Commercial %
			Pred.	Other %
	Neighborhood Description			
	Market Conditions (including support for the above conclusions)			

The neighborhood sections of the URAR and Fannie Mae Form 2055 are identical. A *neighborhood* is defined as a group of complementary land uses, or a congruous grouping of inhabitants, buildings, or business enterprises.[3] It is possible to describe a neighborhood only after the boundaries are defined. Appraisers sometimes try to describe neighborhoods without a clear definition of what a neighborhood is. A good way of describing a neighborhood is to outline it on a zoning map. This enables the appraiser to visualize the geographic limits of the proposed neighborhood and to see the land uses in that neighborhood. Because most zoning map classifications reflect actual uses, they can also be useful for confirming land uses.

Note: Race and the racial composition of the neighborhood are not appraisal factors.

The opening caveat is a cautionary note to the appraiser to be mindful of fair lending and housing rules. See USPAP Advisory Opinion 16, Fair Housing Laws and Appraisal Report Content, for more information.[4]

Neighborhood Characteristics

Location ☐ Urban ☐ Suburban ☐ Rural

Check boxes are provided in this first part of the section for the appraiser to designate the property's location: urban (of the city), suburban (next to a city), or rural (low-density agricultural). An urban location would imply that the comparables are located near the subject. A rural classification would imply that the comparables would not be very close to the subject. When the appraiser completes this section, the attached comparable sales map and street scene validate the listed conclusions. Properties located in an urban setting should show a map with many streets and details. The opposite would be true for properties in rural locations.

In many urban areas before World War II, city leaders hired planners to plan communities' street locations, block widths, lot sizes, street connectivity, and so forth. Cities were developed according to

3. *The Dictionary of Real Estate Appraisal*, 4th ed. (Chicago: Appraisal Institute, 2002), 193.
4. *USPAP Advisory Opinions, 2008-2009 Edition* (Washington, D.C: The Appraisal Foundation, 2008), A-37.

a preordained, approved, and published master plan. This allowed real estate developers to know what type of development was expected of them. Commercial properties were also planned to some detail, but residential properties were planned more carefully than they are in most markets today.

After the war, it became more popular for developers to subdivide land in the outlying areas of cities and design their own communities according to their opinion of the correct street widths, lot sizes, and block widths. These later developments were not as predictable or as similar to each other as pre-war developments. Because of the changes in zoning, density, and lot sizes over the decades, it is sometimes possible to learn a great deal about the subject's area by viewing a map. Zoning maps, in particular, can be used to show whether a property is urban, suburban, or rural, as Exhibits 3, 4, and 5 illustrate.

Exhibit 3. Zoning Map for an Urban Area

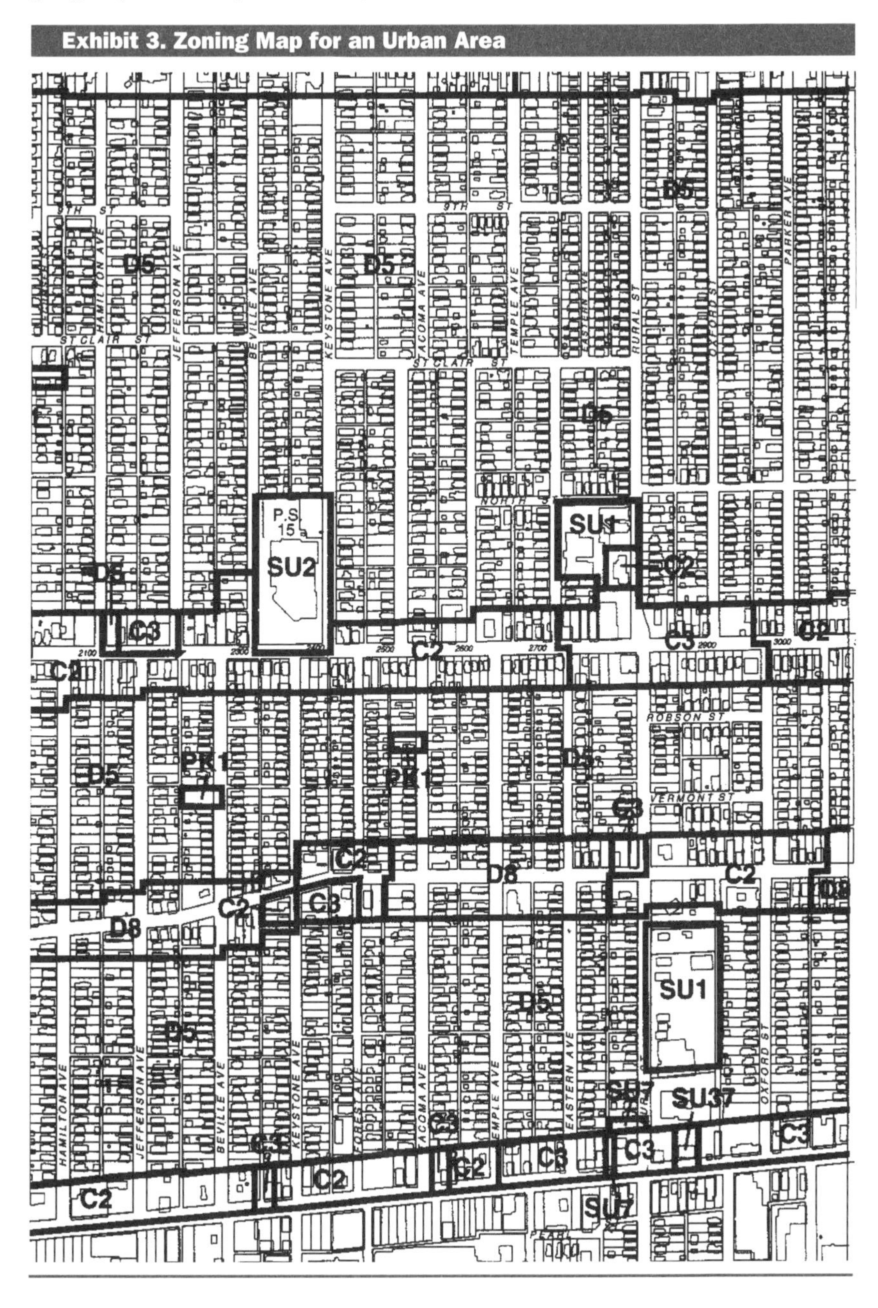

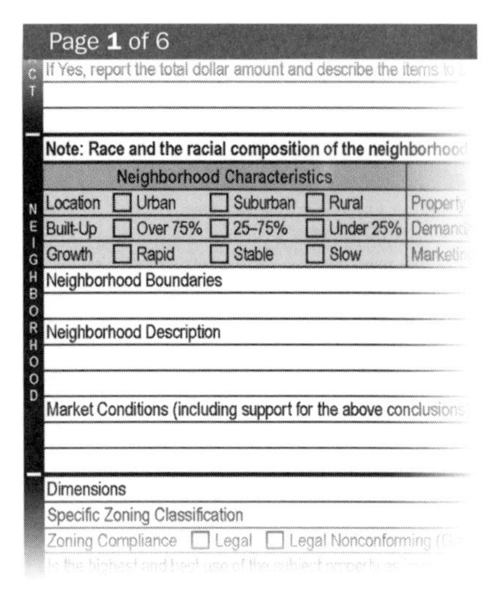
Page **1** of 6

If Yes, report the total dollar amount and describe the items to

Note: Race and the racial composition of the neighborhood

Neighborhood Characteristics				
Location	☐ Urban	☐ Suburban	☐ Rural	Property
Built-Up	☐ Over 75%	☐ 25–75%	☐ Under 25%	Demand
Growth	☐ Rapid	☐ Stable	☐ Slow	Marketing

Neighborhood Boundaries

Neighborhood Description

Market Conditions (including support for the above conclusions)

Dimensions

Specific Zoning Classification

Zoning Compliance ☐ Legal ☐ Legal Nonconforming

Exhibit 4. Zoning Map for a Suburban Area

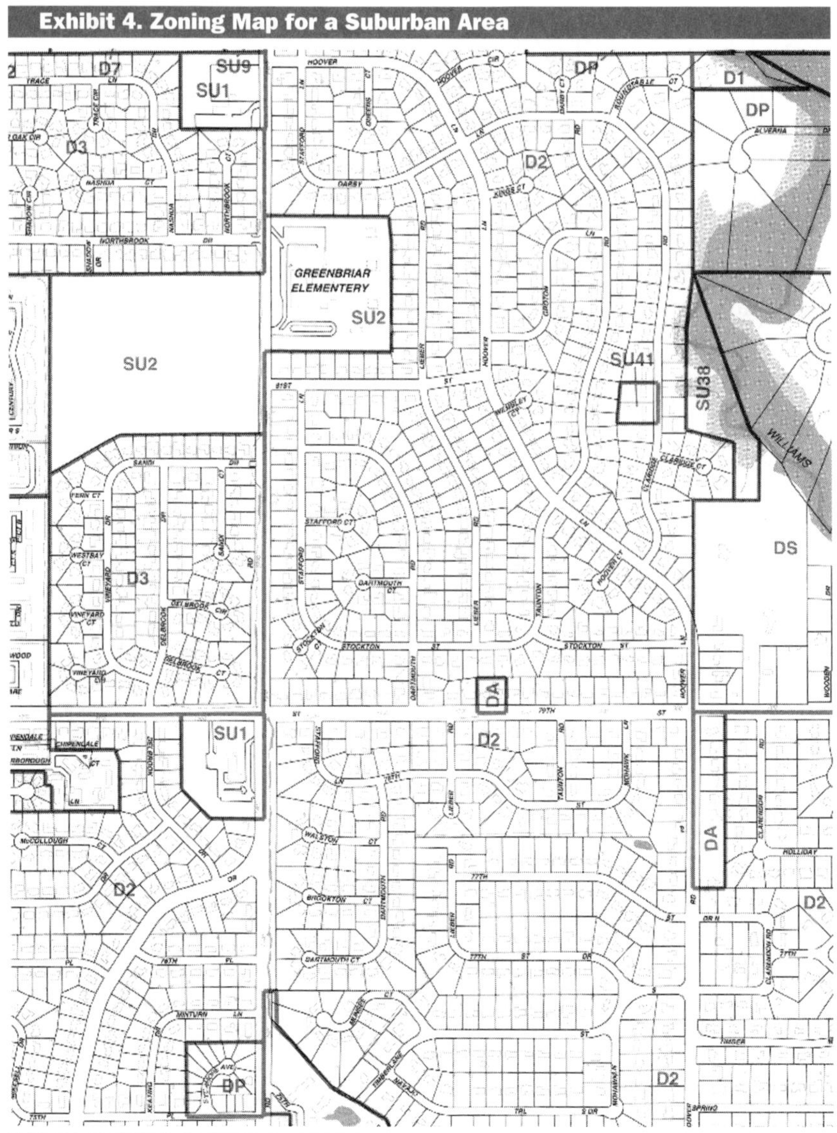

Exhibit 5. Zoning Map for a Rural Area

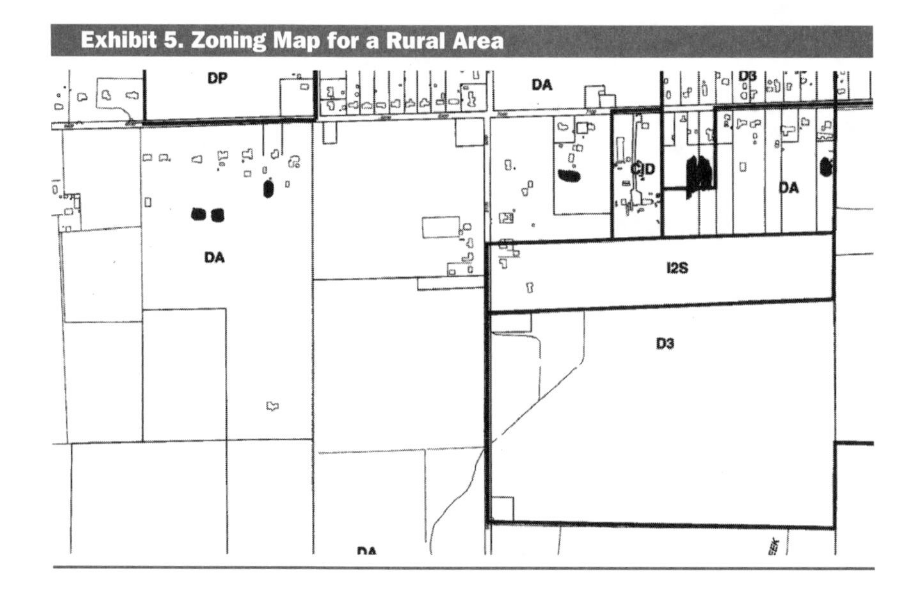

A zoning map is probably the best type of neighborhood map because it shows the majority of the neighborhood land uses in addition to the density of the area. Of course, classifying an area by the zoning maps will not work in all markets.

Built-Up ☐ Over 75% ☐ 25–75% ☐ Under 25%

The next set of check boxes describes the density of the area. Readers of appraisal reports look at their attached location maps to ascertain the density of the streets for consistency. Fannie Mae defines the term "built-up" as the degree of development of a neighborhood, which is the percentage of the available land in the neighborhood that has been improved.

A common interpretation of the correct procedure for determining the extent to which a neighborhood is built up is to compare the percentage of land that is improved with buildings and used for a purpose to the total amount of land available in the neighborhood.

Some appraisers compare the improved land as shown on an aerial map with the amount of land that is not improved with buildings. If a residential subdivision had 100 lots and 100 homes are located on those lots, it would be about 35% built up because the majority of the land is covered with grass, asphalt, or concrete. This is a simplistic interpretation, however, and is probably not in line with the interpretation of most practicing appraisers. This interpretation is also less acceptable to secondary market lenders and, as a result, most review appraisers.

Growth ☐ Rapid ☐ Stable ☐ Slow

The set of check boxes for growth helps describe any change in the area. The term *growth* is interpreted by most to be the rate at which the area is building up with improvements. An established neighborhood would have a stable growth rate if the line were interpreted to mean the rate at which development occurs. If 100% of the land in a neighborhood is developed, the growth rate is zero and will be zero the following year as well as the year after that.

The meaning of the term *growth* is difficult for many appraisers to agree on. *The Dictionary of Real Estate Appraisal* defines the term as a stage in a market area's life cycle in which the market area gains public favor and acceptance.[5] This refers to the life cycle of a market area, which includes the stages of growth, stability, decline, and revitalization.

Some appraisers would make the case that *growth* refers to growth in the defined neighborhood–that is, whether the geographic limits of the neighborhood are increasing or decreasing. When completing this section, most appraisers describe an area that has much or little construction activity.

One-Unit Housing Trends

The next part of the form, which deals with one-unit housing trends, can be misinterpreted by appraisers. This misinterpretation is easily

5. *Dictionary*, 133.

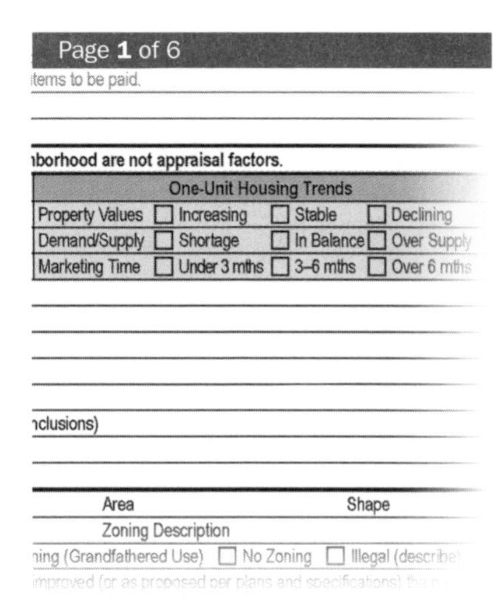
Page 1 of 6

items to be paid.

borhood are not appraisal factors.

One-Unit Housing Trends			
Property Values	☐ Increasing	☐ Stable	☐ Declining
Demand/Supply	☐ Shortage	☐ In Balance	☐ Over Supply
Marketing Time	☐ Under 3 mths	☐ 3–6 mths	☐ Over 6 mths

clusions)

Area Shape

Zoning Description

ning (Grandfathered Use) ☐ No Zoning ☐ Illegal (describe)

mproved (or as proposed per plans and specifications)

understood because the questions are located within the neighborhood section of the form. A neighborhood is defined geographically, but a market can encompass much more or less than a geographical neighborhood. A market has to be analyzed with competing properties that should appeal to the same buyer as the subject. Since this section of the form describes a geographically delineated area, it is difficult to translate it to market analysis, which has different delineations.

Some appraisers have defined *housing trends* here to mean price trends in *all* properties in the neighborhood, rather than just the ones that compete with the subject. However, this is not accurate because a neighborhood often includes single-unit residences as well as apartments, offices, retail properties, and even special-purpose properties. Because the form specifies one-unit housing trends, other uses are eliminated. However, a neighborhood can also include very low-priced and high-priced homes. Market conditions depend on the price segment.

For example, consider a residential property that is located in a golf course community with homes both on and off the golf course. The homes located on the golf course may be oversupplied and the ones off the golf course may be in balance, or vice versa. Such a situation would make this section of the form difficult to complete with any consistency.

Considering the Market Conditions Form (which will be discussed later in this book) as well as the directions for completing the URAR, the appraiser needs to consider this part of the form as pertaining to the subject's neighborhood; if there is a difference between the market and the neighborhood, the appraiser needs to disclose the assumed differences.

Property Values ☐ Increasing ☐ Stable ☐ Declining

The next line and set of check boxes help describe any changes in property value in the subject's neighborhood/market. This data is linked to

1. The Market Conditions Form (Fannie Mae Form 1004MC/Freddie Mac Form 71), which will be discussed in detail in the last section of this book.
2. The supply and demand study on the top of page 2 of the URAR and Form 2055 (above the sales comparison grid), and
3. The market conditions adjustment line in the sales comparison approach grid on page 2 of the URAR and Form 2055 (to be described later).

All of these are focused on supply, demand, and market conditions in the subject's market. The subject's market is defined as competing properties within the subject neighborhood.

Since all three of these sections are focused on the same parameters for analysis, the appraiser must take precautions to ensure against inconsistencies within the same report. The Market Conditions Form is significant and will be the dominant analysis. The supply and demand analysis is very similar to the analysis on the Market Conditions

Form. The data included on the Market Conditions Form should add up to the sales data found on page 2 of the URAR and Form 2055. In some cases, the listing data will also add up to the sales data.

Demand/Supply ☐ Shortage ☐ In Balance ☐ Over Supply
The next line and set of check boxes help describe the neighborhood/market conditions. The information given here should be consistent with that provided on the Market Conditions Form as well as the supply and demand section on page 2 of the URAR and Form 2055. It is advisable to include additional comments here because of the potential for data misinterpretation. Many appraisers used to use their intuition to judge whether a market was oversupplied. This method is unsound and not advised. With all the focus being placed on market conditions, the appraiser will have to develop sound analyses to support the conclusion.

Marketing Time ☐ Under 3 mths ☐ 3–6 mths ☐ Over 6 mths
The section of the form for marketing time helps to describe the neighborhood's market conditions. *Marketing time* is defined as the amount of time a property must be on the market after the effective date of appraisal to expose it to a reasonable number of potential buyers to produce a sale. Marketing time is different from *exposure time*, which is defined as the time that precedes an assumed sale on the effective date of appraisal. Marketing time can be a matter of weeks, months, or years. As was true for supply and demand, this line can also be difficult to complete correctly if the neighborhood includes more than one price range. As a result, marketing time must also be defined to pertain to the neighborhood/market.

One-Unit Housing Price and Age Range

The next section of the form shows the price and age range of all the single-unit homes in the neighborhood, not just the competing properties. If the range is wide–for example, if the subject is located in a golf course community with a wide range of prices–the appraiser will need to explain why the range for the market segment may not actually be as wide as shown.

Understandably, the fact that the prior section on housing trends is based on the market segment rather than the neighborhood and this section as well as those on present land use and neighborhood characteristics are based on neighborhood geography tends to confuse appraisers. If the market and neighborhood are not the same geography, the appraiser must explain the differences. If nothing is stated, it would be a fair assumption that the neighborhood *is* the market.

This section should not include the extremes in property values but should include the most common types of properties found in the neighborhood. Some lenders consider properties valued above the range to be potential overimprovements and properties valued under the indicated range to be potential underimprovements. On the other hand, some appraisers define an *overimprovement* as a property with an improper land-to-building ratio. The land-to-property value ratio

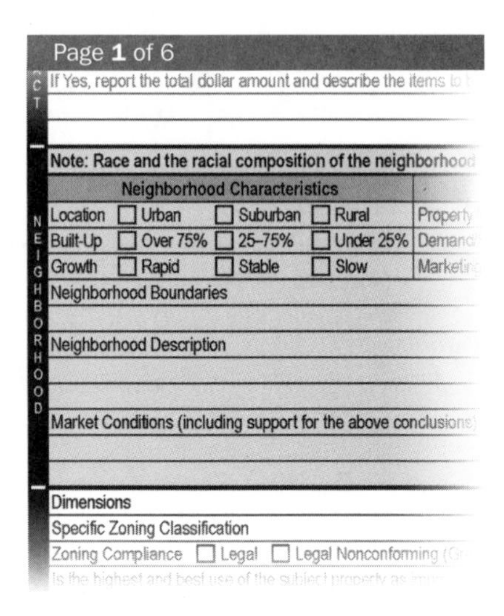
Page 1 of 6

If Yes, report the total dollar amount and describe the items

Note: Race and the racial composition of the neighborho

Neighborhood Characteristics				
Location	☐ Urban	☐ Suburban	☐ Rural	Propert
Built-Up	☐ Over 75%	☐ 25–75%	☐ Under 25%	Demand
Growth	☐ Rapid	☐ Stable	☐ Slow	Marketi

Neighborhood Boundaries

Neighborhood Description

Market Conditions (including support for the above conclusions

Dimensions

Specific Zoning Classification

Zoning Compliance ☐ Legal ☐ Legal Nonconforming

is calculated by dividing the land value (V_L) by the property value (V_O), which includes both the land value (V_L) and building value (V_B).

The land-to-building ratio is calculated by dividing the land value (V_L) by the building value (V_B). Both of these calculations can be used. However, if the land values in an area are compared to the sale prices in the neighborhood, that ratio is aligned with the land-to-property value ratio rather than the land-to-building ratio.

Case in Point

A new house that costs $400,000 is built on a $100,000 lot in an area where the typical land-to-property value ratio is 20%. If an $800,000 house is built on the same lot, the land value would be below the typical lot price ratio and the property would be considered an overimprovement. Conversely, if a $50,000 manufactured home were built on a $100,000 lot, it would be considered an underimprovement.

This point can also be illustrated by a home located in a waterfront community. A $1,000,000 home built on a $200,000 waterfront lot (the land and building ratios are 17%: 83%) may be quite salable in many markets, but if that same $1,000,000 home were built on a $50,000 non-waterfront lot (located across the street from the waterfront lots), it would be an overimprovement and difficult to sell. In this instance, land and building percentages are 5% and 95%.

The analysis of land-to-property value ratios may be the best tool available to develop opinions of the most appropriate improvements for each site. It is clear that in most markets, the appraiser must not assume that one land-to-property value ratio applies to all markets. Research into each market's land-to-property value ratio is required.

Present Land Use %

The next section indicates the present land uses in the area. In most instances, the present land use is also the area's zoning classification. These classifications are also consistent with the definition of a neighborhood, which may include uses other than residential. Zoning maps may provide a good indication of these percentages. Although present land use is a geographic consideration similar to one-unit housing trends, present land use percentages cannot be broken down into markets and submarkets as was illustrated in the one-unit housing trends section.

Neighborhood Boundaries

The next part of the form asks for the location of the neighborhood as well as its size and composition. To complete this section, the appraiser is required to show where the subject is in relation to the surrounding properties. An observant reviewer of the report will place the boundaries on a map, look for any negative factors, and determine whether the neighborhood boundaries are skewed or gerrymandered to exclude these factors. The appraiser must be careful when entering the data in this section because fair housing laws apply. Reviewers can now access very good quality aerial maps to see what is near the subject or any of the comparable sales.

A good piece of advice for the appraiser is to establish the neighborhood boundaries before completing any part of the neighborhood description. It is common for an appraiser to think about a neighborhood, describe it on paper, and later assign a boundary that is inconsistent. The area zoning map is a useful reference tool that shows neighborhood boundaries.

Neighborhood Description

The neighborhood description gives the appraiser the opportunity to clear up any issues about the neighborhood that are relevant to the intended use. It is a good place to clear up any ambiguities that surfaced in completing the prior sections. Again, appraisers should be careful about fair housing rules when adding comments in this section. The appraiser can describe differences in the neighborhood and market or describe the neighborhood in terms other than those that have to do with its rural or suburban character.

Web sites that can help familiarize appraisers with fair housing and fair lending rules that affect the appraisal process are

- *www.appraisalfoundation.org* (for information on Advisory Opinion 16)
- *www.hud.gov* (for information on other partners, fair housing, and fair lending)

Market Conditions (including support for the above conclusions)

The market conditions line prompts the appraiser to support the statements about the neighborhood that were already provided in this section. Discussion and support for market conditions will also be addressed in the supply and demand analysis section of the URAR and Form 2055 as well as on the Market Conditions Form.

Other Neighborhood Issues that May Be Considered and Discussed

Other aspects of a neighborhood that might warrant discussion and consideration in the neighborhood section are:

- The size (width) of the streets.
  Some neighborhood streets may have only 20 feet of pavement, while other nearby neighborhoods have 28 feet. Wider streets mean more capacity for on-street parking and less neighborhood clutter. In some neighborhoods with narrow streets, cars parked on both sides of the street can prevent fire trucks or school buses from passing. In other neighborhoods, visitors and owners park their cars on the grass along the street, which can cause substantial damage to the landscaping. In northern communities, snow removal and storage can be affected by street widths.

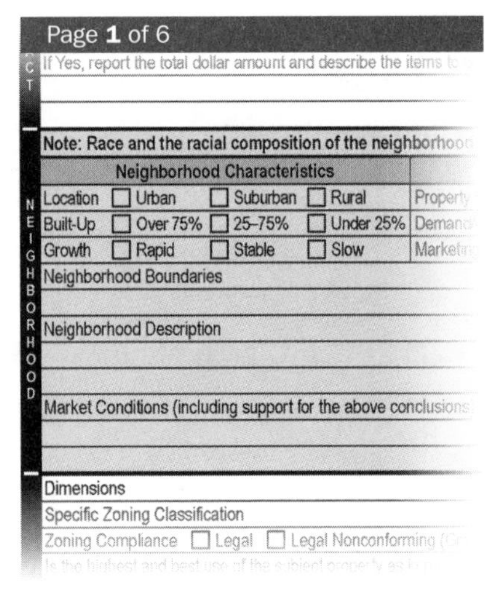
Page 1 of 6

If Yes, report the total dollar amount and describe the items

Note: Race and the racial composition of the neighborho

Neighborhood Characteristics				
Location	☐ Urban	☐ Suburban	☐ Rural	Propert
Built-Up	☐ Over 75%	☐ 25–75%	☐ Under 25%	Demand
Growth	☐ Rapid	☐ Stable	☐ Slow	Marketi

Neighborhood Boundaries

Neighborhood Description

Market Conditions (including support for the above conclusions

Dimensions

Specific Zoning Classification

Zoning Compliance ☐ Legal ☐ Legal Nonconforming

- Neighborhood features such as fountains, medians, or brick walls.
  In many markets, a grass median strip down the center of the street or a fountain in the center of the median, though expensive to maintain, presents a very positive image of the neighborhood. Medians are expensive because they require maintenance and twice as much curbing. Fountains cost a lot to maintain. Brick walls are costly to build but usually do not require much maintenance.
- Streets privately held by the homeowners association.
  The appraiser should verify who is responsible for the maintenance of streets privately held by a homeowners association. If such streets are private and not well funded, they may not be well maintained. When the entity responsible for maintenance cannot be verified, it can lead to serious problems that may affect the future sales of properties in the neighborhood.
- Gravel or unpaved streets.
  Some buyers will not purchase a home next to a gravel street because of the dust, which makes it difficult to keep automobiles clean. This is actually a significant factor for many buyers in many markets.
- Building setback lines that are too close to the street.
  The further the buildings are set back from the road, the less dense the neighborhood appears to be. In some neighborhoods, it is obvious that larger setbacks impact value. A larger setback can be a problem in some markets because it shortens the backyard, which may be undesirable for buyers who desire backyard activities.
- The presence or absence of streetlights.
  In some areas, streetlights are not welcome. On the other hand, if light pollution is not an issue but crime levels are, streetlights may be a positive factor that helps curtail crime. Security can be a factor in urban areas.
- Street configuration and connectivity.
  If the subject is located in a neighborhood where the streets are connected to another neighborhood or subdivision, traffic from one area could funnel onto the subject street. This could create traffic problems, even on an interior street within the subdivision. In some subdivisions, the cut-through traffic can be daunting and impact property values considerably.
- The direction of the wind.
  The existence of asphalt plants, sewer treatment plants, landfills, or other odor-causing facilities may not be obvious on certain days of the year but may seriously inhibit a sale at other times of the year.
- Locations of airports.
  The appraiser should be aware of the location of the local airports and the direction in which takeoffs and landings occur. Airplanes generally take off and land facing the wind, which means that the prevailing wind direction controls the air traffic. Most maps

generally show the direction of the runways. Noise from landings is generally less disturbing than noise from take-offs, which is caused by the engines' thrust. Small planes make little noise when approaching to land, but large jets are a constant source of noise.

- The existence of vacant land nearby.
  It is always a big surprise for a buyer to find out that the vacant field to the rear of the subject is zoned for industrial use or worse. Appraisers should research the zoning classification of all nearby vacant land. In some instances, the appraiser should also be aware of the likelihood of a zoning change in the near future. Although this can only serve as an advisory to the client, the appraiser should be aware of significant problems or probable zoning changes. The inclusion of a zoning map in the report ensures that the appraiser knows the zoning classification of the surrounding land.
- The existence of sidewalks.
  In most markets, neighborhoods with sidewalks are typically more desirable than those without them. Sidewalks are usually built in the right of way to allow for unfettered access by all citizens. Exhibit 6 illustrates a typical modern neighborhood configuration of the right of way, pavement line, and sidewalk.

Exhibit 6 shows the location of the curb, sidewalk, grass strip, and street pavement. This type of configuration is common in most markets. The proximity of the sidewalk to the pavement can have implications for safety. Moreover, it can affect snow storage during the winter months in northern communities. For example, sidewalks are not usable for several months out of the year in some markets because they are covered with snow from the streets. Sidewalks that are placed immediately next to the street pavement can be dangerous for pedestrians.

Exhibit 6. Surveyor Location Report

This report is designed for use by a title insurance company with residential loan policies. No corner markers were set and the location data herein is based on limited accuracy measurements; therefore, no liability will be assumed for any use of data for construction of new improvements or fences.

PROPERTY ADDRESS: 12548 Scottish Terrace Lane Smallburg

PROPERTY DESCRIPTION: Lot 32 Dog Pound Addition in Hancock County

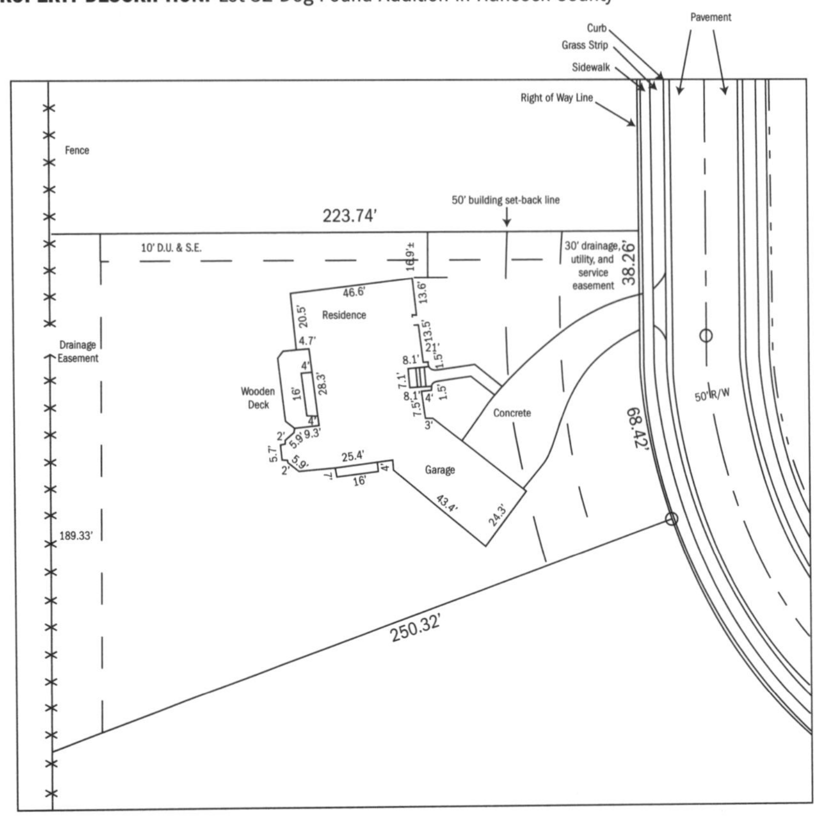

Fannie Mae discusses the neighborhood section of the appraisal report in depth in their 2009 single-family *Selling Guide*, available on their Web site at *www.efanniemae.com*.

To access the guide, type "Selling Guide" in the search box that appears in the top right corner of the home page. The *Selling Guide* can also be accessed by first clicking on "Appraisers" under the "Industry Specialists" heading. Next, click on "Single-Family Guides for free online" under the heading "AllRegs Online." A list of documents will then appear. If pop-ups are blocked, click on "View Support Tips and AllRegs Contact Info" under the "AllRegs Online" heading to access directions for changing the browser settings to allow pop-ups.

The following sections of Subpart B4 of the *Selling Guide* are applicable:

- B4-1, Appraisal Guidelines
- B4-1.4-02, Appraisal Report Review: Urban Properties
- B4-1.4-03, Appraisal Report Review: Property Location
- B4-1.4-04, Appraisal Report Review: Trend of Neighborhood Property Values, Demand/Supply, and Marketing Time

Site Section

Dimensions		Area		Shape		View	
Specific Zoning Classification		Zoning Description					
Zoning Compliance ☐ Legal ☐ Legal Nonconforming (Grandfathered Use) ☐ No Zoning ☐ Illegal (describe)							
Is the highest and best use of the subject property as improved (or as proposed per plans and specifications) the present use? ☐ Yes ☐ No If No, describe							
Utilities Public Other (describe)		Public Other (describe)		Off-site Improvements—Type		Public	Private
Electricity ☐ ☐		Water ☐ ☐		Street		☐	☐
Gas ☐ ☐		Sanitary Sewer ☐ ☐		Alley		☐	☐
FEMA Special Flood Hazard Area ☐ Yes ☐ No FEMA Flood Zone		FEMA Map #		FEMA Map Date			
Are the utilities and off-site improvements typical for the market area? ☐ Yes ☐ No If No, describe							
Are there any adverse site conditions or external factors (easements, encroachments, environmental conditions, land uses, etc.)? ☐ Yes ☐ No If Yes, describe							

The site sections of the URAR and Fannie Mae Form 2055 are identical. Site analysis is an important component of residential property appraisal. Appraisers should evaluate the site independently of the building to ensure that the land value is reasonable and does not exceed the improved property value. A generally accepted appraisal principle is that land must always be valued as though it were vacant and available for redevelopment.

Dimensions

The first line of the site section provides space for the appraiser to list the boundary lines of the subject site. This is easy to complete unless dimensions are not available. If the dimensions are not available, the appraiser must make an assumption about the dimensions and condition the appraisal upon verification. Site access, road frontage, and use as a building site are critical to value, and all of the relevant assumptions should be listed. It is always a surprise in a "cut-out" appraisal to assume a one-acre parcel and have the owner cut out an acre with no frontage or access point. It is improper to indicate "one acre" on this part of the form because it would not constitute a dimension but rather only repeats the next line of the form, which calls for site area. The dimension of one acre could be 10 ft. × 4,356 ft. or 208.71 ft. × 208.71 ft. These figures represent the same area but different sites with different levels of utility.

For loans sold to Fannie Mae, the appraiser is required to report the entire parcel. *Announcement 08-30* states the following:

> **Appraising the Entire Site of a Property**
> The property site should be of a size, shape, and topography that is generally conforming and acceptable in the market area. It also must have comparable utilities, street improvements, adequate vehicular access, and other amenities. Fannie Mae is clarifying that the appraisal must include the actual size of the site and not a hypothetical portion of the site. For example, the appraiser may not appraise only five acres of an unsubdivided 40-acre parcel. The appraised value must reflect the entire 40-acre parcel.[6]

6. Fannie Mae, *Announcement 08-30*, 6-7.

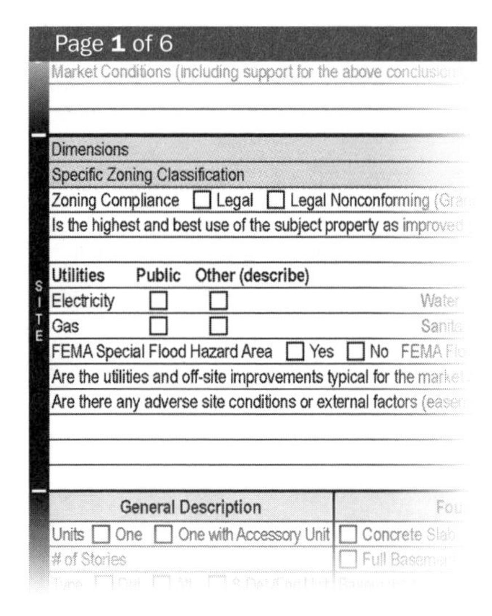
Page 1 of 6
Market Conditions (including support for the above conclusio
Dimensions
Specific Zoning Classification
Zoning Compliance ☐ Legal ☐ Legal Nonconforming
Is the highest and best use of the subject property as improve
Utilities Public Other (describe)
Electricity ☐ ☐ Water
Gas ☐ ☐ Sanit
FEMA Special Flood Hazard Area ☐ Yes ☐ No FEMA
Are the utilities and off-site improvements typical for the mark
Are there any adverse site conditions or external factors (ease
SITE
General Description
Units ☐ One ☐ One with Accessory Unit ☐ Concrete Sla
# of Stories ☐ Full Baseme

Area

The entry for area calls for the appraiser to list the calculated site size. It can be expressed in square feet (sq. ft.) or acres. Moreover, buyers think in terms of square feet of land in some markets, while in other markets they think in terms of acreage. Regardless, the size of the lot is often a major concern. In markets where isolation from neighbors is prized, the additional land included in the subject property may be valued highly. In others, an extra large site may not be an asset as much as it is a larger area to maintain. Additional land is not wanted in some markets.

Shape

The next entry requires the appraiser to describe the shape of the lot, which can easily be accomplished when the lots are rectangular. For irregular lots, however, the directions "see attached drawing" may be more appropriate. For some appraisals, the shape of the lot can be a significant factor and may require the appraiser to determine whether the building improvements fit on the site physically. This is a standard requirement.

Obtaining a copy of a recent land survey report, plot plan, or preliminary title report can reduce the potential for future problems. This recent information yields the site dimensions, approximate location of the improvements on the site, encroachments, and positive or negative easements. In many appraisal situations, the residential appraiser can obtain a copy of the survey, plot plan, or title report that was prepared when the current owners bought the property by asking for it when the appointment is set. To make a copy of the old survey or plot plan drawing at the property owner's residence, the residential appraiser need only carry an old thermal paper fax machine in the car to use as a copy machine. Portable scanners can also do the job. Power converters are available to convert the DC power to AC, which allows the appraiser to have a copy machine right in their vehicle.

Appraisers must be aware that surveyors measure the property to determine if it adds up to the width of the lot including the side yards. As a result, appraisers should use a survey only as a secondary source for building dimensions.

View

The view from the house may be an insignificant feature of a residential appraisal, or it may be the most important feature on the site. Buyers can pay significantly more for a golf course view or lake view. Even a view of a farmscape can be a significant attribute in some markets. For some urban properties, a view of the city skyline may be a positive attribute. Conversely, a negative view can also have a significant effect on the value opinion and must be considered in the appraisal.

Many buyers are reluctant to buy property if it has a view of commercial, industrial, or other types of properties. Other buyers complain about properties located next to schools or churches because of the view of the parking lot or nonresidential building. They also complain about noise, lights, and the extra traffic associated with schools. Many other issues associated with view can be factors that affect value for residential appraisals. In many markets, the higher the price of the home, the more important the view.

Specific Zoning Classification

The next entry requires the appraiser to specifically indicate the zoning classification and type. It is generally not acceptable to simply list "residential" but more correct to list something along the lines of "Residential District R-3" or "Dwelling District #4."

Appraisers should not assume that a property is zoned correctly. All market value appraisals require the appraiser to research zoning classification to develop a value opinion that represents the highest and best use. A mistake in this area can cause significant problems for appraisers. Because zoning classifications are factual, an appraiser who fails to research and report the correct data is highly exposed to legal liability. Reporting the zoning classification for a property usually allows little room for opinion. In most states, zoning classifications often vary from community to community and are not interchangeable. This does not mean that zoning legality is not subject to interpretation, but only that the classification is generally definable.

Zoning Description

The zoning description briefly explains the zoning classification assigned to the previous entry. For example, "R-1"stands for medium-density, single- and two-unit residences. Some appraisers fail to take the time to determine whether the subject property (as improved and used) complies with current zoning ordinances. Ordinances often change after the subject property is built and sometimes require more space in the unit, more parking, and increased minimum lot sizes.

In many jurisdictions, a property that was zoned for its current use before the adoption of the current ordinance is considered a "legal nonconforming" or "grandfathered" use. This usually means that if a property is a "legal nonconforming" use, it can continue to function according to the nonconforming use only if it has been continuously maintained for such a use.

Legal uses, grandfathered uses, exceptions, and variances are all specific to location and an appraiser can get conclusive answers only by researching this information in the locale. It is important for the appraiser to find out the amount of damage and other conditions that must be met to rebuild a structure destroyed by fire so that it meets legal nonconforming use. If more than a certain percentage of a structure is destroyed, a petition for variance is often required to obtain a permit to rebuild. In some cases, a structure destroyed by fire can be rebuilt only within the parameters of the current ordinance and building codes. It is impossible to know the zoning classifications, allowances, and requirements for all the different areas in which an appraiser may be asked to work. However, it is the appraiser's job when performing market value appraisals to develop

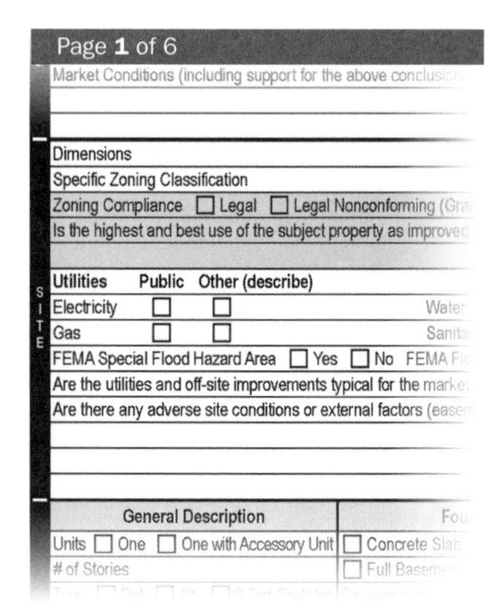
Page 1 of 6

Market Conditions (including support for the above conclusi

Dimensions

Specific Zoning Classification

Zoning Compliance ☐ Legal ☐ Legal Nonconforming (Gra

Is the highest and best use of the subject property as improve

SITE

Utilities	Public	Other (describe)	
Electricity	☐	☐	Wate
Gas	☐	☐	Sanit

FEMA Special Flood Hazard Area ☐ Yes ☐ No FEMA F

Are the utilities and off-site improvements typical for the mark

Are there any adverse site conditions or external factors (ease

General Description	Fou
Units ☐ One ☐ One with Accessory Unit	☐ Concrete Sla
# of Stories	☐ Full Basem

an opinion of highest and best use, which includes researching and analyzing any existing zoning and land use regulations. Sometimes researching the zoning and what is allowed requires more time than any other part of the appraisal.

Zoning Compliance ☐ Legal ☐ Legal Nonconforming (Grandfathered Use) ☐ No Zoning ☐ Illegal (describe)

The section on zoning compliance is very important to investors in real estate as well as to the appraisal process itself. This is an area in which some appraisers need to do more research than they typically do. If a property is not in compliance with the current zoning standards, it can fall into the legal nonconforming or illegal use category. A *legally nonconforming use* constitutes a use that was lawfully established and maintained, but no longer conforms to the use regulations of the current zoning in the zone where it is located.[7]

In some jurisdictions, properties that do not meet the minimum lot size, setback, frontage, or depth requirements are not compliant with development standards. However, this does not necessarily mean that it is a "legal but nonconforming use." In these jurisdictions, property "use" that is in accordance with the zoning ordinance but has lot size or setbacks that do not comply with the zoning ordinance is deemed legal conforming use but is noncompliant with development standards. This may or may not affect the highest and best use opinion, which is where this situation applies most.

Case in Point

An appraiser is performing an appraisal of a house in a platted subdivision in Smallburg, an area zoned single-family residential "R-2." This property is on a 15,000-sq.-ft. site, and the minimum lot size now is 20,000 square feet. Is the subject a legal or legal-but-nonconforming use?

In many jurisdictions, such a subject would qualify as a legal but nonconforming use. In other jurisdictions it would be considered a legal conforming use that is noncompliant with the development standards within that zoning classification. The word "use" is the defining term in this instance.

Does this classification as a legal but nonconforming use affect market value? In this example, it is doubtful that a buyer would know these requirements. For typical buyers who are aware of these legal constraints and base their decisions on these issues, it still may not affect the value.

If a property were not in compliance with the current zoning, including all the previously-mentioned requirements, it would likely be a grandfathered use. It may also possibly be an illegal use or illegal construction.

Is the highest and best use of the subject property as improved (or as proposed per plans and specifications) the present use? ☐ Yes ☐ No If No, describe

The next space on the form is used to indicate whether a better use for the property exists (other than single-unit residential). Because

7. *Dictionary*, 162.

the URAR is a residential form, this could be an issue only if the proposed improvement were to be something other than what the property is being used for now, such as converting a single-unit property into a two-unit property or converting an office to a home. For some appraisals, this question can be the most significant one asked. If the subject property has a highest and best use other than residential, it would be inappropriate to use the URAR form. If the property is currently used for nonresidential purposes but the highest and best use is residential, the URAR may be used.

Another issue that arises with this question pertains to properties that have worthless improvements. These improvements are not worthless because of their quality or condition but because the land value exceeds the improved property value.

Case in Point

An older home located adjacent to a popular lake has a land value (V_L) of $400,000 and an improved value of only $375,000 ($V_O$). In this case, the highest and best use as improved would be to remove the building and sell the land (assuming a demolition cost of less than $25,000). A common mistake is that appraisers miss this step because they do not always apply the cost approach to properties with older improvements. Failure to use the cost approach is not the problem, but failure to develop an opinion of the land value is. It is prudent for appraisers to at least consider the underlying land value in all appraisals to prevent situations in which the land is worth more than the improved property.

If analysis of the property reveals a difference in the highest and best use of the land as though vacant, a discussion of the property's future use is in order. This difference is always an issue for properties that are zoned for nonresidential uses.

In every market value appraisal, the appraiser is expected to research the actual zoning classification, including setback requirements, minimum lot sizes, minimum improvement sizes, required utilities, and other significant factors. In many appraisals, the analyst must also research details of zoning classifications that may be quite elaborate. According to USPAP Standards Rule 1- 3(a), appraisers must identify and analyze the effect on use and value of existing land use regulations, reasonably probable modifications of such land use regulations, economic supply and demand, the physical adaptability of the real estate, and market area trends.[8]

Must the appraiser know the complete zoning code, including all categories and classifications, on every property being appraised? In most appraisals, the appraiser must know the code for the specific property type and its highest and best use but may not need to know the commercial or industrial code for a residential appraisal unless a chance exists for converting it to those other uses. If the subject's value is dependent on some unusual use, then a complete knowl-

8. *Uniform Standards of Professional Appraisal Practice (USPAP)* (Washington, D.C.: The Appraisal Foundation, 2008), U-17.

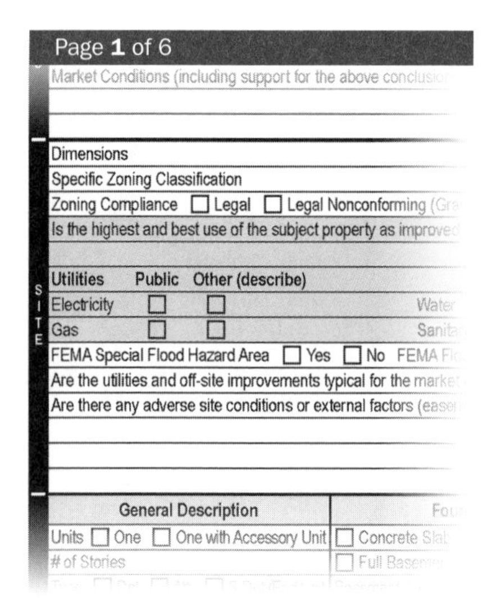
Page 1 of 6

Market Conditions (including support for the above conclusi

Dimensions

Specific Zoning Classification

Zoning Compliance ☐ Legal ☐ Legal Nonconforming (Gr

Is the highest and best use of the subject property as improve

SITE

Utilities Public Other (describe)

Electricity ☐ ☐ Water

Gas ☐ ☐ Sanit

FEMA Special Flood Hazard Area ☐ Yes ☐ No FEMA F

Are the utilities and off-site improvements typical for the marke

Are there any adverse site conditions or external factors (ease

General Description | Fo

Units ☐ One ☐ One with Accessory Unit | ☐ Concrete Sla

# of Stories | ☐ Full Basem

edge of the zoning code may be necessary. In most cases, just the phone number of the city employees who know the rules is required.

Another common mistake that appraisers make is to assume that if the property exists, it must be legal. This assumption can lead to trouble.

Case in Point

The subject is a 19-year-old residence located on a five-acre parcel in Blue Creek Township outside the city limits of Bigville. The planning and zoning is handled by the county, which requires at least five acres and at least 75 feet of road frontage on a county-owned right of way. The owner of the property originally owned 10 acres, but after a couple of years sold off the southern five acres located along the road to his cousin, who built a house on the southern part. The cousin held back an easement to his house from the county road and now owns a house without the mandatory 75 feet of road frontage. This was deemed an illegal use by the local planning commission due to the lack of the requisite road frontage.

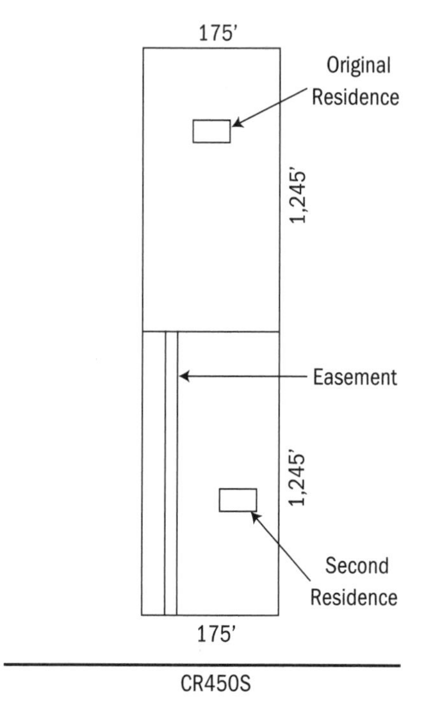

How does an appraiser value a property that fits this description? Highest and best use analysis requires a legal use, which this is not. The appraiser must determine what alternatives, penalties, or remedies are available and make an adjustment for the cost to cure the problem. It is possible that in some jurisdictions the improvement would not be usable, but more commonly a fine would be imposed or a subdivision plat would be required.

Utilities

The utilities section requires the appraiser to indicate if the utilities are public or qualify as "other." This assumes that the utilities are available and connected to the subject improvements. Utilities are provided by public, public-private, or private companies. Most appraisers consider utilities to be public even if they are privately owned but publicly regulated, such as in the following situations:

- An electric company that is a "for-profit" company but is regulated by the state.
- A sewer utility run by a government agency with appointed officials as leaders.
  If the utility is owned by the city, the classification should be clear. Utilities may be owned by governments or quasi-governmental entities or may even be privately owned by publicly regulated entities.
- A gas company that is a stock company regulated by the state.
  If the gas is liquid petroleum and is trucked in, it is considered to be owned by a private entity.

Some site issues that appraisers must be aware of in this area include:

- The location of available public sewer and water lines for properties that are connected to wells and have septic systems.
  Some lenders require connection to sewers if the lines are within a certain number of feet of the residence. If so, the appraiser should consider the impact on value of the cost of connection and the increase (if any) in value from the connection to the sewers. The appraiser can assume a connection to public sewers and/or water lines but should also add value if the market shows that an adjustment is warranted. Assuming that the subject is connected but not adjusting for it in the analysis is an appraisal error.
- The location of an on-site septic system.
  Septic systems or septic fields located in identified flood hazard areas are not allowed in some markets. As a result, they would not be approved for replacement if they fail. In some cases, septic systems have been found to be located on an adjacent property or in the public right of way.
- The distance between the subject's water well-head and the septic system.
  Most counties have codes to regulate this.

Appraisers should verify the status of the utilities as much as possible. It should not be assumed that a property is connected to a public sewer or water supply unless a source can support that assumption. Occasionally, an owner in a subdivision served by public utilities will not connect because of the cost. In other instances, properties are not connected to sewer lines and lack septic systems as well. These properties pose a significant environmental hazard that could become the appraiser's problem. As a result, appraisers should perform the necessary research to ensure that they become as knowledgeable as possible about the utilities that serve the subject property.

Off-site Improvements–Type

The off-site improvements section requires the appraiser to report the type and ownership of the public-access right of ways that are

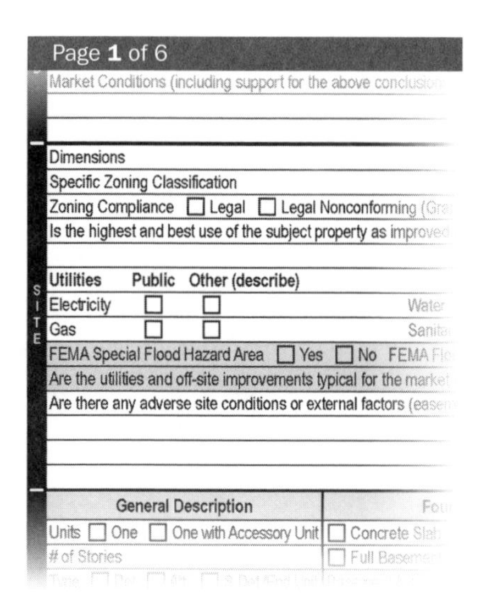
Page 1 of 6
Market Conditions (including support for the above conclusio

Dimensions
Specific Zoning Classification
Zoning Compliance ☐ Legal ☐ Legal Nonconforming
Is the highest and best use of the subject property as improve

SITE

Utilities	Public	Other (describe)	
Electricity	☐	☐	Water
Gas	☐	☐	Sanit

FEMA Special Flood Hazard Area ☐ Yes ☐ No FEMA
Are the utilities and off-site improvements typical for the mark
Are there any adverse site conditions or external factors

General Description	Fou
Units ☐ One ☐ One with Accessory Unit	☐ Concrete Slab
# of Stories	☐ Full Basem

adjacent to the subject property. This feature usually does not serve an important function in the valuation; nevertheless, it is still reported. If the streets are private, a discussion of the entity responsible for their maintenance as well as legal access to the subject site is required. There must be some provision for the maintenance of private streets. Appraisers should not assume that streets are public without looking at the survey or plat. Some subdivisions have private streets that were built to public standards, and the only way to know that they are private is to look at the plat. If a sign says "private," the streets are probably not public and not maintained by the municipality. If the entrance is gated, the streets are usually private. This issue can have a significant effect on the value conclusion. If private streets lack a provision for maintenance, it can pose a big problem at the time of the subject property's resale when the streets fall into disrepair.

Rural areas commonly have private, unmarked roads. These roads do not fall within a city or county maintenance and are left up to homeowners to maintain. Appraisers must be diligent in finding out about any such private roads.

FEMA Special Flood Hazard Area ☐ Yes ☐ No FEMA Flood Zone ____ FEMA Map # ____ FEMA Map Date

The FEMA flood hazard section of the form requires the appraiser to comment on the subject's location in relation to identified flood hazard areas. If the subject property is located in a flood hazard area and the improvement is not high enough above the flood level, it may require flood insurance for mortgage purposes. The Statement of Assumptions and Limiting Conditions located on page 4 of both forms states that

> The appraiser has examined the available flood maps that are provided by the Federal Emergency Management Agency (or other data sources) and has noted in this appraisal report whether any portion of the subject site is located in an identified Special Flood Hazard Area. Because the appraiser is not a surveyor, he or she makes no guarantees, express or implied, regarding this determination.

This statement means that the appraiser is responsible for noting whether any portion of the site is located in a flood hazard area, which can create problems for appraisers in areas where maps are not specific enough for this requirement. This problem can be compounded by the fact that the flood hazard maps are geographically drawn, but the determination of the property located in the flood hazard area is topographically determined. It is quite possible for a property to be mapped in a flood hazard area but not actually located at an elevation where flooding is likely.

If the subject property, or at least the building area, is located in a FEMA flood hazard area and the community is participating in the federal program, the subject may be a legal nonconforming use. If the appraiser indicates that the subject is in the flood hazard area, he or she should consider whether the legal nonconforming use box should also be checked. This leads to the question of whether an appraiser finding a subject in a flood hazard area must make an adjustment for that additional cost of ownership. For example, if the homeowner must pay $300 per year in additional cost for the flood insurance, the appraiser could logically convert it to a $3,000 adjustment ($300/0. 10 = $3,000). However, the market may not recognize such an adjustment. In some cases, buyers may be unaware of this issue until just before closing, when the lender issues the final commitment and stipulates a flood insurance requirement. In such instances, the buyer must decide whether to buy that property with the additional cost or cancel the purchase. It is essential that the appraiser perform the research to determine whether the market recognizes this continuing cost as a basis for a positive or negative adjustment in the market.

Are the utilities and off-site improvements typical for the market area? ☐ Yes ☐ No If No, describe

If the subject receives its water from a private well and treats its waste via a private septic system but the rest of the market receives public water and sewer service, can the appraiser say that the utilities are typical? Moreover, will this affect the property's value? In markets where corporate transferees make up the majority of buyers, this can be problematic because locals may know and accept septic systems but non-residents may fear septic failures and reject properties because of it. In other agricultural markets, the septic system may be the accepted market standard. If the broker inputs "public water and sewer" as search criteria in a computerized multiple listing service (MLS) system, the properties on well and septic systems will not come up. It is the appraiser's job to know which utilities serve the subject (as reported by the owner or broker) as well as which utility services are typical and accepted by the market.

If the subject is located on a gravel road that is the only such street in the county, is this typical? If the subject is not on an "all-weather" road, the mortgage loan may not be acceptable to all lenders. It is important to verify who maintains these roads. The cost of road maintenance can have a significant impact on the property values in the area if owners must pay taxes for public and private road maintenance. Some buyers will not purchase a property that abuts a gravel road because of the dust.

Is the subject an urban property that has adequate off-site parking? Residences can be unsalable in some markets because of the lack of adequate parking. This may be a significant issue for attached homes and condos in many markets. In markets characterized by high density or cul-de-sacs, the lack of driveway parking can create overflow parking in the street and on grassy areas.

In other markets, the existence or lack of sidewalks has a significant impact on value. For buyers who are pedestrians, the existence of sidewalks or multipurpose paths may present an issue as well.

Page 1 of 6
Market Conditions (including support for the above conclusio
Dimensions
Specific Zoning Classification
Zoning Compliance ☐ Legal ☐ Legal Nonconforming (Gra
Is the highest and best use of the subject property as improved
SITE
Utilities Public Other (describe)
Electricity ☐ ☐ Water
Gas ☐ ☐ Sanita
FEMA Special Flood Hazard Area ☐ Yes ☐ No FEMA Fl
Are the utilities and off-site improvements typical for the marke
Are there any adverse site conditions or external factors (ease
General Description | Fou
Units ☐ One ☐ One with Accessory Unit | ☐ Concrete Slab
# of Stories | ☐ Full Basemen

Are there any adverse site conditions or external factors (easements, encroachments, environmental conditions, land uses, etc.)? ☐ Yes ☐ No If Yes, describe

A single question about adverse site conditions and external factors brings up many other questions associated with the following issues:

Topography and Drainage

An appraisal involving a walk-through inspection in which the appraiser has full access to the site allows for the assessment of these factors. However, a curbside appraisal would make these factors difficult to assess. Nonetheless, these valuation issues are significant. If a site has negative drainage, the basement may be wet and the house may have mold, which can promote termite damage. Appraisers who only view the property from the street may not be able to ascertain these subtle problems.

Easements

Some appraisers do not thoroughly research the existence of easements, which creates a major problem because an easement can have a devastating effect on property value. For instance, an easement that cuts through the center of a building site may render the site unbuildable. Furthermore, an easement that prohibits plantings or other forms of landscaping may preclude some landscaping plans. Also, an ingress-egress easement from another property could cause a significant loss in privacy for a property, having a negative effect on market value.

Soil Types, Settlement Problems, and Underground Geological Problems

Subsidence is a common problem in some markets. Not all soils are solid enough to support a building. Septic systems can function only with certain soil types, and the water table must be sufficient to supply a well.

> To obtain more information on soil types, settlement problems, and underground geological problems, visit the U.S. Geological Survey Web site at *www.usgs.gov.*

Appraisers must know their areas geographically and geologically. Geography (proximity) and geology (earth composition) can have a significant impact on the value conclusion. For example, an appraiser prepares an appraisal report on a property near a rock quarry but is unaware of the blasting that happens there each day at 3:00 p.m. The blasting has caused the house to settle 3 inches. Just because the appraiser may have never seen such an issue does not mean that it is not an important factor in value.

Fannie Mae discusses the site section of the appraisal report in depth in their 2009 single-family *Selling Guide*, which is available on their Web site at *www.efanniemae.com*.

To access the guide, type "Selling Guide" in the search box that appears in the top right corner of the home page. The *Selling Guide* can also be accessed by first clicking on "Appraisers" under the "Industry Specialists" heading. Next, click on "Single-Family Guides for free online" under the heading "AllRegs Online." A list of documents will then appear. If pop-ups are blocked, click on "View Support Tips and AllRegs Contact Info" under the "AllRegs Online" heading to access directions for changing the browser settings to allow pop-ups.

The following sections of Subpart B4 of the *Selling Guide* are applicable:

- Section B4-1.4-05, Appraisal Report Review: Site Analysis Parameters
- Section B4-1.4-06, Appraisal Report Review: Subject Property Zoning

Improvements Section of the URAR

General Description	Foundation	Exterior Description materials/condition	Interior materials/condition
Units ☐ One ☐ One with Accessory Unit	☐ Concrete Slab ☐ Crawl Space	Foundation Walls	Floors
# of Stories	☐ Full Basement ☐ Partial Basement	Exterior Walls	Walls
Type ☐ Det. ☐ Att. ☐ S-Det./End Unit	Basement Area sq. ft.	Roof Surface	Trim/Finish
☐ Existing ☐ Proposed ☐ Under Const.	Basement Finish %	Gutters & Downspouts	Bath Floor
Design (Style)	☐ Outside Entry/Exit ☐ Sump Pump	Window Type	Bath Wainscot
Year Built	Evidence of ☐ Infestation	Storm Sash/Insulated	Car Storage ☐ None
Effective Age (Yrs)	☐ Dampness ☐ Settlement	Screens	☐ Driveway # of Cars
Attic ☐ None	Heating ☐ FWA ☐ HWBB ☐ Radiant	Amenities ☐ Woodstove(s) #	Driveway Surface
☐ Drop Stair ☐ Stairs	☐ Other Fuel	☐ Fireplace(s) # ☐ Fence	☐ Garage # of Cars
☐ Floor ☐ Scuttle	Cooling ☐ Central Air Conditioning	☐ Patio/Deck ☐ Porch	☐ Carport # of Cars
☐ Finished ☐ Heated	☐ Individual ☐ Other	☐ Pool ☐ Other	☐ Att. ☐ Det. ☐ Built-in
Appliances ☐ Refrigerator ☐ Range/Oven ☐ Dishwasher ☐ Disposal ☐ Microwave ☐ Washer/Dryer ☐ Other (describe)			
Finished area **above** grade contains: Rooms Bedrooms Bath(s) Square Feet of Gross Living Area Above Grade			
Additional features (special energy efficient items, etc.)			
Describe the condition of the property (including needed repairs, deterioration, renovations, remodeling, etc.).			
Are there any physical deficiencies or adverse conditions that affect the livability, soundness, or structural integrity of the property? ☐ Yes ☐ No If Yes, describe			
Does the property generally conform to the neighborhood (functional utility, style, condition, use, construction, etc.)? ☐ Yes ☐ No If No, describe			

IMPROVEMENTS

The improvements sections of the URAR and Form 2055 have numerous differences, so addressing them at the same time would be difficult. This necessitates a separate commentary for each form. The URAR will be discussed first.

General Description

Units ☐ One ☐ One with Accessory Unit

The first part of the improvements section on the URAR requires the appraiser to indicate whether the subject is a single unit or a single unit with an accessory apartment. An accessory unit may or may not be legal and always requires a discussion of zoning and highest and best use.

Fannie Mae addresses the topic of a single unit versus a single unit with an accessory unit in their 2009 single-family *Selling Guide*, Subpart B4, Underwriting Property, B4-1.4-06, Appraisal Report Review: Subject Property Zoning.

> **Introduction**
> This topic contains information on Appraisal Report Review: Subject Property Zoning.
>
> - Subject Property Zoning
> - Permissible Use of Land
> - Highest and Best Use
>
> **Subject Property Zoning**
> Lenders must ensure that the specific zoning class has been reported in the appraisal, along with a general statement as to what the zoning permits.

The appraisal must include a statement that the subject property presents a legal, conforming; legal, nonconforming (grandfathered) use; or an illegal use under the zoning regulations; or whether there is no local zoning.

Permissible Use of Land
Fannie Mae does not purchase or securitize mortgage loans on properties if the improvements do not constitute a legally permissible use of the land.

Certain exceptions to this policy are made provided the property is appraised and underwritten in accordance with the special requirements imposed as a condition to agreeing to make the exception:

Property Type	Loan Eligible for Purchase or Securitization by Fannie Mae?
A property that is subject to certain land-use regulations, such as coastal tideland or wetland laws that create setback lines or other provisions that prevent the reconstruction or maintenance of the property improvements if they are damaged or destroyed.	No.
A property that represents a legal, but nonconforming, use of the land and the appraisal analysis reflects any adverse effect that the nonconforming use has on the value and marketability of the property.	Yes, if the mortgage is secured by a one- to four-unit property or a unit in a PUD project.
A property where the improvements from a project that represents a legal, but nonconforming, use of the land only can be rebuilt to current density in the event of partial or full destruction.	Yes, Fannie Mae will purchase or securitize a condo unit mortgage or co-op share loan, provided the mortgage file includes either a copy of the applicable zoning regulations or a letter from the local zoning authority that authorizes reconstruction to current density.
A one- or two-unit property that includes an illegal additional unit or accessory apartment (sometimes referred to as a mother-in-law, mother-daughter, or granny unit).	Yes, provided that: · The illegal use conforms to the subject neighborhood and to the market. The property is appraised based upon its current use. · The borrower qualifies for the mortgage without considering any rental income from the illegal unit. · The appraisal must report that the improvements represent an illegal use. · The appraisal report must demonstrate that the improvements are typical for the market through an analysis of at least three comparable properties that have the same illegal use. · The lender ensures that the existence of the illegal additional unit will not jeopardize any future hazard insurance claim that might need to be filed for the property.
A three- to four-unit property that includes an illegal accessory apartment.	No.

Highest and Best Use
If the current improvements clearly do not represent the highest and best use of the site as an improved site, the appraiser must so indicate on the appraisal report. Fannie Mae will not purchase or securitize a mortgage that does not represent the highest and best use of the site.[9]

Based on this statement, Fannie Mae will buy mortgages that include a current use as an illegal mother-in-law apartment if the valuation is made based on the legal use (single unit). The appraiser is required to report the illegal use and show that the improvements are typical for the market. This permits a lender to make such a loan but does not require the applicant to evict the tenant or allow the appraiser to include a value for the second, illegal unit.

9. Fannie Mae, *Selling Guide* (single-family) (April 1, 2009), 464-466. Available at *www.efanniemae.com*. Direct link: *https://www.efanniemae.com/sf/guides/ssg/sg/pdf/sg0309.pdf*.

Page **1** of 6

General Description	Fou
Units ☐ One ☐ One with Accessory Unit	☐ Concrete Slab
# of Stories	☐ Full Basement
Type ☐ Det. ☐ Att. ☐ S-Det/End Unit	Basement Area
☐ Existing ☐ Proposed ☐ Under Const.	Basement Finish
Design (Style)	☐ Outside Entry/
Year Built	Evidence of ☐
Effective Age (Yrs)	☐ Dampness ☐
Attic ☐ None	Heating ☐ FWA
☐ Drop Stair ☐ Stairs	☐ Other
☐ Floor ☐ Scuttle	Cooling ☐ Centr
☐ Finished ☐ Heated	☐ Individual

IMPROVEMENTS

Appliances ☐Refrigerator ☐Range/Oven ☐Dishwasher

Finished area **above** grade contains: Rooms

Additional features (special energy efficient items, etc.)

Describe the condition of the property (including needed repairs

Are there any physical deficiencies or adverse conditions that

Does the property generally conform to the neighborhood (func

Freddie Mac Form 70 March 2005

Case in Point

The subject of an appraisal is the fee simple interest in a 30,000-sq.-ft. site improved with a 2,900-sq.-ft. residence and an 800-sq.-ft. apartment over the detached garage. The zoning in this area requires at least 75 feet of road frontage per property, and this site has 100 feet. The zoning was first passed by the city council in 1964, but this house was built in 1924. The apartment over the garage was used as a caretaker's apartment from 1924 to 1929 and then was used as a rental unit from 1929 to 1975. From 1975 until three years ago, the apartment over the garage was used as storage for lawn chairs, off-season clothes, and old bicycles, as gleaned from prior MLS listing sheets. The zoning ordinance states that if any "legal nonconforming" use is vacated for longer than 12 months, the owner loses the right to reestablish its use. Last year, the new owner of this property spent $25,000 to remodel the apartment (without a permit) and immediately rented it out for $600 per month. The appraisal is dated today and the apartment is still being rented and is still illegal in the jurisdiction where it is located.

In this situation, the appraiser can value the property only within a legal use, so the apartment must be judged as nonconforming and illegal. The appraiser must ignore the income derived from the apartment and the value that it adds, but the lender can still make the loan without requiring the owner to vacate the use. It is important for an appraiser to know the zoning laws well in each area because this use may not be legal as a rental in some jurisdictions but would be legal if it were used as a professional studio or home office. In other words, the apartment may have no value as a second dwelling unit but could be used by the owner for his or her own purposes. A good question for an appraiser to research is whether the unit adds value if it can only be used by the occupant of the main residence. In many jurisdictions, legal nonconforming uses can be rebuilt if they meet certain conditions or if they get a variance from the code. If the subject is a legal but nonconforming use, the appraiser must speak to the requirements for rebuilding that improvement and reestablishing the use after a fire, flood, or other major destruction.

Because of changes in zoning rules over the years, it is not uncommon to find that the majority (50%+) of single-unit homes are legal but nonconforming uses or are noncompliant with development standards such as those for setback and lot size.

When completing the general description section, it is always a good idea to consider what a single-unit or two- to four-unit residential property actually is. This may be difficult, as questions such as the following may arise:

- Is a building that has two, three, or four units included in a single structure a two- to four-unit home?
- Is a building that has two, three, or four units included in a single structure a condominium?
- Is a property that has two dwelling units on a single site a two-unit property?
- Is a property that has two dwelling units on the site a two-unit property if

  1) the site could be divided into two parcels and

2) the sales of the two net more than a sale of a two-unit home on one parcel?

Many appraisers struggle with these questions when determining the type of property they are valuing.

Case in Point

Exhibit 7 shows a drawing of an attached residential property in Bigville for which the following zoning and market characteristics apply:

- Zoning in this part of the city requires 6,000-sq.-ft. lots with at least 45 feet of road frontage on a dedicated right of way.
- Each dwelling unit must have 850 square feet of finished living space.
- Single-unit attached homes similar to the ones depicted in Exhibit 7 sell for $115,000 each.
- Two-unit properties with attached units such as this sell for $180,000.
- Selling costs are all based on percentages, so two small sales are equal to the percentage of selling costs for one larger sale.
- Any platted lot or parcel in this zoning classification and in the subject's addition can be divided at will if it meets the previously listed zoning requirements.
- No impediments to selling individual units exist. A party wall agreement is commonly used to establish and maintain a plan for maintenance and dispute resolution.

Exhibit 7. Attached Residential Property in Bigville

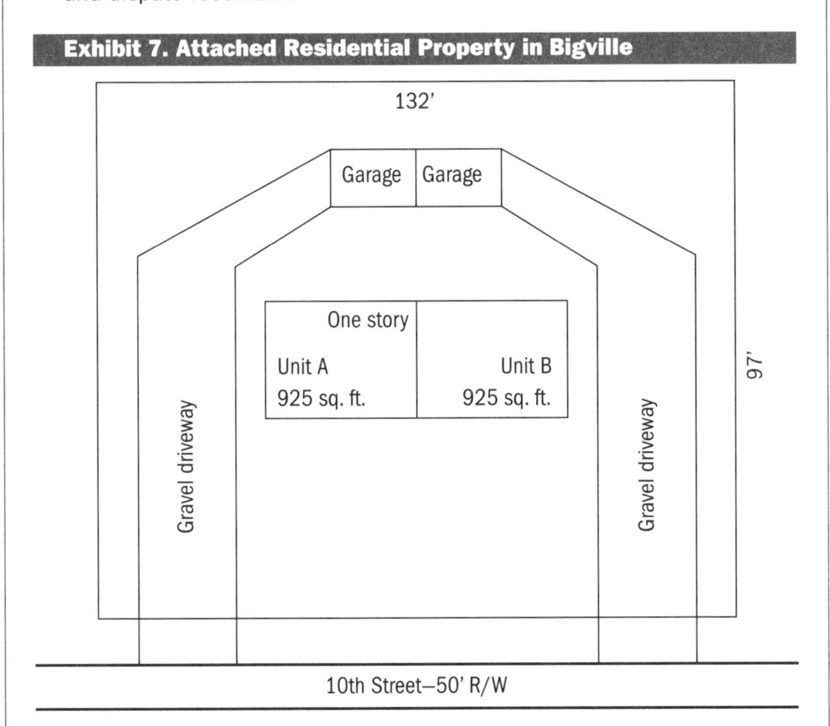

Is the property illustrated in Exhibit 7 a single-unit home or a two-unit home? Because it appears that the market will pay more for the two units as single-unit residences than as a single-owner, two-unit residence, and since it is allowed by the zoning ordinance, the answer to this question is that the property is two single-unit homes that should be split down the middle and sold as two parcels. This represents the highest and best use. Typically, the market would already show other comparable uses.

Page **1** of 6

General Description	Fou
Units ☐ One ☐ One with Accessory Unit	☐ Concrete Slab
# of Stories	☐ Full Basement
Type ☐ Det. ☐ Att. ☐ S-Det./End Unit	Basement Area
☐ Existing ☐ Proposed ☐ Under Const.	Basement Finish
Design (Style)	☐ Outside Entry/
Year Built	Evidence of ☐ In
Effective Age (Yrs)	☐ Dampness ☐
Attic ☐ None	Heating ☐ FWA ☐
☐ Drop Stair ☐ Stairs	☐ Other
☐ Floor ☐ Scuttle	Cooling ☐ Centr
☐ Finished ☐ Heated	☐ Individual

IMPROVEMENTS

Appliances ☐Refrigerator ☐Range/Oven ☐Dishwasher ☐

Finished area **above** grade contains: Rooms

Additional features (special energy efficient items, etc.)

Describe the condition of the property (including needed repairs

Are there any physical deficiencies or adverse conditions that a

Does the property generally conform to the neighborhood (func

Freddie Mac Form 70 March 2005

Defining what constitutes a two-unit home versus two single-unit homes is always a question of highest and best use that requires the appraiser to know the zoning requirements for the property's area as well as the market demand for two-unit homes versus attached single-unit homes.

of Stories

The next line requires the appraiser to list the number of stories in the building. This is usually easy to ascertain and will match the floor plan configuration listed later in the report.

Type ☐ Det. ☐ Att. ☐ S-Det./End Unit

The next line requires the appraiser to check whether the subject unit is attached, detached, or an attached end unit. In this instance, the word "attachment" does not mean "condominium." A home that is attached on both sides but that includes a small lot is an attached, single-unit home. Appraisers must be familiar with the rights in realty and the property that they are appraising. Most avoid using attached home comparables with detached homes and vice versa. If the subject is an attached home, the lot will often be as wide as the building plus additional land in the front and rear. In some cases, the lot size may be equivalent in area to the first floor's foundation.

Detached end units may sell for a little more in some markets and should be identified as such in this section. End units have more land and afford more privacy as shown in Exhibit 8, a diagram of a typical townhouse project in which the units are attached on two sides. The lot size is along the party walls and runs from the right of way to the alley.

Exhibit 8. Typical Townhouse Development

50' Right of Way with 30' Pavement

#1	#2	#3	#4	#5	#6
2-Story Townhouse	2-Story Townhouse	2-Story Townhouse	2-Story Townhouse	2-Story Townhouse	2-Story Townhouse

Alley

☐ Existing ☐ Proposed ☐ Under Const.

The next section of the general description enables the appraiser to indicate whether the appraisal is of an existing improved property, a property proposed for construction, or a property under construction. If the subject is proposed for construction or is under construction, a check box at the bottom of page 2 of this form is usually marked to indicate that the value is subject to completion of the construction.

Design (Style)

The design (style) line calls for the appraiser to indicate the architectural style of the property. Architectural style can be an important factor in single-unit residential markets. Whether a home is Southern colonial, English Tudor, or New England salt box may have an effect on value in some markets. It is also very common for a popular modern design to have a positive impact on value but not have a specific name. If that is the case, it becomes more important to find comparables with the same nondescript but popular design. Conversely, design trends are sometimes temporary and designs that were once trendy may fade in popularity. Once this happens, the style "dates" the property and eventually results in a decrease in value due to functional obsolescence.

The height of the residence can be a significant design issue in some markets. The taller the home, the more impressive it is. A two-story residence with a steep roof pitch may appear to be larger than a one-story or two-story house with a lower roof pitch. Builders will sometimes not build the basements or crawl spaces as deep into the ground as usual in order to make the house and part of the basement floor extend higher up. This makes the house appear to be taller and more imposing.

Year Built

The year built is an obvious piece of information necessary for an appraisal report. The year built is the actual age, not the effective age. For most appraisals, this fact should be easy to confirm. For appraisals in which the date of construction is not known, the appraiser should indicate that the reported date is only an estimate.

Effective Age (Yrs)

Actual age is the difference in years from the date of construction and the effective date of the appraisal. *Effective age* is the numerical age estimate of the improvement based on a comparison with the condition of the other improved properties with which the subject competes. If one building is better maintained than other buildings in this market area, the effective age of that building may be less than its actual age. If a building is poorly maintained, its effective age may be greater than its actual age. If a building has received typical maintenance, its effective age and actual age may be the same.[10]

An improved property that is 20 years old but has much deferred maintenance may have an effective age of 30 years. Conversely, a property that has a 30-year-old improvement but has been remodeled substantially may have an effective age of only 20 years. This definition implies that a home that is 75 years old and in average condition for its market has an effective age of 75 years. The effective age rating is always subjective and is frequently a point of disagreement among appraisers. Many appraisers cannot even agree on what the term "effective age" means, much less what the appropriate number should be. The only appraisal use for these terms is in the cost approach.

These definitions of actual age and effective age imply that a five-year-old home with standard maintenance has an effective age of five

---

10. *The Appraisal of Real Estate*, 13th ed. (Chicago: Appraisal Institute, 2008), 412.

Page **1** of 6

Foundation		Exterior Descriptio
☐ Concrete Slab ☐ Crawl Space		Foundation Walls
☐ Full Basement ☐ Partial Basement		Exterior Walls
Basement Area	sq. ft.	Roof Surface
Basement Finish	%	Gutters & Downspo
☐ Outside Entry/Exit ☐ Sump Pump		Window Type
Evidence of ☐ Infestation		Storm Sash/Insula
☐ Dampness ☐ Settlement		Screens
Heating ☐ FWA ☐ HWBB ☐ Radiant		Amenities
☐ Other	Fuel	☐ Fireplace(s) #
Cooling ☐ Central Air Conditioning		☐ Patio/Deck
☐ Individual	☐ Other	☐ Pool

ven ☐Dishwasher ☐Disposal ☐Microwave ☐Washer/Dryer

Rooms Bedrooms Bath(s)

ent items, etc.)

cluding needed repairs, deterioration, renovations, remodeling, et

verse conditions that affect the livability, soundness, or structural i

he neighborhood (functional utility, style, condition, use, construct

Page 1 of 6

years and a 25-year-old home with standard maintenance has an effective age of 25 years. More significantly, they imply that a 75-year-old home that has had standard maintenance has an effective age of 75.

Other relevant terms in this discussion of actual and effective age are "economic life" and "remaining economic life." *Economic life* is the period over which improvements to real property contribute to property value.[11] *Remaining economic life* is the estimated period during which improvements will continue to contribute to property value, or an estimate of the number of years remaining in the economic life of the structure or structural components as of the date of the appraisal. Remaining economic life is used in the age-life method of estimating depreciation.[12]

A building that is in average condition has typical maintenance compared to the homes in the market in which it competes, so a 75-year-old home that has some deferred maintenance should be labeled as "average." If a 30-year-old old home has had similar maintenance as the homes it competes with, its effective age and chronological age are the same and the rating should also be "average." A 75-year-old home that has been well maintained or recently remodeled cannot compete with 10- to 20-year-old homes because it does not have the same functional utility. Because of design and functional issues, a remodeled 75-year-old home competes with other remodeled 75-year-old homes rather than new homes. This issue is covered in more depth in the cost approach to value section, where it is applicable.

Foundation

☐ Concrete Slab ☐ Crawl Space

☐ Full Basement ☐ Partial Basement

Basement Area ________ sq. ft.

Basement Finish _______ %

More than one of the boxes in the foundation section of the form are usually checked. This section requires the appraiser to indicate whether the subject improvement includes a basement, and if so, its area in square feet. The presence of basements varies according to the geographic region in which the property is located. The valuation of basement areas can be a challenge for appraisers because of the large adjustments that may result. Many appraisers have difficulty convincing intended users of the value of basements because they can cause such large overall and net adjustments. As a result, some appraisers underestimate the value of basements. Basement finishing is classified by a percentage based on the finished area in relation to the total basement area. For example, a basement that has an area of 1,000 square feet with 950 finished square feet would be classified as 95% finished.

☐ Outside Entry/Exit ☐ Sump Pump

The outside entry or exit can be an attribute for a property, but it also may be a requirement for homes with finished basements that

11. *Dictionary*, 92.
12. Ibid., 242.

include sleeping rooms. State, county, and city building codes may require a second point of ingress or egress from the basement if bedrooms are part of the floor plan. This is usually a code issue, and the appraiser should know the requirements when discussing the highest and best use. In many markets, a walkout basement yields a better market appeal because of the natural light that it affords. Easy access to the front or rear lawn can also be a big positive for such a property.

Evidence of ☐ Infestation ☐ Dampness ☐ Settlement

If a sump pump is found in the subject's basement or crawl space, the sump pump box should be checked. Dampness is a significant concern in many markets because of the mold problem associated with it. Damp crawl spaces can be one of the most significant threats to the life of the improvement, as it can cause wood rot in the floor joists, rafters, and roof underlayment. Moisture in crawl spaces often goes unnoticed, and high humidity can permeate the house up to and including the attic. Although water in the basement can be a problem, it is usually detected quickly. Not all houses need sump pumps. Drains may lead to an area that is lower than the foundation perimeter drains rather than into a sump pump pit if the property has such a feature.

Exterior Description ____materials/condition

Foundation Walls

Appraisers cannot assume to know the type and material of which the foundation is made. Foundations may be made of wood, piers, or other materials. In completing this section, the appraiser is responsible for noting any observable deficiencies. The appraiser needs to know what type of foundation is acceptable to the market. Property owners may be disappointed if this is not reported correctly.

Case in Point

An appraiser accepts an appraisal assignment for a five-year-old, bi-level (raised ranch) residence with a two-car attached garage on a 1⁄4-acre site. The home is vacant, and the broker provided access via a lock box. The appraiser performs a walk-through and then goes outside to measure the residence. She finds that vinyl siding covers the entire exterior except for the area a few inches above the ground, which is covered with a thin sheet of metal flashing. This sheet metal band conceals the foundation area. The appraiser is curious because the foundation cannot be seen anywhere on the structure. She is determined to find out why the owners covered up the foundation. After 20 minutes of searching, she finds that every part of the foundation is covered with vinyl siding, sheet metal, or drywall on the interior. She finds a small, uncovered section under the staircase, which is viewable if she lies down on the floor and looks up. She discovers that the foundation is made of wood and that the owners have been hiding it.

If this condition is acceptable in the market, the appraiser's precaution was unnecessary; however, if buyers are reluctant to purchase houses with wood foundations, this effort could be necessary to render a competent value opinion.

Page 1 of 6

Exterior Description	materials/condition	Interior
Foundation Walls		Floors
Exterior Walls		Walls
Roof Surface		Trim/Finish
Gutters & Downspouts		Bath Floor
Window Type		Bath Wainscot
Storm Sash/Insulated		Car Storage
Screens		☐ Driveway
Amenities	☐ Woodstove(s) #	Driveway Surf
☐ Fireplace(s) #	☐ Fence	☐ Garage
☐ Patio/Deck	☐ Porch	☐ Carport
☐ Pool	☐ Other	☐ Att. ☐

ave ☐Washer/Dryer ☐Other (describe)

Bath(s) Square Feet of Gross Living Area

ations, remodeling, etc.).

ndness, or structural integrity of the property? ☐ Yes ☐ No

idition, use, construction, etc.)? ☐ Yes ☐ No If No, describe

e 1 of 6 Fannie Mae Fo

Some lenders and insurers have standards that require a certain amount of the foundation to be exposed or that prohibit the exterior siding from touching the ground. If the siding covers the exterior walls and extends into the soil, it could pose a big problem for lenders.

Exterior Walls

The exterior wall type can indicate the quality of the home's construction. Vinyl siding is acceptable in some markets but not in others. Moreover, wood siding that needs repainting every few years is the only type of siding accepted by some markets, while in other markets it is considered a detriment. In many markets, too much of the same siding material on one house may also be a detriment. In cases like this, builders generally install 50% of one type of siding on the house and 50% of another type. This is a market-specific issue and local brokers should be consulted to help develop an opinion of what is acceptable to the market and what is not. Interviewing more than one local broker is recommended to prevent their possible bias from becoming the appraiser's. The adjustments for one type of siding over another can be extracted from a paired sales analysis. If no obsolescence exists, the difference in the cost of one type versus another can be used as a basis for adjustment.

Roof Surface

The next section of the report requires the appraiser to indicate the type of roof covering in place, which may be asphalt shingles, slate, tiles, rolled asphalt paper, copper sheets, mopped asphalt, and so on. The purpose of this entry is to describe the improvement and give an indication of its quality. The steepness of the roof (roof pitch) also gives an indication of the quality of the improvement. The appraiser may have to get additional advice on the condition and remaining life of the roof surface. If an appraisal is done for mortgage collateral assessment, the condition of the roof is important because it is usually expensive to replace roof shingles and an owner may not have the money for this capital expense during the first few years of ownership.

Gutters & Downspouts

Working gutters are needed in many properties to keep the foundation area of the building dry, which prevents moisture from penetrating into the basement or crawl space. The next section of the form more or less requires the appraiser to observe and note the materials used for guttering.

Gutters that do not work properly can result in surrounding areas of exposed gravel or trenches where the water running over the gutters washes away the topsoil but leaves a trench or gravel patch. This erodes the topsoil around the structure and may cause negative drainage toward the foundation. Problems associated with negative drainage around the foundation are made worse by the lack of gutters or by gutters that are rusted through or have been plugged up with leaves.

Window Type

The appraiser lists the type, material, and condition of the windows in the next section. Windows can be a minor feature of a residence. However, in some older home markets, houses with new energy-efficient windows are more valuable than homes with old windows that leak, stick, and cannot be cleaned easily. The type, material, and condition of the windows can amount to a several-thousand-dollar difference in value if the market observes and notes the difference.

Storm Sash/Insulated

Next, the appraiser observes, notes, and reports on the type of secondary windows as well as their condition and materials. This may entail simple storm windows over the primary windows or double-glazed "thermo-break" vacuum seal windows.

Screens

The presence of screens, though not big cost items, must also be noted. The appraiser must look at the windows to see if they are in place. This feature is not an issue in all markets.

Interior ____materials/condition

Floors
Walls
Trim/Finish
Bath Floor
Bath Wainscot

The next section requires the appraiser to indicate the interior finishes and their condition(s). Typical finishes include carpet and drywall or plaster.

Attic **☐ None**
☐ Drop Stair **☐ Stairs**
☐ Floor **☐ Scuttle**
☐ Finished **☐ Heated**

The attic section requires the appraiser to indicate if the subject has an attic and whether it is finished. If the attic is easily accessed, finished, and heated and cooled, many appraisers consider it to be living area and include it in the gross living area (GLA). If this is the case, the appraiser should not add it here unless the improvements are more definitive and are described in detail on an attached page. Some states have regulations on how to measure attic space and require the use of ANSI (American National Standards Institute) standards.

Heating **☐ FWA (forced warm air)**
☐ HWBB (hot water, baseboard) **☐ Radiant**
☐ Other
Fuel

Appraisers are expected to observe, note, and report the type of heating used in the residence, and may need to comment on the market

Page 1 of 6

	Foundation		Exterior Descripti
nit	☐ Concrete Slab ☐ Crawl Space		Foundation Walls
	☐ Full Basement ☐ Partial Basement		Exterior Walls
nit	Basement Area	sq. ft.	Roof Surface
st.	Basement Finish	%	Gutters & Downsp
	☐ Outside Entry/Exit ☐ Sump Pump		Window Type
	Evidence of ☐ Infestation		Storm Sash/Insulat
	☐ Dampness ☐ Settlement		Screens
	Heating ☐ FWA ☐ HWBB ☐ Radiant		Amenities
	☐ Other	Fuel	☐ Fireplace(s) #
	Cooling ☐ Central Air Conditioning		☐ Patio/Deck
	☐ Individual	☐ Other	☐ Pool

ven ☐Dishwasher ☐Disposal ☐Microwave ☐Washer/Dryer

Rooms Bedrooms Bath(s)

ent items, etc.)

cluding needed repairs, deterioration, renovations, remodeling, etc

verse conditions that affect the livability, soundness, or structural in

he neighborhood (functional utility, style, condition, use, construct

Page 1 of 6

acceptability of each type. In some markets, only gas forced air units are acceptable, and any other type will cause functional obsolescence. In others, electric forced air or heat pumps may be the only acceptable system. A few questions to a local real estate broker should determine what is acceptable for the property's market. Appraisers must be careful not to assume that an acceptable system in one price range of homes is acceptable for all price ranges. Electric baseboard heat may be market acceptable in the $100,000 to $150,000 price range but not in the $400,000 to $500,000 range. Also, the heating system is of secondary importance to the cooling system in some markets.

Cooling

☐ Central Air Conditioning

☐ Individual ☐ Other

Here again, the appraiser should observe, note, and report the type of cooling system and, if need be, comment on its functional utility. The condition of these items should be included in the overall condition rating of the improvement. Air conditioning is considered a luxury in some markets and may not be required. However, in other markets it is considered to be a necessity and its lack is a source of functional obsolescence.

Amenities

☐ Wood Stove(s) #

☐ Fireplace(s) # **☐ Fence**

☐ Patio/Deck **☐ Porch**

☐ Pool **☐ Other**

Check boxes for amenities indicate distinguishing features of the property. Any boxes checked in this section would also be listed in the sales comparison adjustment grid on the next page of the form.

Car Storage

☐ None

☐ Driveway ________________ # of Cars

Driveway Surface

☐ Garage ________________ # of Cars

☐ Carport ________________ # of Cars

☐ Att. ☐ Det. ☐ Built-in

Car storage is an important asset for many properties. In some urban properties, the existence of off-street parking can be a major asset for the subject. If a property is located in an area with limited on-street parking, a garage or even a space on the property to park a vehicle can be of great value. In some instances when parking spaces are at a premium, on-site parking may even produce income for the property owner. In some areas, especially northern climates, enclosed garages are a necessity. In some southern states, a carport may be all that is needed.

Car storage structures can be classified according to construction type.

- An attached garage is a common construction type in many markets. It is a garage that is attached to one or more sides of the residence structure. The chief advantage of this type of garage is the lower construction cost owing to the common wall. In colder climates, the attached garage provides an insulation "air lock." It also provides a partially insulated-heated car storage area, which may help facilitate starting a car in the winter.
- Another common type of garage is the detached garage, which is separated from the house. This type of garage offers the advantage of fire safety. A vehicle fire that occurs in an attached garage can often spread to the residence to cause greater loss, whereas a detached garage is spaced at a safe distance from the house. A disadvantage of the detached garage is that it does not provide extra insulation for the house. Residents of homes with detached garages are also exposed to the elements because they must exit the house to get to the garage, which can be a disadvantage in some markets. In many markets, detached garages are unpopular choices in new construction.
- In some markets, properties have a common garage built into the residence. A built-in garage has living area on at least one side and above. This type of garage does not provide the safety of separation from the residence in the event of a fire, but it does provide an air lock for the residence and the garage should stay warmer in the winter months. It also permits the resident to walk directly from the garage into the residence, which is an advantage during inclement weather.
- A basement garage can also be found in some markets. These garages are similar to built-in garages, but they are an integral part of the basement. The cost of a basement and a basement garage are nearly the same and can be treated similarly. The most common problem discovered in appraisals of properties that feature basement garages is double counting the space in the cost and sales comparison approach. If the building has a basement garage and the appraiser measures and includes all the space in the basement area and then dedicates an amount to the garage, he or she is essentially counting the space twice. To avoid this mistake, it would be prudent to dedicate a portion of the basement area to the garage and consider the garage and basement as segregated space throughout the analysis. Basement garages can be unpopular in some markets because the resident must climb steps to get to the main part of the house.
- Carports and *porte cocheres* are open, roofed structures that provide the least amount of shelter for vehicles. They may be all that is needed in some markets and climates. However, in other areas and markets, they may be inadequate for most buyers who seek a warm enclosed place to store a vehicle.

Page **1** of 6

General Description	Fou
Units ☐ One ☐ One with Accessory Unit	☐ Concrete Slab
# of Stories	☐ Full Basement
Type ☐ Det. ☐ Att. ☐ S-Det./End Unit	Basement Area
☐ Existing ☐ Proposed ☐ Under Const.	Basement Finish
Design (Style)	☐ Outside Entry/E
Year Built	Evidence of ☐ In
Effective Age (Yrs)	☐ Dampness ☐
Attic ☐ None	Heating ☐ FWA ☐
☐ Drop Stair ☐ Stairs	☐ Other
☐ Floor ☐ Scuttle	Cooling ☐ Centr
☐ Finished ☐ Heated	☐ Individual

IMPROVEMENTS

Appliances ☐ Refrigerator ☐ Range/Oven ☐ Dishwasher ☐

Finished area **above** grade contains: Rooms

Additional features (special energy efficient items, etc.)

Describe the condition of the property (including needed repair

Are there any physical deficiencies or adverse conditions that a

Does the property generally conform to the neighborhood (func

Freddie Mac Form 70 March 2005

- In some areas, driveways may be the only available areas for parking. In some urban markets, the availability of an open space on the site for parking a car may be a significant asset, especially when on-street parking is scarce. Access to the site without the need to move another car is important. Sometimes brokers list a property as having four-car, on-site parking, but it can be misleading because the cars are stacked two deep and the front row cannot be moved without moving the second row.

Appliances

☐ Refrigerator ☐ Range/Oven ☐ Dishwasher

☐ Disposal ☐ Microwave ☐ Washer/Dryer

☐ Other (describe)

In the next section, the appraiser lists the appliances, which may include those that are built in and considered to be real estate as well as any personal property included in the appraisal. If the appliances are personal property, USPAP requires that the appraiser identify them and lenders generally want the appraiser to show their contributory value. Appliances are incidental in some properties, while in others they can add significantly to value. USPAP Standards Rule 1-2(e) states that when developing a real property appraisal, an appraiser must identify the characteristics of the property that are relevant to the type and definition of value and intended use of the appraisal, including any personal property, trade fixtures, or intangible items that are not real property but are included in the appraisal.[13]

Finished area *above* grade contains:

___ Rooms ___ Bedrooms _____Bath(s) _____ Square Feet of Gross Living Area Above Grade

Here, the appraiser indicates the room count and configuration as well as the amount of gross living area. To be considered living area, the floored area of a section of a residence must be finished, heated, and cooled commensurate with the main part of the residence as well as located above the grade level of the surrounding earth.

Gross living area is a term commonly used in residential properties. This measurement is nearly always made by measuring the outside walls of the dwelling with a tape measure. Any part of a floored area that is below the ground is almost always considered to be basement area. This rule causes much consternation in the real estate business when brokers, owners, and less technically oriented persons want finished basements considered as part of the GLA. In most markets, the basement area costs less to finish than the above-grade area (even if it is equal quality), and since most markets are driven by and limited by the cost of construction, the construction costs are a major factor. Some appraisers are under pressure to make their reports conform to a set of standard guidelines, so they are reluctant to adjust an adequate amount for basements. In this

13. *USPAP*, U-16.

way, they are undervaluing this feature of the home to stay within these guidelines.

In most markets and according to some lenders' guidelines, the finished floored above-grade area must have a ceiling height of at least seven feet for a space to be included in gross living area calculations. However, the following exceptions apply:

- An area situated under minimal obstructions, such as ceiling beams and HVAC duct work.
  In these areas, the minimum ceiling height must be between 6 and 6.5 feet.
- A stairwell that has a low ceiling because another staircase lies above it.
- A room with a sloped ceiling, in which case at least half of the finished area must have a ceiling height of at least seven feet.

Areas where the finished space has a ceiling height of less than five feet may not be included in living area. (In markets where the gross living area is set by the tax assessor's office, this standard is relaxed or modified.)

For most lenders, openings to the upper floors that expose the floor below cannot be included in the GLA for the second or third floors, with the exception of the staircases. This allows the appraiser to include the area around a center hall staircase but not to include the unfinished second- or third-floor areas for properties with cathedral or vaulted ceilings. Although this feature of a home cannot be figured into the GLA, it does not preclude the appraiser from adding value for it.

Garages and other unfinished or finished areas of lesser quality cannot be included in the GLA. GLA is always a finished area, and in most markets it is heated and cooled. Debates always occur about well-finished, enclosed porches or room extensions that the owner insists constitutes living area. If the area is well finished, heated, and cooled and the appraiser calls it a living area and adds value based on $50/sq. ft., or if the appraiser calls the area a porch but adds value at $50/sq. ft., it is still the same.

The analysis of the local market is very important. For example, a converted garage–even when well-finished–results in a lot of added square footage but may be excessive for a particular market and result in an overimprovement and less return. Also, the property loses the garage, which may penalize the property more than the added GLA.

Porches, patios, decks, and other like areas that are not enclosed cannot be included in the GLA unless they are suitable for year-round occupancy. It is important to not count this area twice. Some appraisers have been known to classify the enclosed porch as living area and then also add it to the porch line.

While it is important to be consistent with local practice, it is more important to be consistent with the data source from which the standards are derived. If the county assessor's records are the source of GLA for the comparable sales, for example, appraisers must adjust their figures to conform to that standard.

Page **1** of 6

IMPROVEMENTS

General Description		Fou
Units ☐ One ☐ One with Accessory Unit		☐ Concrete Slab
# of Stories		☐ Full Basement
Type ☐ Det. ☐ Att. ☐ S-Det/End Unit		Basement Area
☐ Existing ☐ Proposed ☐ Under Const.		Basement Finish
Design (Style)		☐ Outside Entry/
Year Built		Evidence of ☐ In
Effective Age (Yrs)		☐ Dampness ☐
Attic	☐ None	Heating ☐ FWA
☐ Drop Stair	☐ Stairs	☐ Other
☐ Floor	☐ Scuttle	Cooling ☐ Centr
☐ Finished	☐ Heated	☐ Individual

Appliances ☐Refrigerator ☐Range/Oven ☐Dishwasher ☐

Finished area **above** grade contains: Rooms

Additional features (special energy efficient items, etc.)

Describe the condition of the property (including needed repair

Are there any physical deficiencies or adverse conditions that a

Does the property generally conform to the neighborhood (fun

Freddie Mac Form 70 March 2005

Additional features (special energy efficient items, etc.)

Here, the appraiser lists any special features deemed appropriate, including interior finish items, exterior or site amenities not already listed, or possibly a more descriptive listing of some of the features included in the check boxes.

Describe the condition of the property (including needed repairs, deterioration, renovations, remodeling, etc.).

The form's short request to describe the condition of the property has huge consequences. It requires the appraiser to list all repairs needed and deferred maintenance as well as any recent updates or renovations to the property. If an appraiser chooses to describe the property as being in above-average condition, this section serves to support that assessment. Conversely, if the appraiser does not list any recent updates or problems, it implies that the subject is in average condition (compared to the other properties with which it competes). If the appraiser lists nothing here, it would be hard to believe that a property would be in above-average condition (good) or below-average condition (fair). Appraisal reviewers have been known to look at this line to see if the property condition listed on the report is suspect. If the appraiser says that the property is in better-than-average condition (good), there should be evidence of recent repairs made or updating of the property listed in this section.

A common challenge for appraisers is deciding whether to list deficiencies or needed repairs. In the case of mortgage appraisals, the underwriter will nearly always require that needed repairs listed by the appraiser be taken care of. This section of the form calls for the appraiser to list all needed repairs, deterioration, or remodeling. Most appraisers are guided by the intended use of the appraisal report when determining which repairs should be listed.

Fannie Mae addresses improvement condition in its single-family *Selling Guide*, Section B4-1.4-15, Appraisal Report Review: Property Condition of the Improvements:

> **Introduction**
> This topic contains information on property condition of the improvements.
>
> - Property Condition
> - Infestation, Dampness, or Settlement
> - As-Is Condition of the Subject Property
> - Physical Deficiencies That Affect Soundness, Structural Integrity, and Livability of the Subject Property
> - Property Condition Disclosure to Borrower
>
> **Property Condition**
> Lenders must take the necessary steps to ensure that a property meets Fannie Mae's condition requirements as outlined in this subsection.
>
> The following table provides the requirements for property condition.

✔ **Requirement**

☐ Based on the factual data of the improvement analysis, the appraisal report must express an opinion about the condition of the improvements.

☐ Appraisals based on interior and exterior inspections must include complete visual inspections of the accessible areas of the property.

Note: Appraisers are not responsible for hidden or unapparent conditions.

☐ Appraisal reports must reflect adverse conditions that were apparent during the inspection or discovered while performing research–such as, but not limited to, needed repairs, deterioration, or the presence of hazardous wastes, toxic substances, or adverse environmental conditions.

☐ Detrimental conditions of the improvements must be reported in the appraisal even if the conditions are typical for competing properties.

☐ The appraisal must consider and describe the overall quality and condition of the property.

☐ The appraisal must identify:

- Items that require immediate repair, and
- Items where maintenance may have been deferred, which may or may not require immediate repair.

The appraisal comments section must address needed repairs and physical, functional, or external inadequacies.

Infestation, Dampness, or Settlement

If the appraisal indicates evidence of wood-boring insects, dampness, or settlement, the appraisal must comment on the effect on the marketability and the value of the subject property.

The lender must either provide satisfactory evidence that the condition was corrected or submit a professionally prepared report, indicating–based on an inspection of the property–that the condition does not pose any threat of structural damage to the improvements.

As-Is Condition of the Subject Property

Fannie Mae permits appraisals to be based on the as-is condition of the property, provided existing conditions are minor and do not affect the livability, soundness, or structural integrity of the property, and the appraiser's opinion of value reflects the existence of these conditions.

Minor conditions and deferred maintenance are typically due to normal wear and tear from the aging process and the occupancy of the property.

Note: While such conditions generally do not rise to the level of a required repair, they must be reported.

Examples of minor conditions and deferred maintenance include worn floor finishes or carpet, minor plumbing leaks, holes in window screens, or cracked window glass.

Physical Deficiencies That Affect Soundness, Structural Integrity, and Livability of the Subject Property

The appraisal report must identify and describe physical deficiencies that could affect a property's soundness, structural integrity, or livability, or improvements that are incomplete. The property must be appraised subject to completion of the specific alterations or repairs.

If the appraiser is not qualified to evaluate the alterations or repairs needed, the appraisal must identify and describe the deficiencies and the property must be appraised subject to a satisfactory inspection by a qualified professional. The appraisal may have to be revised based upon the results of the inspection. If so, the report must indicate the impact, if any, on the final opinion of value. The lender must review the revised appraisal report to ensure that no physical deficiencies or conditions that would affect the livability, soundness, or structural integrity of the property are indicated. The lender must ensure that material conditions are repaired before loan delivery.

If a property has incomplete improvements, the alterations or repairs must be performed. The lender must obtain a completion report from an appraiser before loan delivery.

Property Condition Disclosure to Borrower

The lender must disclose all known property condition issues to the borrower so that the borrower may take necessary actions to address such issues.[14]

14. Fannie Mae, *Selling Guide*, 474-476.

Page 1 of 6

General Description	Fou
Units ☐ One ☐ One with Accessory Unit	☐ Concrete Slab
# of Stories	☐ Full Basement
Type ☐ Det. ☐ Att. ☐ S-Det./End Unit	Basement Area
☐ Existing ☐ Proposed ☐ Under Const.	Basement Finish
Design (Style)	☐ Outside Entry/
Year Built	Evidence of ☐
Effective Age (Yrs)	☐ Dampness ☐
Attic ☐ None	Heating ☐ FWA
☐ Drop Stair ☐ Stairs	☐ Other
☐ Floor ☐ Scuttle	Cooling ☐ Centr
☐ Finished ☐ Heated	☐ Individual

IMPROVEMENTS

Appliances ☐ Refrigerator ☐ Range/Oven ☐ Dishwasher ☐

Finished area above grade contains: Rooms

Additional features (special energy efficient items, etc.)

Describe the condition of the property (including needed repairs

Are there any physical deficiencies or adverse conditions that

Does the property generally conform to the neighborhood (func

Freddie Mac Form 70 March 2005

The Debate Over "Property Condition Ratings"

Rating the condition of the improvements is controversial for some appraisers. The issue in question is whether an appraiser should rate the quality and condition of the subject improvements in accordance with all housing in a geographic area (usually a city or town) or only the properties with which the subject competes. In the past, appraisers were asked to label all properties for condition and quality based on a comparison to the properties with which they competed. This practice was misunderstood and misused by many appraisers for many years.

In the 1993 revision of the URAR, Fannie Mae stated that it had removed the rating grids that used the classifications "good, average, fair, and poor" to promote "meaningful comments instead of marking 'relative' ratings." The rating grids for these terms on the URAR were removed as of that date, but it did not eliminate the need for appraisers to assess the condition of the subject using a rating classification for comparison purposes. Appraisers were still required to enter something on the sales comparison grid on the line for quality and condition of the subject as well as the comparable sales. The current 2005 URAR form omits the rating grids but still necessitates that the appraiser recognize the property's condition and then report it to the client in a meaningful way.

The words *quality* and *condition* are assumed to refer to the improvements, although they could also pertain to site improvements. To help appraisers understand the question, it is necessary to define the terms. A *quality and condition survey* is an analysis of the quality and condition of building components that distinguishes among deferred maintenance items (those in need of immediate repair), short-lived items (those that must be repaired or replaced in the future), and items that are expected to last for the remaining economic life of the building.[15] The *observed condition* is the condition of a property ascertained from an appropriate inspection.[16] An *improvement condition* (as defined by the author) is a rating that reflects the amount of wear and tear or diminished utility observed on an improvement or component of an improvement due to the passage of time, or a rating of the degree of wear and tear that an improvement has endured or the extent of its needed updates. This rating, when applied to a structure, compares it to properties that compete for the same buyer as the subject.

15. *Dictionary*, 227.
16. Ibid., 199.

Case in Point

The subject property is improved with an 80-year-old home located in a neighborhood that is improved with 70- to 90-year-old homes similar to the subject. This neighborhood is also considered to be the subject's market segment. The majority of the homes in the market sell at prices ranging from $125,000 to $150,000. The subject and many of the houses in the market have the following physical conditions:

- Roof shingles that are about 15 years old and will need to be replaced in 5 to 10 years.
- 18-year-old aluminum gutters that are dented and sag in one area. They are functional but may need respiking soon.
- An 11-year-old furnace that will need to be replaced in 10 to 15 years.
- A 21-year-old water heater that needs to be replaced now.
- Original windows that are 80 years old, do not open and close very well, and are fitted with storm windows on the outside.
- Interior and exterior doors that are original and functional but are dented, cracked, and have several layers of paint on them.
- Interior walls that are lathe and plaster coated and have cracks and bulges in many areas. Though not perfect, they are salable in this market. Also, some of the paint (probably lead-based) is chipped.
- Exterior walls that are wood slats nailed to the 2 x 4s have been painted numerous times. The paint (probably lead-based) is chipping.
- A wooden front porch that is structurally sound but has a broken lattice and sagging steps.
- Electrical wiring that was replaced throughout the house eight years ago when a new circuit breaker box was installed. A minimal number of electrical outlets are found in each room.
- Original plumbing lines with most fixtures having been replaced over the years.
- A kitchen and bathrooms that were remodeled 26 years ago with new cabinets, countertops, sinks, and toilets. The tub surrounds in the bathrooms were replaced five years ago.

Other older homes that are priced similarly to the subject and are located in the immediate area also have similar levels of maintenance. The competing properties do not exhibit the same problems, but they do exhibit deficiencies that are similar in the cost of repair.

If the appraiser compares this home to all homes in its geographic market, it will be rated as inferior to the competition, which includes newer and brand-new homes. However, if the appraiser compares the home to those with which it competes (older homes priced at $125,000 to $150,000), it would be rated as "average." The dilemma is that some lenders will not make a loan on a property if the appraiser rates it in fair or poor condition. This home is very typical in many markets, and for lenders to refuse to make a loan on the property because of the fair rating would be wrong. Most appraisers would compare the subject to the homes with which it competes and would rate it as being in average condition while listing the deficiencies and repairs needed. In this case, these would include replacing the water heater.

Page 1 of 6

General Description	Fo
Units ☐ One ☐ One with Accessory Unit	☐ Concrete Slab
# of Stories	☐ Full Basement
Type ☐ Det. ☐ Att. ☐ S-Det/End Unit	Basement Area
☐ Existing ☐ Proposed ☐ Under Const.	Basement Finish
Design (Style)	☐ Outside Entry
Year Built	Evidence of ☐
Effective Age (Yrs)	☐ Dampness ☐
Attic ☐ None	Heating ☐ FWA
☐ Drop Stair ☐ Stairs	☐ Other
☐ Floor ☐ Scuttle	Cooling ☐ Cent
☐ Finished ☐ Heated	☐ Individual

IMPROVEMENTS

Appliances ☐ Refrigerator ☐ Range/Oven ☐ Dishwasher ☐

Finished area **above** grade contains: Rooms

Additional features (special energy efficient items, etc.)

Describe the condition of the property (including needed repairs

Are there any physical deficiencies or adverse conditions that a

Does the property generally conform to the neighborhood (func

Freddie Mac Form 70 March 2005

If an appraiser accepts the notion that the condition rating means comparing a property to those with which it competes, the question arises as to what the appraiser is to do when appraising a recently completed "new" home. Many appraisers will rate the home as being in good condition. This would be an erroneous rating, considering that a new home cannot be rated as "above average" if it is compared to other newer homes. In such a situation, the appraiser's logic must prevail. The new home must also be rated as "average" as compared to the homes with which it competes, which are probably also new.

Are there any physical deficiencies or adverse conditions that affect the livability, soundness, or structural integrity of the property? ☐ Yes ☐ No If Yes, describe

The open check boxes at the second-to-last part of page 1 require the appraiser to describe how the previously-listed problems or instances of deferred maintenance affect the subject's livability, soundness, or structural integrity. This requires the appraiser to indicate whether the previously-noted items are significant to the property value or utility. If an appraiser checks "no" when repairs are noted, this will increase liability for the appraiser while possibly allowing the lender to ignore the repair for the purposes of underwriting the loan. Appraisers should consider the implications of this section of the form from a liability standpoint.

Does the property generally conform to the neighborhood (functional utility, style, condition, use, construction, etc.)? ☐ Yes ☐ No If No, describe

The last part of page 1 requires the appraiser to report whether the subject conforms to its environment. If some problem exists, it would necessitate an absolute "Yes" or "No" answer and some explanation. More comment will be required if the answer is "No" than if the answer is "Yes." This could pose a difficult question if the property does not conform to the neighborhood, has numerous functional problems, or is in less-than-average condition. If the property is nonconforming for any of these reasons, the appraiser must explain why and analyze the impact on value due to the lack of conformity. Repossessed properties, properties with unusual designs, and properties with lesser or superior-quality construction commonly warrant a "no" answer. This question may be quite perplexing to an appraiser if the subject is atypical.

Improvements Section of Form 2055

IMPROVEMENTS

Source(s) Used for Physical Characteristics of Property ☐ Appraisal Files ☐ MLS ☐ Assessment and Tax Records ☐ Prior Inspection ☐ Property Owner
☐ Other (describe) Data Source(s) for Gross Living Area

General Description	General Description	Heating / Cooling	Amenities	Car Storage
Units ☐One ☐One with Accessory Unit	☐Concrete Slab ☐ Crawl Space	☐ FWA ☐ HWBB	☐ Fireplace(s) #	☐ None
# of Stories	☐Full Basement ☐ Finished	☐ Radiant	☐ Woodstove(s) #	☐ Driveway # of Cars
Type ☐Det. ☐Att. ☐S-Det./End Unit	☐Partial Basement ☐Finished	☐ Other	☐ Patio/Deck	Driveway Surface
☐Existing ☐ Proposed ☐ Under Const.	Exterior Walls	Fuel	☐ Porch	☐ Garage # of Cars
Design (Style)	Roof Surface	☐ Central Air Conditioning	☐ Pool	☐ Carport # of Cars
Year Built	Gutters & Downspouts	☐ Individual	☐ Fence	☐ Attached ☐ Detached
Effective Age (Yrs)	Window Type	☐ Other	☐ Other	☐Built-in

Appliances ☐Refrigerator ☐Range/Oven ☐Dishwasher ☐Disposal ☐Microwave ☐Washer/Dryer ☐Other (describe)

Finished area **above** grade contains: Rooms Bedrooms Bath(s) Square Feet of Gross Living Area Above Grade

Additional features (special energy efficient items, etc.)

Describe the condition of the property and data source(s) (including apparent needed repairs, deterioration, renovations, remodeling, etc.).

Are there any apparent physical deficiencies or adverse conditions that affect the livability, soundness, or structural integrity of the property? ☐ Yes ☐ No
If Yes, describe

Does the property generally conform to the neighborhood (functional utility, style, condition, use, construction, etc.)? ☐ Yes ☐ No If No, describe

The following discussion addresses only those sections of the improvements section of Form 2055 that are different from the URAR or that require a different response.

Source(s) Used for Physical Characteristics of Property

☐ Appraisal Files ☐ MLS ☐ Assessment and Tax Records

☐ Prior Inspection ☐ Property Owner

☐ Other (describe)

Data Source(s) for Gross Living Area

The appraiser is asked to indicate the source of the improvement information on the subject property. The response substantiates the reliability of the description of improvements. This differs from the URAR form, which assumes that data about the subject has been obtained from a complete inspection of the subject. The size of the residence can be obtained from a different source. It is common for appraisers to obtain as much data as they can about the subject from the limited exterior inspection and/or an old entry from the MLS and then use the county assessor's or auditor's records to get information about its size. In the case of exterior-only inspections, it is important for appraisers to have a consistent source of data for the subject and comparables.

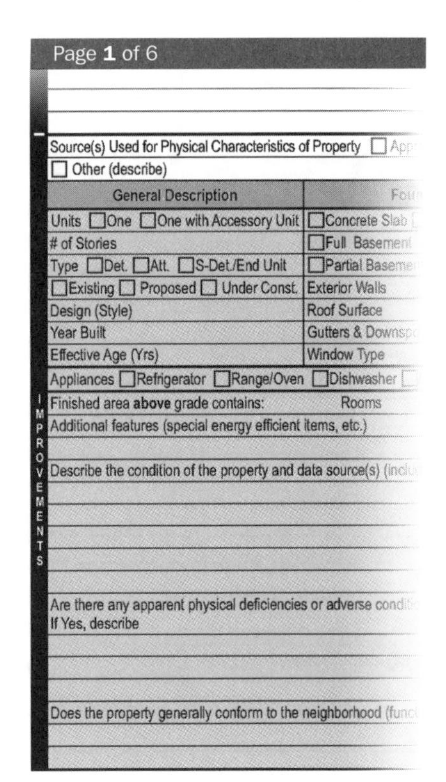

Page **1** of 6

IMPROVEMENTS

Source(s) Used for Physical Characteristics of Property ☐

☐ Other (describe)

General Description	
Units ☐One ☐One with Accessory Unit	☐Concrete Slab
# of Stories	☐Full Basement
Type ☐Det. ☐Att. ☐S-Det./End Unit	☐Partial Basement
☐Existing ☐ Proposed ☐ Under Const.	Exterior Walls
Design (Style)	Roof Surface
Year Built	Gutters & Downspouts
Effective Age (Yrs)	Window Type

Appliances ☐Refrigerator ☐Range/Oven ☐Dishwasher ☐

Finished area **above** grade contains: Rooms

Additional features (special energy efficient items, etc.)

Describe the condition of the property and data source(s)

Are there any apparent physical deficiencies or adverse conditions

If Yes, describe

Does the property generally conform to the neighborhood

General Description

The general description section of Form 2055 is similar to the URAR except in the following aspects:

- The percentage of basement finishing is difficult to estimate, so the form asks only whether the basement is finished or not.
- The outside entry, sump pump, evidence of infestation, and dampness or settlement are all aspects that are hard to ascertain in an exterior-only inspection, so these features have been removed.
- The composition of the foundation walls cannot be known from an exterior-only inspection appraisal, so this feature has been removed.
- The interior finish is not generally known to an appraiser who performs an exterior-only inspection, so it has been omitted.

Appliances

Although the appliances are listed on both forms, an exterior-only inspection cannot establish whether appliances are built in or removable. An appraiser could include personal property on this part of the form, but USPAP would require some additional discussion.

Describe the condition of the property and data source(s) (including apparent needed repairs, deterioration, renovations, remodeling, etc.).

Note the addition of the words “data sources” and “apparent,” which appear here in Form 2055 but not the URAR.

Are there any apparent physical deficiencies or adverse conditions that affect the livability, soundness, or structural integrity of the property?

☐ Yes ☐ No If Yes, describe

The addition of the word *apparent* to the question tailors it to an exterior-only inspection appraisal report. It is difficult to determine if any physical deficiencies or adverse conditions affect the property’s livability, soundness, or structural integrity from 50 feet away from the improvement. In this exterior-only appraisal report, the word *apparent* implies that the appraiser can comment only on the items that are visible from a distance.

Fannie Mae discusses the improvements section of the appraisal report in depth in their 2009 single-family *Selling Guide*, available on their Web Site at *www.efanniemae.com*. Sections B4-1.4-10 through B4-1.4-15 are applicable.

To access the guide, type "Selling Guide" in the search box that appears in the top right corner of the home page. The *Selling Guide* can also be accessed by first clicking on "Appraisers" under the "Industry Specialists" heading. Next, click on "Single-Family Guides for free online" under the heading "AllRegs Online." A list of documents will then appear. If pop-ups are blocked, click on "View Support Tips and AllRegs Contact Info" under the "AllRegs Online" heading to access directions for changing the browser settings to allow pop-ups.

Uniform Residential Appraisal Report

File #

SALES COMPARISON APPROACH

There are comparable properties currently offered for sale in the subject neighborhood ranging in price from $ to $.

There are comparable sales in the subject neighborhood within the past twelve months ranging in sale price from $ to $.

FEATURE	SUBJECT	COMPARABLE SALE # 1		COMPARABLE SALE # 2		COMPARABLE SALE # 3	
Address							
Proximity to Subject							
Sale Price	$		$		$		$
Sale Price/Gross Liv. Area	$ sq. ft.	$ sq. ft.		$ sq. ft.		$ sq. ft.	
Data Source(s)							
Verification Source(s)							
VALUE ADJUSTMENTS	DESCRIPTION	DESCRIPTION	+(-) $ Adjustment	DESCRIPTION	+(-) $ Adjustment	DESCRIPTION	+(-) $ Adjustment
Sale or Financing Concessions							
Date of Sale/Time							
Location							
Leasehold/Fee Simple							
Site							
View							
Design (Style)							
Quality of Construction							
Actual Age							
Condition							
Above Grade	Total Bdrms. Baths	Total Bdrms. Baths		Total Bdrms. Baths		Total Bdrms. Baths	
Room Count							
Gross Living Area	sq. ft.	sq. ft.		sq. ft.		sq. ft.	
Basement & Finished Rooms Below Grade							
Functional Utility							
Heating/Cooling							
Energy Efficient Items							
Garage/Carport							
Porch/Patio/Deck							
Net Adjustment (Total)		☐ + ☐ -	$	☐ + ☐ -	$	☐ + ☐ -	$
Adjusted Sale Price of Comparables		Net Adj. % Gross Adj. %	$	Net Adj. % Gross Adj. %	$	Net Adj. % Gross Adj. %	$

I ☐ did ☐ did not research the sale or transfer history of the subject property and comparable sales. If not, explain

My research ☐ did ☐ did not reveal any prior sales or transfers of the subject property for the three years prior to the effective date of this appraisal.

Data source(s)

My research ☐ did ☐ did not reveal any prior sales or transfers of the comparable sales for the year prior to the date of sale of the comparable sale.

Data source(s)

Report the results of the research and analysis of the prior sale or transfer history of the subject property and comparable sales (report additional prior sales on page 3).

ITEM	SUBJECT	COMPARABLE SALE # 1	COMPARABLE SALE # 2	COMPARABLE SALE # 3
Date of Prior Sale/Transfer				
Price of Prior Sale/Transfer				
Data Source(s)				
Effective Date of Data Source(s)				

Analysis of prior sale or transfer history of the subject property and comparable sales

Summary of Sales Comparison Approach

Indicated Value by Sales Comparison Approach $

RECONCILIATION

Indicated Value by: Sales Comparison Approach $ Cost Approach (if developed) $ Income Approach (if developed) $

This appraisal is made ☐ "as is", ☐ subject to completion per plans and specifications on the basis of a hypothetical condition that the improvements have been completed, ☐ subject to the following repairs or alterations on the basis of a hypothetical condition that the repairs or alterations have been completed, or ☐ subject to the following required inspection based on the extraordinary assumption that the condition or deficiency does not require alteration or repair:

Based on a complete visual inspection of the interior and exterior areas of the subject property, defined scope of work, statement of assumptions and limiting conditions, and appraiser's certification, my (our) opinion of the market value, as defined, of the real property that is the subject of this report is $, as of , which is the date of inspection and the effective date of this appraisal.

Freddie Mac Form 70 March 2005 Page 2 of 6 Fannie Mae Form 1004 March 2005

Sales Comparison Approach and Reconciliation

The sales comparison sections of the URAR and Form 2055 are the same and will be discussed together.

Sales Comparison Approach Section: Supply and Demand Analysis

There are	comparable properties currently offered for sale in the subject neighborhood ranging in price from $	to $	.
There are	comparable sales in the subject neighborhood within the past twelve months ranging in sale price from $	to $	.

There are ___ comparable properties currently offered for sale in the subject neighborhood ranging in price from $_____ to $______.

There are ___ comparable sales in the subject neighborhood within the past twelve months ranging in sale price from $_____ to $______.

The first section of page 2 of the URAR and Form 2055 allots space for reporting the current supply and demand analysis of the subject's neighborhood/market, considering only those properties that compete with the subject. This gives the appraiser and client an indication of the supply and demand factors that exist in the subject's market and influence value as of the date of the report. It does not ask for a forecast of future supply and demand but requests data on the current state of the market only.

In analyzing supply and demand, the appraisal industry follows the lead of many other industries that compare inventory to the annual sales rate. The first step in the analysis is to define the market, which is accomplished by defining the potential buyer of the subject property. After a potential buyer is defined, the appraiser determines the significant attributes of the property for the subject's market. After the most significant attributes for the subject are established, the appraiser can search the database to determine the supply of homes on the market and the annual rate of sales for the last 12 months. This exercise is very similar to the work that must be done to complete the Market Conditions Form, which will be discussed in the last section of this book. Exhibit 9 provides an example of how this task could be accomplished in most markets.

Exhibit 9 shows a 12-month supply of homes on the market. This number is based on a comparison of the historical sales rate and the current number of listings extracted from the market using the same criteria for listings and sales, which would indicate an oversupply in most markets. This search does not take into account builder sales

Exhibit 9. MLS Grid for Researching Market Supply and Demand

Item	Subject Attributes	Search Criteria	Rationale
Location	Union Township	Union Township	Locational search criteria may represent the taxing district, school system, or other factors
Zip code	12345	12345	Further delineates the location
Year built	1995	1990–2000	Brackets the subject and eliminates noncomparable properties
Design	2-story	2-story	Delineates the market more
Living area	2,236 sq. ft.	2,000 to 2,500 sq. ft.	Delineates the market to ensure that only comparable properties are counted
Basement	No	No	Eliminates noncompetitive properties
Garage	3-car, attached	3-car, attached	Eliminates noncompetitive properties
Attachment	Detached	Detached	Eliminates noncompetitive properties
Bedrooms	4	3-5	Eliminates noncompetitive properties

Results:

Active listings (current): 12

Closed sales (0-12 months ago): 12

Pending sales (current): 4

Ratio: 1 sale per month

Inventory: 12-month supply

and "for sale by owners" (FSBOs), but it errs on both sides in that listings and sales are ignored. As a result, the ratios would not be affected much in most markets.

This supply and demand analysis is not a tool that appraisers can use without knowledge of other comparison data. For example, unless appraisers perform this analysis often enough to know that a 12-month supply is standard or signals a downturn in the market, they can get the wrong impression. However, supply and demand analysis is a great tool for appraisers who need to be informed of their market's activity if they hone their skills by using it frequently.

Some MLS computer programs can retrieve additional data, such as the average sale price in the price range, number of days on the market (DOM), home size, and list-price-to-sale-price ratio. Supply and demand analysis is not easy in markets without an MLS. Some MLS systems require two searches: one for listings and one for sales. The analysis required for this part of the form is very similar to the required analysis for the Market Conditions Form, which will be discussed at the end of this book. The main difference is that the Market Conditions Form asks for comparable sales within three- and six-month windows rather than for an entire year, as is the case here.

Sales Comparison Process, Logic, and Purpose

The sales comparison approach to market value is an analysis of historical sales or current listings of similar properties and may include analysis of prior sales or listings of the subject. The approach is based on the assumption that an opinion of value can be developed based on the logic of comparison of the subject with recently sold or currently listed similar properties. For example, if a comparable property sells for $X and is slightly superior to the subject, the subject property should be worth a little less than the comparable. Conversely, if a comparable property sells for $X and is slightly inferior to the subject, the subject property should be worth a little more than the comparable. This logic is easily understood by the public, investors, and appraisers alike.

Adjustment grid analysis using comparable sales and listings relies on historical sales and current listings of similar properties to support an estimate of value. To use this approach, three or more properties that are identical to the subject in every way must be found. Otherwise, adjustments are needed. The sales dates for these comparable properties should be as close as possible to the effective date of the appraisal and the conditions of sale should meet all the requirements listed in the definition of market value. Based on the sale prices of these identical properties, it can be inferred that the subject would also sell for a similar price.

The process of developing an opinion of market value using the sales comparison approach becomes more complicated if identical comparable sales are not found. For this reason, an adjustment process has evolved to overcome this deficiency. In this process, nonidentical sales are "made comparable" by making monetary adjustments to the sale prices of the comparables to compensate for the physical or financial differences between the subject and the comparables. Of course, an appraiser who uses comparable listings (in addition to closed sales) is analyzing the current competition, which still provides good answers. However, this data must be tempered by the fact that the property is unsold. Listings usually do not sell for more than the list price, but they can and often do sell for less. As a result, current listings do not suggest to the appraiser what the subject is worth, but they can (after adjustment) suggest what it is *not* worth.

One significant advantage of using comparable listings is the accuracy with which they can be reported to the database. Obtaining accurate sale prices of comparable sales is difficult in some markets because some brokers enter the prices in the database and exaggerate them to prevent appraisal problems later. These brokers almost never exaggerate the list price because it only increases the difficulty of selling the subject. Pricing a listing is an important part of any real estate marketing effort. List prices are almost always correctly listed by the brokers, although sale prices are sometimes wrong.

Analyzing current listings is almost always a good idea in market value appraisals because these listings are the options available to potential buyers. It is assumed that the comparable sales were the best buys on the market at the time of their sale. However, listings represent the market better than historical sales. The problem with listings is that they may be overpriced and never sell for the amount asked.

The appraiser can also look at prior sales or listings of the subject property. This analysis can be done if the subject has been on the market recently and the appraiser can compensate for changes in the market and/or the property. Analysis of sales and current listings of the subject is a requirement for almost all appraisals. When undertaking this task, the appraiser should consider the following:

- Sales concessions included in the initial sale
- Motivations of the buyers and sellers in the initial sale
- Changes in the property due to recent upgrades or needed repairs
- Changes in the age of the improvement
- Market value trends that may be easy or nearly impossible to track

Exhibit 10 illustrates the sales comparison process.

Exhibit 10. The Sales Comparison Process

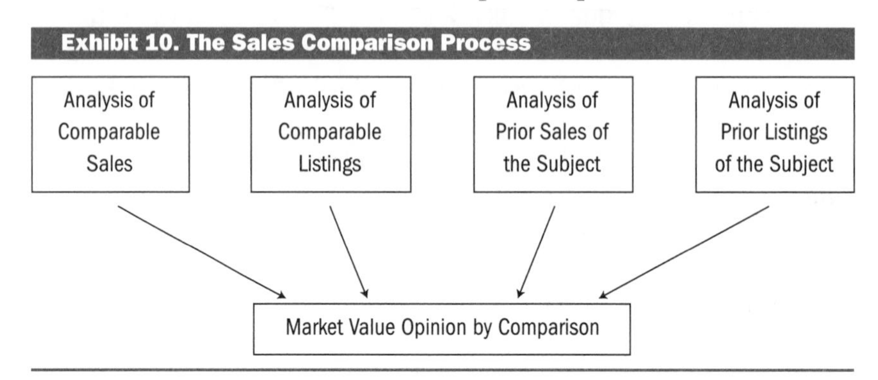

Logic

If a comparable sale has a feature that is superior to the subject, it is assumed that it should have sold for more because of it. Subtracting a dollar amount from the comparable's price to reflect that difference makes the subject and comparable similar. Most appraisers do not struggle with recognizing the need for adjustment but do struggle with figuring out how much to adjust for.

Adjustments made on a dollar basis seem to make sense for residential property appraisals for which the data is usually much better than nonresidential properties. While such dollar-based adjustments are made on residential appraisals, the data may be so poor for some commercial or farm appraisals that only an analysis based on a percentage of value, price per acre, or price per square foot makes sense. This is why most residential appraisals are based on the gross price and not the price per square foot as is the case with office buildings, retail centers, and industrial buildings. In agricultural markets, nearly all properties are analyzed based on a price per acre because the data might include a 75-acre sale and a 500-acre sale in the same data set. It is very difficult to adjust on a gross basis with such diverse data.

Fannie Mae's single-family *Selling Guide* provides the following applicable comments in section B4-1.4-16, Appraisal Report Review: Sales Comparison Approach:

> **Introduction**
> This topic contains information on the sales comparison approach to value.
>
> - Three-Year Prior Sales History
> - Sources of Comparable Market Data
> - General Requirements

- Rural Properties
- Properties in Established Subdivisions, Condos, or PUDs
- Properties in New or Recently Converted Subdivisions, Condos, or PUDs

Three-Year Prior Sales History

The Uniform Standards of Professional Appraisal Practice (USPAP) require appraisers to report a minimum three-year prior sales history for the subject property.

The appraiser must comply with the minimum requirements of USPAP.

Sources of Comparable Market Data

Data and/or verification source(s) for each comparable sale must be reported on the appraisal report form.

Single or multiple sources for data and verifications are acceptable provided they adequately verify the comparable sales.

When comparable sales data is provided by parties that have a financial interest in either the sale or financing of the subject property, the data must be reverified with a party that does not have a financial interest in the subject transaction.

General Requirements

The table below provides general requirements for selecting comparable sales.

✔	Requirement
☐	Influences that may affect value based on market evidence–such as closed sales, contract sales, and offerings or listings of the most comparable properties for sale in the market area, market studies, etc.–must be researched, analyzed, and considered in the appraisal report.
☐	A minimum of three comparable sales must be reported as part of the sales comparison approach to value. More than three comparable sales may be submitted to support the opinion of market value provided at least three are actual settled or closed sales.
☐	Properties that are not truly comparable to the subject property or are in competing neighborhoods are acceptable as comparable sales provided the reason for the use of these sales as comparables is adequately documented and explained. The appraisal must include a discussion of how a competing neighborhood is comparable to the subject neighborhood. **Note:** In some situations, sales of properties that are not truly comparable or sales of properties that are located in competing neighborhoods may simply be the best comparables available and the most appropriate for the appraisal analysis.
☐	Comparable sales that have been settled or closed within the last 12 months should be used in the appraisal. Older comparable sales that are the best indicator of value for the subject property can be used if appropriate. Comparable sales that are more than six months old must be accompanied by an appraiser explanation for use. For example, if the subject property is located in a rural area that has minimal sales activity, the appraiser may not be able to locate three truly comparable sales that sold in the last 12 months. In this case, the appraiser may use older comparable sales as long as he or she explains why they are being used.
☐	The subject property can be used as a fourth comparable sale or as supporting data if it was previously sold and closed or settled.
☐	Contract offerings and current listings can be used as supporting data if appropriate.

Rural Properties

Rural properties often have large lot sizes and rural locations can be relatively undeveloped; therefore, there may be a shortage (or absence) of recent truly comparable sales in the immediate vicinity of a subject property that is in a rural location.

Comparable sales located a considerable distance from the subject property can be used if they represent the best indicator of value for the subject property.

The appraisal must include an explanation of why the particular comparables were selected.

Properties in Established Subdivisions, Condos, or PUDs

Comparable sales from within the same subdivision or project as the subject property must be used if the subdivision or project has resale activity.

Resale activity from within the subdivision or project is the best indicator of value for properties in that subdivision or project.

Note: Use of comparable properties located outside of the established subject neighborhood must be explained in the appraisal analysis.

Properties in New or Recently Converted Subdivisions, Condos, or PUDs
The subject property must be compared to other properties in its general market area as well as to properties within the subject subdivision or project.

The appraiser must select one comparable sale from the subject subdivision or project and one comparable sale from outside the subject subdivision or project. The third comparable sale can be from inside or outside of the subject subdivision or project, provided it is a good indicator of value for the subject property.

Note: Sales or resales from within the subject subdivision or project are preferable to sales from outside the subdivision or project provided the developer or builder of the subject property is not involved in the transactions.[1]

It appears that Fannie Mae is suggesting that the use of comparable listings and pending sales is acceptable but not as a substitute for the minimum of three closed sales (see next section). Comparable listings and pending sales should not replace comparable sales, but they are preferred in markets where closed sales are scarce or dissimilar to the subject.

Case in Point

Exhibit 11 shows an example of an adjustment grid for a single-unit home. The grid uses a series of dollar adjustments, however

- The date of sale/time adjustment is based on a percentage of the sale price.
- The site/view adjustments are also based on a percentage of the sale price.
- Other adjustments are based on a flat dollar amount or ratio that runs across the grid.

In other words, the date of sale and site/view adjustments are based on percentages of the gross sale price, but the adjustment for differences in GLA is based on a flat rate of $37 per square foot, regardless of the sale price. These percentage adjustments are not incorrect, they just differ from the way that many appraisers make adjustments. Using a ratio instead of a lump sum can have advantages and disadvantages but is usually accurate based on extraction and application methods. If the appraiser extracts the data on a percentage basis and applies it on a percentage basis, the analysis is logical. However, if the data is extracted on a percentage basis and applied a different way, it is illogical.

1. Fannie Mae, *Selling Guide* (single-family) (April 1, 2009), 476-479. Available at *www.efanniemae.com*. Direct link: *https://www.efanniemae.com/sf/guides/ssg/sg/pdf/sg0309.pdf*.

Exhibit 11. Adjustments for Three Comparables in Smallburg

<table>
<tr><th></th><th>Adjustment Rate</th><th>Subject</th><th>Comparable</th><th>1</th><th>Comparable</th><th>2</th><th>Comparable</th><th>3</th></tr>
<tr><td>Address</td><td></td><td>622 Lake Blvd.
Smallville</td><td>666 Johnson Road
Smallville</td><td></td><td>569 Lakeview Road
Smallville</td><td></td><td>987 Beech Road
Smallville</td><td></td></tr>
<tr><td>Proximity to subject</td><td></td><td>Windlake</td><td>Same platted addition</td><td></td><td>Same platted addition</td><td></td><td>Same platted addition</td><td></td></tr>
<tr><td>Sale price</td><td></td><td></td><td></td><td>$299,000</td><td></td><td>$290,000</td><td></td><td>$286,000</td></tr>
<tr><td>Sale price/gross liv. area</td><td></td><td></td><td></td><td>$ 99.67</td><td></td><td>$ 95.84</td><td></td><td>$ 96.95</td></tr>
<tr><td>Data source(s)</td><td></td><td>Inspection</td><td>MLS 338324</td><td></td><td>MLS 339249</td><td></td><td>MLS 339223</td><td></td></tr>
<tr><td>Verification source(s)</td><td></td><td></td><td>Confirmed with deed record</td><td></td><td>Confirmed with deed record</td><td></td><td>Confirmed with deed record</td><td></td></tr>
<tr><td>Value Adjustments</td><td></td><td>Description</td><td>Description</td><td>+(−) $ Adj.</td><td>Description</td><td>+(−) $ Adj.</td><td>Description</td><td>+(−) $ Adj.</td></tr>
<tr><td>Sales or financing concessions</td><td></td><td></td><td>New mortgage no concessions</td><td>–</td><td>New mortgage no concessions</td><td>–</td><td>New mortgage no concessions</td><td>–</td></tr>
<tr><td>Date of sale/time (months)</td><td>3.0%</td><td></td><td>3 months ago</td><td>2,200</td><td>5 months ago</td><td>3,600</td><td>4 months ago</td><td>2,900</td></tr>
<tr><td>Location</td><td></td><td>Windlake</td><td>Windlake</td><td>–</td><td>Windlake</td><td>–</td><td>Windlake</td><td>–</td></tr>
<tr><td>Leasehold/fee simple</td><td></td><td>Fee simple</td><td>Fee simple</td><td>–</td><td>Fee simple</td><td>–</td><td>Fee simple</td><td>–</td></tr>
<tr><td>Site</td><td></td><td>90 x 137</td><td>90 x 170</td><td>(3,000)</td><td>128 x 146</td><td>(5,800)</td><td>155 x 140</td><td>(5,700)</td></tr>
<tr><td>View</td><td></td><td>Lake front</td><td>Lake front</td><td>–</td><td>Lake front</td><td>–</td><td>Lake front</td><td>–</td></tr>
<tr><td>Design (style)</td><td></td><td>1-story/ranch</td><td>1-story/ranch</td><td>–</td><td>1-story/ranch</td><td>–</td><td>1-story/ranch</td><td>–</td></tr>
<tr><td>Quality of construction</td><td></td><td>Brick/frame/avg.</td><td>Brick/frame/avg.</td><td>–</td><td>Brick/frame/avg.</td><td>–</td><td>Brick/frame/avg.</td><td>–</td></tr>
<tr><td>Actual age</td><td>$ 2,500</td><td>5 years</td><td>7 years</td><td>5,000</td><td>7 years</td><td>5,000</td><td>2 years</td><td>(7,500)</td></tr>
<tr><td>Condition</td><td></td><td>Average</td><td>Average</td><td>–</td><td>Average</td><td>–</td><td>Average</td><td>–</td></tr>
<tr><td>Above grade room count</td><td></td><td>Total | Bdrms. | Baths
10 | 4 | 3.5</td><td>Total | Bdrms. | Baths
12 | 4 | 3.5</td><td>–</td><td>Total | Bdrms. | Baths
9 | 4 | 3.5</td><td>–</td><td>Total | Bdrms. | Baths
9 | 4 | 3.5</td><td>–</td></tr>
<tr><td>Gross living area</td><td>$ 37</td><td>3,504</td><td>3,000</td><td>18,600</td><td>3,026</td><td>17,700</td><td>2,950</td><td>20,500</td></tr>
<tr><td>Basement & finished</td><td>$ 15</td><td>654</td><td>1,127</td><td>(7,100)</td><td>1,706</td><td>(15,800)</td><td>900</td><td>(3,700)</td></tr>
<tr><td>rooms below grade</td><td>$ 10</td><td>0</td><td>800</td><td>(8,000)</td><td>1,200</td><td>(12,000)</td><td>600</td><td>(6,000)</td></tr>
<tr><td>Functional utility</td><td></td><td>Average</td><td>Average</td><td>–</td><td>Average</td><td>–</td><td>Average</td><td>–</td></tr>
<tr><td>Energy-efficient items</td><td></td><td>Standard</td><td>Equal</td><td>–</td><td>Equal</td><td>–</td><td>Equal</td><td>–</td></tr>
<tr><td>Heating and cooling</td><td></td><td>GFA/cent. AC</td><td>GFA/cent. AC</td><td>–</td><td>GFA/cent. AC</td><td>–</td><td>GFA/cent. AC</td><td>–</td></tr>
<tr><td>Garage/carport</td><td></td><td>3-car/att./gar.</td><td>3-car/att./gar.</td><td>–</td><td>3-car/att./gar.</td><td>–</td><td>3-car/att./gar.</td><td>–</td></tr>
<tr><td>Porches, patios, etc.</td><td></td><td>Scr. porch</td><td>Deck</td><td>5,000</td><td>Deck</td><td>5,000</td><td>Scr. porch</td><td>–</td></tr>
<tr><td>Other</td><td></td><td>1 fireplace</td><td>1 fireplace</td><td>–</td><td>1 fireplace</td><td>–</td><td>1 fireplace</td><td>–</td></tr>
<tr><td></td><td></td><td>None</td><td>In-ground pool</td><td>(25,000)</td><td>None</td><td>–</td><td>None</td><td>–</td></tr>
<tr><td>Net adjustment</td><td></td><td></td><td></td><td>(12,300)</td><td></td><td>(2,300)</td><td></td><td>500</td></tr>
<tr><td>Adjusted sale price of comparable</td><td></td><td></td><td></td><td>$286,700</td><td></td><td>$287,700</td><td></td><td>$286,500</td></tr>
</table>

When choosing comparable sales to present in the report, it is important to remember that appraisers also sign a statement to certify the results. These statements appear on pages 5 and 6 of both the URAR and Form 2055. Reviewers of the appraisal report should pay particular attention to the following statements, which appear on both of the forms:

> 6. I researched, verified, analyzed, and reported on the prior sales of the comparable sales for a minimum of one year prior to the date of sale of the comparable sale, unless otherwise indicated in this report.
>
> 7. I selected and used comparable sales that are locationally, physically, and functionally the most similar to the subject property.
>
> 8. I have not used comparable sales that were the result of combining a land sale with the contract purchase price of a home that has been built or will be built on the land.
>
> 9. I have reported adjustments to the comparable sales that reflect the market's reaction to the differences between the subject property and the comparable sales.
>
> 10. I verified, from a disinterested source, all information in this report that was provided by parties who have a financial interest in the sale or financing of the subject property.

How significant are these statements? They may not be very significant to an appraiser who gets the market value opinion correct, who does not mislead the client, and whose report results in a satisfied client and intended user. If the clients are not satisfied, however, the statements of certification could become significant in any litigation against the appraiser.

What Is a Comparable?

Are all closed sales and current listings as well as all prior market activity of the subject indications of market value? The answer is clearly no, but this raises the issue of what constitutes a valid comparable to be used in a market value appraisal. To address this, keep in mind that the final opinion of value in a market value appraisal is supposed to be the amount of U.S. dollars that the property would bring if it were exposed to the market immediately before the effective date of appraisal (see the discussion of exposure time in USPAP Standards Rule 1-2(c)). Other conditions that must be met are listed in *The Dictionary of Real Estate Appraisal*'s definition of *market value*. Effectively, the main question that the appraiser should ask is, "What would the seller be able to get for a sale price if the property was for sale now?" In other words, "If there was a 'For Sale' sign in the front yard of the subject property, what would a buyer pay for it?" To that end, the appraiser should be looking for clues as to how the market will react to the property. Some common clues are comparable sales, comparable listings, or prior listings or sales of the subject.

Line-by-Line Discussion

To help appraisers understand the most complicated part of the appraisal process, a line-by-line discussion of the grid follows. This part of the form can be completed in many different ways; the following discussion shows only one way to do it. Appraisers may have different and better ways of completing these forms that are equally correct.

Sales Comparison Approach Section: Sales Comparison Grid Identification Data

FEATURE	SUBJECT	COMPARABLE SALE # 1		COMPARABLE SALE # 2		COMPARABLE SALE # 3	
Address							
Proximity to Subject							
Sale Price	$		$		$		$
Sale Price/Gross Liv. Area	$ sq. ft.	$ sq. ft.		$ sq. ft.		$ sq. ft.	
Data Source(s)							
Verification Source(s)							

Address

For nearly all residential assignments, the address section of the sales comparison grid includes sufficient detail to locate the comparable sale properties. The legal description establishes the exact location and lot size of each comparable, but the address is usually sufficient for this purpose. The appraiser should take care to get the address correct. If it is wrong, a review appraiser may not be able to find the comparable and may think the data was created and not reported. To eliminate the problem of review appraisers not being able to find the comparable sales, many appraisers also list the MLS numbers or other identifying numbers.

Proximity to Subject

The second line of the sales comparison grid indicates the distance of the comparable sales from the subject property. For many lenders, the maximum distance between the comparable sales and the subject property is one mile, unless the appraiser is able to make a good case for why closer comparables were not available. If the subject is located in an urban area, it may be difficult to convince a skeptical underwriter that closer sales were not available. Appraisers should remember that the subject location map could indicate the type of neighborhood in which the subject is located. If an appraiser reports that the subject is located in a low-population area but the location map shows high-density streets, the underwriter's or client's questioning of the lack of proximate sales would be well founded. If, on the other hand, the map shows a low-density area of only one street per mile, it would be an excellent indication of why the comparable sales were not closer. Appraisers' exhibits often show conflicting information, which causes problems. Mortgage underwriters can now use computer mapping programs to determine the density of the area surrounding the subject.

Most appraisers know that sales that are not comparable are often located within one mile of the subject. Conversely, other sales located more than a mile away may be most comparable to the subject. Lenders and investors tend to look at the one-mile line as a signal of a possible problem, so additional consideration on the appraiser's part is needed. Some lenders use software to evaluate sales and listing data in every neighborhood in the United States, which enables them to determine if better comparable sales are available.

Page 2 of 6

There are comparable properties currently offered for s

There are comparable sales in the subject neighborho

FEATURE	SUBJECT	COMPA
Address		
Proximity to Subject		
Sale Price	$	
Sale Price/Gross Liv. Area	$ sq. ft.	$
Data Source(s)		
Verification Source(s)		
VALUE ADJUSTMENTS	DESCRIPTION	DESCRIPTI
Sale or Financing Concessions		
Date of Sale/Time		
Location		
Leasehold/Fee Simple		
Site		
View		
Design (Style)		
Quality of Construction		
Actual Age		
Condition		
Above Grade Room Count	Total Bdrms. Baths	Total Bdrms
Gross Living Area	sq. ft.	
Basement & Finished Rooms Below Grade		
Functional Utility		
Heating/Cooling		
Energy Efficient Items		
Garage/Carport		
Porch/Patio/Deck		
Net Adjustment (Total)		☐ + ☐
Adjusted Sale Price of Comparables		Net Adj. Gross Adj.

SALES COMPARISON APPROACH

I ☐ did ☐ did not research the sale or transfer history of the

My research ☐ did ☐ did not reveal any prior sales o

Sale Price

The next line provides space for the appraiser to list the gross sale price of each comparable. The gross sale price is the amount that appears on the top line of the closing statement and includes the price before selling expense deductions are made. The gross sale price is usually the one reported by all involved in the transaction; it can be different from the net sale price, which would reflect deductions for many expenses.

For comparable sales, the sale price is not the list price but the price negotiated by the buyer and seller for the transfer of the rights in realty from the seller to buyer. It can be the same as the list price in some sales, but often it is slightly less. If the sale price is more than the list price, the appraiser is responsible for finding out why and should research the situation and reconcile the market factors that caused it. This does not mean that there would never be any legitimate reasons for such an event to occur, only that more market research by the appraiser would be appropriate. Most sales with sale prices above list prices have some sales or financing concessions included.

If an appraiser is using this grid or a similar grid for comparable listings, it is important for the intended users and review appraisers to be able to verify the list prices. The appraiser should not reduce the list price by a normal or typical sale-to-list-price ratio. If the comparable is a current listing, the appraiser should list the actual current asking price and then address the fact that it is normal for properties to sell for less than their asking prices in the section set aside for additional comments on page 3 of both forms. If an appraiser uses the list price after reduction for the sale-to-list-price ratio, it must be well identified to prevent the review appraiser from being misled. Since list prices may lower over time, it is important for appraisers to keep a copy of the listing in the file in case this information is challenged.

Sale Price/Gross Liv. Area

The line for sale price per GLA provides space for the appraiser to list the price per square foot of GLA (including land). This price includes the price paid for the land, porches, patios, and pools. The gross sale price also reflects basements and garages, but the square feet of GLA does not include this space in the calculation. The price per square foot of GLA including land will be skewed in some analyses for which the comparable sales have basements, large lots, or other significant features that the subject does not have. Some appraisers use the price per square foot of GLA in analyses of homes that are much larger than the typical home, which may disguise the property as an overimprovement.

Data Source(s)

The data source indicates where the data came from. Inadequate data can show the appraiser's lack of diligence in researching possible data sources. In markets where the data is not very well organized, such as markets that lack an MLS, this line provides the appraiser an opportunity to show the intended users the resources that were available.

Case in Point

Ronnie Researcher is an appraiser in Scott County. He received a request for an appraisal and report on the Reagan Ranch (10 acres) in Redford County, which is one county west of Scott County. In this state, sales data is not public information. Ronnie belongs to the Scott County MLS system, which includes farm and ranch listings and comparable sales in all of Scott and Blue Counties. Some of the members also get listings and report sales in Redford County (see Exhibit 12).

About 40% of the market data in Redford County comes from the brokers located in Hanks County, which is located one county west of Redford County. Another 40% comes from Scott County, and the rest is brokered by agents from other counties to the north and south that do not belong to any MLS. As a result, some sales in Redford County are in the Scott County MLS, others are in the Hanks County MLS, and a small number are from other areas that lack any reporting vehicle. An appraiser who performs appraisals in Redford County must belong to both MLS systems to get the benefit of most of the data. However, because one of the counties is not the primary area from which most of the appraisal assignments come, belonging to two MLS systems can be an onerous expense for most appraisers.

Exhibit 12. Five-County MLS Breakdown

Hanks County	Ford County	Redford County	Blue County	Scott County
With MLS services	Uses MLS from Hanks County ←	← Reagan No MLS here	Uses MLS from Scott County →	With MLS services Home of Ronnie Researcher, appraiser

To ensure that no confusion exists about the data source that the appraiser used in this situation, Ronnie Researcher must show where he looked for the data. The data source line in the report tells the review appraiser where to look to confirm that data. This example shows why some underwriters may think appraisers have data available but are not presenting it. If Ronnie Researcher belonged to only one MLS system, he could not truthfully state that comparable sales that are the *most* locationally, physically, and functionally similar to the subject were selected and used in this case, as is stated in Certification 7 on page 5 of the URAR and Form 2055. Diligence in researching comparables is very important.

Page 2 of 6

There are comparable properties currently offered for sa...
There are comparable sales in the subject neighborhoo...

FEATURE	SUBJECT	COMPA...
Address		
Proximity to Subject		
Sale Price	$	
Sale Price/Gross Liv. Area	$ sq. ft.	$
Data Source(s)		
Verification Source(s)		
VALUE ADJUSTMENTS	DESCRIPTION	DESCRIPTI...
Sale or Financing Concessions		
Date of Sale/Time		
Location		
Leasehold/Fee Simple		
Site		
View		
Design (Style)		
Quality of Construction		
Actual Age		
Condition		
Above Grade Room Count	Total Bdrms. Baths	Total Bdrms
Gross Living Area	sq. ft.	
Basement & Finished Rooms Below Grade		
Functional Utility		
Heating/Cooling		
Energy Efficient Items		
Garage/Carport		
Porch/Patio/Deck		
Net Adjustment (Total)		☐ + ☐
Adjusted Sale Price of Comparables		Net Adj. Gross Adj.

SALES COMPARISON APPROACH

I ☐ did ☐ did not research the sale or transfer history of the s...

My research ☐ did ☐ did not reveal any prior sales or ...

In most markets, appraisers are not able to obtain data for all the sales that occur. They have to work hard to get data, and the research is open-ended.

To help review appraisers find the same data on which the appraisal report was based, it is usually advisable for appraisers to list the MLS number or deed number for data that comes from an MLS system.

Case in Point

Jimmy James is an appraiser in Jamestown. He was asked to appraise a house on Jamison Street for Jimmy Bob's Mortgage Company. He did a fairly good job of research and analysis, wrote a report, and sent it to Jimmy Bob. All went well until Jimmy James got a call from a lender saying that the underwriter had rejected the appraisal after a third-party appraiser performed a review. The review appraiser indicated that the appraiser had made up data, and Sale 3 located at 12345 N. Michigan Street did not exist. There was no property located at that address.

The mortgage company threatened to sue Jimmy because he lost the loan as well as credibility with that lender. Jimmy was dismayed because he had never made up data during his career. He went back into the file to find out what happened. After he pulled the file, he found out that the MLS reported that the sale involved a property located at 12354 N. Michigan Street, not 12345 N. Michigan Street. He had made a typographical error when he entered it on the form.

The reviewer did not catch that error and accused him of making up the data. Adding the MLS number would have prevented this error because the reviewer could have found the sale data and would have recognized the error immediately.

Although many appraisers and some clients believe that the MLS database is designed for the retrieval of information to support appraisals, this is not the case. For most markets, the MLS is designed for real estate brokers to market real property more effectively. This must be remembered when looking at MLS data. Agents rarely include negative information–such as that a house backs up to the interstate, is located in a noisy area, or has some other problem making it undesirable to a buyer–in the descriptive comments on the MLS data sheets. Many agents operate according to the philosophy, "If you can't say something nice, don't say anything at all." Keep in mind that brokers are hired and often legally obligated to facilitate the sale, and this includes advertising the property in the best possible light. For this reason, appraisers should in some cases perform more research to support their opinions.

Verification Source(s)

The verification source line asks the appraiser to show that the data was verified. Some appraisers do not verify the data and are surprised when a review appraiser finds one or two of the three sales to be erroneous. Appraisers who use the minimum amount of data should confirm that data to a reasonable degree. What constitutes a reasonable degree depends on the market, the number of comparables used, and the reliability of the data. In markets where the MLS is notoriously inaccurate, verification may include the following:

- A phone call to the
  - Listing agent
  - Selling agent
  - Buyer
  - Seller
  - County auditor's or assessor's office that has access to public records
- An Internet search of public records to verify price
- An Internet or file search of newspaper articles that publish real estate prices
- A file search of the appraiser's own records

The standard of data confirmation is the minimum amount that provides for a correct and accurate analysis. This means that appraisers who rely on three comparable sales only will find themselves in trouble if one or two of the sales are flawed. Appraisers who use five or six sales or listings as comparables have a lower standard of confirmation because any error in the data will not impact the conclusion as much.

The standard for verification is much higher when minimum data is available or the appraiser relies on minimum data. In contrast, an automated valuation model (AVM) does not verify the sales data, but the computer may use 75 pieces of data to draw conclusions. This issue is results-oriented. Standard verification requires whatever it takes the make sure the information is correct. The appraiser must use individual judgment to decide when enough is enough.

Appraisers who face the problem of inadequate comparable sales may be forced to use sales that appear to be uncomparable to develop the opinion of value. Comparables that are derived from a different market segment can lead to excessive adjustments. In such cases, the adjustment rates used may overwhelmingly influence the value conclusion. As a result, it is important for all appraisers to have a logical basis for their adjustments. However, an appraiser may have a logical argument for an adjustment but still be wrong. The rationale and amount of adjustment is often a point of discussion and debate for many appraisals.

For a long time, it has been considered best appraisal practice for appraisers to find comparable sales and listings that are both inferior and superior to the subject overall. This enables the appraiser to perform a paired data analysis–that is, matched pairs–to extract rates of adjustment. To validate the adjustment for size, it is best to find a larger residence and a smaller one for comparison. Underwriters are correct when they ask an appraiser to bracket the subject's sale price whenever possible. The words "whenever possible" are important here. If the subject were thought to be an overimprovement, bracketing the subject would not be possible. Appraisers must be able to recognize and compensate if the subject is an overimprovement, and the lack of sales above the market value opinion indicated could be evidence of that. All properties do not necessarily have to have higher- and lower-priced comparables, but appraisers should question the situation when they cannot find any comparables priced as high as the subject's value opinion. It should also be noted that "bracketing" the subject does not mean bracketing a target value but rather bracketing the subject's attributes (size, age of improvement, lot size, etc.).

Sales Comparison Approach Section: Sales Comparison Grid Elements of Comparison

SALES COMPARISON AP

VALUE ADJUSTMENTS	DESCRIPTION	DESCRIPTION	+(-) $ Adjustment	DESCRIPTION	+(-) $ Adjustment	DESCRIPTION	+(-) $ Adjustment
Sale or Financing Concessions							
Date of Sale/Time							
Location							
Leasehold/Fee Simple							
Site							
View							
Design (Style)							
Quality of Construction							
Actual Age							
Condition							
Above Grade Room Count	Total Bdrms. Baths	Total Bdrms. Baths		Total Bdrms. Baths		Total Bdrms. Baths	
Gross Living Area	sq. ft.	sq. ft.		sq. ft.		sq. ft.	
Basement & Finished Rooms Below Grade							
Functional Utility							
Heating/Cooling							
Energy Efficient Items							
Garage/Carport							
Porch/Patio/Deck							
Net Adjustment (Total)		☐+ ☐-	$	☐+ ☐-	$	☐+ ☐-	$
Adjusted Sale Price of Comparables		Net Adj. % Gross Adj. %	$	Net Adj. % Gross Adj. %	$	Net Adj. % Gross Adj. %	$

Sales or Financing Concessions

The next line requires the appraiser to make adjustments for any increase in the sale price of the comparable that is attributable to the sellers giving favorable financing or paying financing costs for the buyer. This adjustment should make the subject's value estimate equal to the definition of value attached to the appraisal. Essentially, the problem with financing concessions is that no limit exists as to how much can be added to a price for concessions.

Case in Point

A broker indicated the sale price for Comparable Sale 1 to be $164,500, and the property closed three weeks ago. The home is nearly identical to the subject and is in the same platted subdivision. The list price was $159,900, and the home was on the market for 90 days before the offer came in. The offer included a provision that the seller pay $7,000 in closing costs, points, and other financing costs for the buyer. The agent reported that the seller was agreeable to these extra costs because she was willing to sell the property for $155,000 to $158,000 and this arrangement enabled her to net similar amounts.

A broker indicated the sale price for Comparable Sale 2 to be $174,500, and the property closed six weeks ago. The home is nearly identical to the subject and is in the same platted subdivision. The list price was $159,900, and the home was on the market for 90 days before the offer came in. The offer included a provision that the seller pay $7,000 in closing costs, points, and a $10,000 decorating allowance for the buyer. The agent reported that the seller was agreeable to these extra costs because he was willing to sell the property for $155,000 to $158,000 and this arrangement enabled him to net similar amounts.

A broker indicated the sale price of Comparable Sale 3 to be $184,500, and the property closed three weeks ago. The home is nearly identical to the subject and is in the same platted subdivision. The list price was $159,900, and the home was on the market for 90 days before the offer came in. The offer included a provision that the sellers take back a $27,000 "forgivable second mortgage." The buyer signed the mortgage. However, the seller gave the mortgage back to the buyer outside the closing office, and the buyer tore it up. No other copies of the mortgage were made, and it was never recorded. The agent reported that the sellers were agreeable to these extra costs because they were willing to sell the property for between $155,000 and $158,000, enabling them to net similar amounts.

As this example shows, the correct sale price for all three comparables is $157,500. The effect on the appraisal and the value conclusion is substantial unless the appraiser makes adjustments to compensate for these special financing arrangements. Because unlimited concessions can be included, the appraiser must draw the line somewhere. The line is drawn by most lenders at $0 concessions paid by the seller.

According to this scenario, the adjustment is made only to the comparable sales for the favorable financing included in the comparable's sale price. These comments should not be misinterpreted to imply that financing concessions included in the sale price of the subject property necessitate an adjustment. After all, the assignment is not to appraise the subject's price but to appraise the subject property (rights in realty) as of the effective date of appraisal. If the subject benefits from seller-paid financing costs or other favorable terms such as contracts or assumptions, it is more likely that the subject's sale price may be difficult to support with cash equivalent–adjusted prices. However, this does not require an adjustment. Only financing concessions included with the comparable sales must be adjusted for on this line.

There are comparable properties currently offered for s...
There are comparable sales in the subject neighborho...

FEATURE	SUBJECT	COMP...
Address		
Proximity to Subject		
Sale Price	$	
Sale Price/Gross Liv. Area	$ sq. ft.	$
Data Source(s)		
Verification Source(s)		
VALUE ADJUSTMENTS	DESCRIPTION	DESCRIPT...
Sale or Financing Concessions		
Date of Sale/Time		
Location		
Leasehold/Fee Simple		
Site		
View		
Design (Style)		
Quality of Construction		
Actual Age		
Condition		
Above Grade	Total / Bdrms. / Baths	Total / Bdrms.
Room Count		
Gross Living Area	sq. ft.	
Basement & Finished Rooms Below Grade		
Functional Utility		
Heating/Cooling		
Energy Efficient Items		
Garage/Carport		
Porch/Patio/Deck		
Net Adjustment (Total)		☐ + ☐
Adjusted Sale Price of Comparables		Net Adj. Gross Adj.

SALES COMPARISON APPROACH

I ☐ did ☐ did not research the sale or transfer history of the...

My research ☐ did ☐ did not reveal any prior sales or trans...

Methods of Extracting and Supporting Adjustments for Sales or Financing Concessions

Income Capitalization Approach

For financing concessions that involve a discounted interest rate on a seller financing package, the adjustment is more complicated because no simple lump sum amount stated in a contract will be readily accessible to the appraiser. When evaluating discounted interest rates given to a buyer such as a sub-market conditional sales contract or a purchase money mortgage, the common technique is to calculate the present value of the mortgage loan at the stated terms and compare it to the present value of the mortgage at the market rate.

Sales Comparison Approach

The sales comparison approach is the most obvious approach for this situation, but it is the hardest to use. For this approach, the appraiser must find sales that included this favorable financing as well as nearly identical sales that did not include it. The technique is easy to understand and use, but the data is nearly impossible to find in most markets because the terms vary so much.

Other

Some appraisers ask the buyer how much weight they attributed to the financing given in the sale. If they did not give it much consideration, then logic would dictate that it did not have much of an impact on price. The difficulty with this technique is that buyers cannot often be found and they may not really understand the question or be concerned about providing an accurate response.

Most appraisers use a dollar-for-dollar adjustment when the amount of the concession is a cash payment or allowance such as seller-paid closing costs and allowances. If a seller pays $1,000 on behalf of the buyer, the appraiser would compensate with a lower discount on the list price or in many cases add the $1,000 to the price, even if the adjusted price exceeds the list price.

Date of Sale/Time

One-Unit Housing Trends			
Property Values	☐ Increasing	☐ Stable	☐ Declining
Demand/Supply	☐ Shortage	☐ In Balance	☐ Over Supply
Marketing Time	☐ Under 3 mths	☐ 3–6 mths	☐ Over 6 mths

Unless otherwise explained, the date of sale/time line should correlate to the "One-Unit Housing Trends" section of the neighborhood analysis on page 1 of the URAR and Form 2055. For example, if prices are stable in the neighborhood analysis, it is probably incorrect to make date of sale adjustments here without a lengthy explanation. To extract and support an adjustment for the date of sale/time, the following techniques are used for the cost approach and the sales comparison approach, respectively.

Methods of Extracting and Supporting Adjustments for Date of Sale/Time

Cost Approach

An easy way to support an adjustment for the date of sale or time is to correlate the adjustment rate to the rate of inflation in building costs. For example, if building costs are increasing at 3% compounded each year and the rate of depreciation is 1.5% per year, the net increase per year should be 1.5%. This technique is easy but may not be correct in areas where the increase in land values is more than the increase in the rate of inflation in building costs or in situations involving external obsolescence. This nets an unrealistic rate in some markets because of an imbalance in supply and demand that pushes prices up at very high rates or pushes prices down very rapidly. This technique is not usable in many areas of the United States and does not work at all in markets that suffer from poor economic conditions (buyer's markets). Gauging whether this technique is usable in a particular market involves studying cost and appreciation rates in tandem.

Sales Comparison Approach

The sales comparison approach is a good way to extract and support the adjustment for date of sale and is based on sales and resales of the same property over time. This method must include several properties because there will be extenuating circumstances for price changes other than price appreciation. The underlying logic is that if a comparable property sold for $X three years ago and $Y today, the rate of change for that sale and resale should be indicative of how fast property values are changing in that market and should indicate the amount of adjustment required for comparable sales today. Exhibit 13 shows how to extract such an adjustment.

Exhibit 13. Extraction from Comparable Sales

Appreciation Analysis	Sale 1	Date	Sale 2	Date	Sale 3	Date	Sale 4	Date
Initial sale price & date	$258,000	36 mos. ago	$209,000	48 mos. ago	$225,000	50 mos. ago	$289,000	5 mos. ago
Less seller concessions	$-		$(3,500)		$-		$-	
Adjusted initial sale price	$258,000		$205,500		$225,000		$289,000	
Second sale price & date	$290,000	1 mo. ago	$235,000	2 mos. ago	$265,000	Now	$296,000	Now
Less seller concessions	$(3,500)		$-		$-		$-	
Adjusted second sale price	$286,500		$235,000		$265,000		$296,000	
Difference (price and months)	$28,500	35	$29,500	46	$40,000	50	$7,000	5
Less improvements after sale	$-		$-		$(3,500)		$-	
Deferred maintenance needed	$-		$3,500		$-		$-	
Net difference in sale prices	$28,500		$33,000		$36,500		7,000	
% increase or decrease overall	11.05%	35	16.06%	46	16.22%	50	2.42%	5
Amt. of apprec. or deprec./yr. (%)	3.79%		4.19%		3.89%		5.81%	

As shown in Exhibit 13, raw numbers may indicate one amount while the net result may be different after adjustments for concessions, improvements, or lack of maintenance. This extracted rate may or may not apply to another market in this area. This analysis can also be flawed if the owners of the property invest a certain amount of money in the property but the investment is insufficient and the property value does not increase. In some cases, a small investment can yield a significant increase in the sale price, which will also skew this analysis. This analysis provides one example, but

Page 2 of 6

There are comparable properties currently offered fo

There are comparable sales in the subject neighborho

FEATURE	SUBJECT	COMP
Address		
Proximity to Subject		
Sale Price	$	
Sale Price/Gross Liv. Area	$ sq. ft.	$
Data Source(s)		
Verification Source(s)		
VALUE ADJUSTMENTS	DESCRIPTION	DESCRIPT
Sale or Financing Concessions		
Date of Sale/Time		
Location		
Leasehold/Fee Simple		
Site		
View		
Design (Style)		
Quality of Construction		
Actual Age		
Condition		
Above Grade Room Count	Total Bdrms. Baths	Total Bdrms
Gross Living Area	sq. ft.	
Basement & Finished Rooms Below Grade		
Functional Utility		
Heating/Cooling		
Energy Efficient Items		
Garage/Carport		
Porch/Patio/Deck		
Net Adjustment (Total)		☐ + ☐
Adjusted Sale Price of Comparables		Net Adj. Gross Adj.

I ☐ did ☐ did not research the sale or transfer history of the

SALES COMPARISON APPROACH

of course prior sales history can be analyzed in many other ways. This analysis is based on straight-line calculations and can also be done using an HP-12C calculator on a compound basis. The compound rate is usually a little less. It should be noted that the sale and resale of the same property may also be skewed a little because the improvement is a little older in the second sale than the first.

Location

A common saying in the real estate business is "the three most important attributes of real estate are location, location, and location." Few real estate practitioners would argue this point. The popularity of a location drives the demand side of the market, which drives prices up or down and affects maintenance levels, homeownership rates, and eventually the outward appearance of the entire neighborhood. Attributes that appraisers should consider when evaluating neighborhoods for the selection of comparables include

- The size, age, quality, and condition of the homes in the neighborhood.
  The most significant locational attribute readily apparent to the appraiser is usually the size, age, quality, and condition of the homes in the neighborhood. Some appraisers quantify neighborhood comparability by comparing the average sale price of the home sales in the neighborhood, so a comparable sale located in a different project is comparable to the subject if the average sale price of the homes in that area is similar to the subject's. The MLS database can usually provide an average sale price for most data sets, facilitating this determination.
- Neighborhood crime rates and level of police protection.
  Issues of crime and police protection can be sensitive when it comes to residential mortgage appraisal. Many appraisers are aware of these issues and use competitive comparables but then do not report the crime statistics. Appraisers who choose to report this data for the subject's market may need to report the same data for competing markets. USPAP Advisory Opinion 16 on fair housing laws and appraisal report content addresses this issue. Appraisers must exercise care in this area. Crime statistics can be misleading in some cases, and the market often does not recognize this.
- The level of government involvement in neighborhood issues, such as planning, zoning, and code enforcement.
  Excessive government involvement may be a detriment in some markets. A government that has imposed numerous controls on land use, nuisances, or other problems for property owners but does not enforce them may cause some diminution of market value. In many markets, the lack of an enforceable zoning code invites negative land uses, which can affect the market value negatively.
- The availability of utilities.
  Utility availability is also a significant issue in many markets. In markets where transferees make up the most common buyers,

the lack of public water and sewer utilities may be a big problem. Many appraisers refrain from using comparable sales with different levels of utilities. Public sewer systems are a positive factor environmentally. Septic systems sometimes cause health problems that are difficult to correct. Private wells are tested for water quality in many areas when the property is transferred but may not be checked again for many years. Public water supplies are generally checked daily or more often for quality per EPA regulations.

- Homeowners association rules, dues, and amenities.
  Homeowners associations also constitute a significant locational attribute. If a residential property has a homeowners association that owns an 18-hole golf course for residents, it could be a significant positive attribute if the typical buyer is a golfer. If the typical buyer is not a golfer, however, the maintenance dues for this feature may be prohibitive.
- Street widths, building setbacks, and side yard requirements.
  Street widths, building setbacks, and side yard requirements can also make or break a neighborhood–especially in high-density urban areas. Large setbacks can create a less crowded feel in the area, and larger side yards provide greater separation from house to house for noise insulation as well as allow space for garages. In other markets, adding a garage at the rear of a site is not possible because of inadequate side yards and the lack of an alley. If garages are desired in a market, they can be hard to add without the necessary space for a driveway.
- Other.
  For a factor to affect the buyer's attitudes, it needs to be known by the buyer. If the issue is hidden inside a residence, such as in the case of a bad floor plan, the impact is probably minimal. The issue has to be known to buyers to affect their decisions as well as the neighborhood's competitive status.

Methods of Extracting and Supporting Adjustments for Location

Cost Approach

Location is most often aligned with land value. As a result, many appraisers use the land value of the subject for comparing the land value of the comparable sales. If the subject has a land value (V_L) of $75,000, and the land value of the comparable (V_L) is $90,000, the adjustment would be -$15,000. Otherwise, the cost approach does not have any significance in supporting this element of comparison.

Sales Comparison Approach

The sales comparison approach is the most common extraction method of adjusting for location. It requires the appraiser to find identical homes that are at different locations and compare the prices of one location versus another. The resulting adjustment yields what is needed for the sales comparison analysis. It is possible that some of the differences in price could be attributed to other issues such as conditions of sale, but that would probably be true for all matched pair extractions. The use of more than one matched pair helps to

Page 2 of 6

There are comparable properties currently offered fo...
There are comparable sales in the subject neighborho...

SALES COMPARISON APPROACH

FEATURE	SUBJECT			COMP...	
Address					
Proximity to Subject					
Sale Price	$				
Sale Price/Gross Liv. Area	$		sq. ft.	$	
Data Source(s)					
Verification Source(s)					
VALUE ADJUSTMENTS	DESCRIPTION			DESCRIPT...	
Sale or Financing Concessions					
Date of Sale/Time					
Location					
Leasehold/Fee Simple					
Site					
View					
Design (Style)					
Quality of Construction					
Actual Age					
Condition					
Above Grade	Total	Bdrms.	Baths	Total	Bdrms.
Room Count					
Gross Living Area			sq. ft.		
Basement & Finished Rooms Below Grade					
Functional Utility					
Heating/Cooling					
Energy Efficient Items					
Garage/Carport					
Porch/Patio/Deck					
Net Adjustment (Total)				☐ + ☐	
Adjusted Sale Price of Comparables				Net Adj. Gross Adj.	

I ☐ did ☐ did not research the sale or transfer history of the...

My research ☐ did ☐ did not reveal any prior sales or trans...

isolate these adjustments without the impact of unusual terms.

Some appraisers also use the median price in one neighborhood versus the median price in the other for this adjustment. While this method is logical, the data requirements for it are too high. The appraiser would probably need 30 sales in each neighborhood to minimize the outliers. With modern computer databases, this analysis is much more possible now than in years past when this data was difficult to research.

Leasehold/Fee Simple

The subject residence may be built on leased land. In such instances, the interest (rights) most similar to the building value would be the leasehold. If the land was leased and a residence built on it, the property interest used with this form would be the leasehold. Most secondary market lenders do not loan on vacant land, so the only interest they will loan is the leasehold. Analysis of leasehold interests for residential properties is similar to that for nonresidential properties. This type of analysis also assumes that the value of the leasehold is the value of the fee simple less the leased fee value. The income from the lease is capitalized via a "leased fee" capitalization rate. The capital (lump sum) value of the leased fee is subtracted from the fee simple value to get the leasehold value.

Methods of Extracting and Supporting Adjustments for Leasehold/Fee Simple

Income Capitalization Approach

The income capitalization approach is one of the main ways to evaluate leased fee and leasehold interest in income property. The income that a property derives from the land lease can be converted to the leased fee interest. The income from the property less the land lease can also be capitalized, which would represent the leasehold interest. The leased fee value can be subtracted from the fee simple to get an estimate of the leasehold interest. This may not be the way that buyers think in some markets, but it is the method that Fannie Mae suggests for appraisers. The income used in this calculation would be the net income from the lease. There may or may not be expenses associated with this lease, so the appraiser should be careful to do some research to investigate. The capitalization (R) is the ratio of the leased fee net income to the value of the leased fee; it can be obtained from sales of leased fee in which the appraiser takes the net income and divides it by the sale price = $I_{LF} / V_{LF} = R_{LF}$.

Sales Comparison Approach

The easiest way to evaluate a leasehold interest is to find sales of similar interests. In markets where real estate is commonly segregated this way, finding comparable sales is not difficult and is the preferred method. In other markets where this type of partitioning of the rights in realty is uncommon, such data may not be available. To evaluate the leasehold interest, an appraiser may have to make phone calls to poll local brokers. In the absence of conclusive data to the contrary, the leasehold interest can be the fee simple interest less the leased fee.

Other

Other methods of performing leasehold/fee simple analysis include using multipliers (a variation of the income capitalization approach), capitalizing the lease payments, and subtracting the value of the lease payment from the fee simple.

Site

Most appraisers use the site line to compensate for the site size. Site size is important to buyers of single-unit properties in some markets. Size is usually listed as the actual size and not as "equal," "inferior," or "superior." Some appraisers do not calculate the site size or even list the dimensions for the comparables; however, this practice should be avoided. Size also includes consideration for

- Insulation from nearby neighbors.
  Insulation is a privacy issue. Larger sites usually mean greater distances from neighbors.
- On-site parking.
  In many markets, the availability of off-street parking is important.
- Availability of land to install pools, tennis courts, and other on-site amenities.
  In higher end markets, on-site amenities are very important.
- Oversized additional parcels.
  In some appraisals, an oversized site may facilitate the highest and best use of an additional parcel. For this type of appraisal, it may be advisable to perform an analysis of the two or more parcels on separate reports or it may include an analysis of Parcel A and Parcel B on the same report, with supporting sales and possibly absorption data. Whatever way the appraiser chooses to report this information, the extra land may be significant and probably should not simply be added to this line as though it added value commensurate with vacant lot prices.

Case in Point

A subject property includes a five-year-old, single-unit residence on 22 acres in the rural area just outside of Smallburg. Most of the area is rolling land too steep to farm. The minimum lot size prescribed by zoning is five acres, but the market appears to demand approximately 10 acres to provide separation from neighbors. In the sales comparison analysis, the only comparable sales found in this market included more than five acres and less than 15 acres. Because of the location of the residence on the parcel, the appraiser believes that it is made up of two parcels: one 12-acre parcel with the existing house on one parcel and one 10-acre parcel of vacant land. To facilitate the appraisal of this property, the appraiser prepared a form appraisal report on the house with 12 acres as part of a short narrative report that also included the vacant 10 acres. The appraisal report featured Parcel A with the house and Parcel B with the vacant 10 acres, which may or may not be allowed by some lenders.

Page 2 of 6

There are comparable properties currently offered fo

There are comparable sales in the subject neighborho

FEATURE	SUBJECT	COMP
Address		
Proximity to Subject		
Sale Price	$	
Sale Price/Gross Liv. Area	$ sq. ft.	$
Data Source(s)		
Verification Source(s)		
VALUE ADJUSTMENTS	DESCRIPTION	DESCRIPT
Sale or Financing Concessions		
Date of Sale/Time		
Location		
Leasehold/Fee Simple		
Site		
View		
Design (Style)		
Quality of Construction		
Actual Age		
Condition		
Above Grade Room Count	Total / Bdrms. / Baths	Total / Bdrms
Gross Living Area	sq. ft.	
Basement & Finished Rooms Below Grade		
Functional Utility		
Heating/Cooling		
Energy Efficient Items		
Garage/Carport		
Porch/Patio/Deck		
Net Adjustment (Total)		☐ + ☐
Adjusted Sale Price of Comparables		Net Adj. Gross Adj.

SALES COMPARISON APPROACH

I ☐ did ☐ did not research the sale or transfer history of the

My research ☐ did ☐ did not reveal any prior sales or tra

See Fannie Mae's *Announcement 08-30* for instructions on appraisals of less than the entire site. To access *Announcement 08-30* on Fannie Mae's Web site at *www.efanniemae.com*, type "Announcement 08-30" in the search box that appears in the top right corner of the home page. The announcement can also be accessed by first clicking on "Appraisers" under the "Industry Specialists" heading on the home page. Next, click on "Single-Family Guides for free online" under the heading "AllRegs Online." A list of documents will then appear. If pop-ups are blocked, click on "View Support Tips and AllRegs Contact Info" under the "AllRegs Online" heading to access directions for changing the browser settings to allow pop-ups. Click on the "Announcements and Letters" file folder. Then click on the "2008 Announcements and Letters" file folder and the "Ann. 08-30" file.

Methods of Extracting and Supporting Adjustments for Site

Sales Comparison Approach

Most appraisers use the sales comparison approach to support an adjustment for site size. This paired data analysis or sales extraction technique involves finding land sales of one size and comparing them to another set of sales of similar land sizes. Using only one pair of sales is ineffective because the buyer's and seller's motivations may be different or they may have some unknown reason for buying one site rather than another. The comparison of improved property sales with small lots versus improved property sales with large lots could give a great indication of the correct adjustment.

View

The view from the site can be significant in single-unit home appraisals if the subject property is in a price range that values this amenity. It is also possible that in some price ranges the view is one of the least important features of a property. If a property is located at the high end of the value spectrum and the typical buyer seeks to create an image of prestige, he or she may pay a significant price to live on a lake or golf course or in the penthouse of a condominium building. Appraisers are expected to discuss positive and negative views of the subject with respect to the comparables. For example, an appraiser who does not pay much attention to comparable sales while photographing them may not see that one property sold at a discount because it has a view of a landfill and another property sold at a premium because it has a lake view.

Some appraisers are challenged by comparing properties located next to a golf course or a lake to properties that lack those features, and such an analysis can lead to errors. It is a valid argument that the motivation of a lakefront property buyer may not be the same as that of a non-lakefront property buyer and may not reflect the same value considerations. In most markets, appraisers try to avoid comparing lakefront or golf course lots to properties located away from these amenities, but it may not be possible when data is limited. Sometimes three recent sales of properties located off the golf course and three older sales of properties located on the golf course are enough to satisfy the underwriters. If the appraiser were making adjustments based on overall land values, an individual adjustment for view would be double-counting.

Method of Extracting and Supporting Adjustments for View

Sales Comparison Approach

Most appraisers use the sales comparison approach to support an adjustment for site view. The technique used is a paired data analysis or sales extraction technique that involves finding sales of land with one view and comparing them to another set of sales with similar views. Using a single paired sale as an indication of this adjustment rate would be inadequate.

Overall Land Value (V_L) Comparison

Some appraisers adjust for location, site size, and view on one line based on the overall land value rather than the many possible attributes. For example, instead of adjusting for lot size in one direction and for traffic counts in the opposite direction, an appraiser would adjust based on overall land value, which includes lot size, traffic counts, location within the block, view, utilities available, and many other attributes. The appraiser estimates the value of the subject's and the comparable's land. Comparing each comparable's estimated land value with the subject's land value results in an adjustment. Many appraisers like this technique because they do not have to raise adjustments for one item and then lower them for another; this keeps the gross adjustments lower and makes the report more acceptable to most underwriters.

Case in Point

Refer to Exhibit 14. The subject's land value is $75,000. Also, Comparable Sales 1 and 3 each have land values (V_L) of $75,000. Comparable Sale 2 has an $80,000 land value ($V_L$). This situation requires the appraiser to develop a land value opinion for the subject and all of the comparables. If no adjustment is made, the assumption is that the subject's land value and the comparables are equal. Comparable Sale 3 provides a fairly good example of why many appraisers like this method. This parcel is much larger, but it is an unplatted lot. In this market, an unplatted, one-acre lot has similar value to a 0.25-acre platted lot. If a size adjustment and an offsetting platted lot adjustment were made, the value would be the same as if no adjustment were made at all. Accompanying explanation should be included in the narrative section because an underwriter or review appraiser may not understand the lack of an adjustment for both items.

Page 2 of 6

There are	comparable properties currently offered for s
There are	comparable sales in the subject neighborhoo

FEATURE	SUBJECT			COMP
Address				
Proximity to Subject				
Sale Price	$			
Sale Price/Gross Liv. Area	$	sq. ft.		$
Data Source(s)				
Verification Source(s)				
VALUE ADJUSTMENTS	DESCRIPTION			DESCRIPTI
Sale or Financing Concessions				
Date of Sale/Time				
Location				
Leasehold/Fee Simple				
Site				
View				
Design (Style)				
Quality of Construction				
Actual Age				
Condition				
Above Grade	Total	Bdrms.	Baths	Total Bdrms
Room Count				
Gross Living Area		sq. ft.		
Basement & Finished Rooms Below Grade				
Functional Utility				
Heating/Cooling				
Energy Efficient Items				
Garage/Carport				
Porch/Patio/Deck				
Net Adjustment (Total)				☐ + ☐
Adjusted Sale Price of Comparables				Net Adj. Gross Adj.

I ☐ did ☐ did not research the sale or transfer history of the

My research ☐ did ☐ did not reveal any prior sales or tr

SALES COMPARISON APPROACH

Exhibit 14. Adjustment of Overall Land Value Based on Three Comparables

	Subject	Comparable 1		Comparable 2		Comparable 3	
Address	288 Elm Tree Lane, Bigville	5689 Keller Road, Bigville		1235 Johnson Road, Smallburg		5112 W. Moores Road, Smallburg	
Proximity to subject	Thorp Acres	0.3 mile		0.5 mile		1 mile	
Sale price		$315,000		$320,800		$315,000	
Data source(s)	Inspection	MLS 456789		MLS 249815		MLS 22356	
Verification source(s)		Confirmed with listing agent		Confirmed with listing agent		Confirmed with listing agent	
Value Adjustments	**Description**	**Description**	**+/– $ Adj.**	**Description**	**+/– $ Adj.**	**Description**	**+/– $ Adj.**
Sales or financing concessions		New mortgage no concessions	–	New mortgage no concessions	–	New mortgage no concessions	–
Date of sale/time	Now	6 months ago	–	6 months ago	–	5 months ago	–
Location	Thorp Acres	Keller Green	–	Keller Green	–	Unplatted	–
Leasehold/fee simple	Fee simple	Fee simple	-0-	Fee simple	-5,000	Fee simple	-0-
Site	0.25 acre	0.25 acre	–	0.35 acre	–	1 acre	–
View	Residential	Residential	–	Residential	–	Residential	–
Design (style)	2-story/ colonial	2-story/ contemp.	–	2-story/ Cape Cod	–	2-story/ contemp.	–
Quality of construction	Brick/frame/ avg.	Brick/frame/ avg.	–	Brick/frame/ avg.	–	Brick/frame/ avg.	–
Actual age	8	8	–	8	–	8	–
Condition	Average	Average	–	Average	–	Average	–
Above grade room count	Total | Bdrms | Baths 8 | 4 | 2.5	Total | Bdrms | Baths 8 | 4 | 2.5	–	Total | Bdrms | Baths 9 | 4 | 2.5	–	Total | Bdrms | Baths 9 | 4 | 2.5	–
Gross living area	2,400	2,400	–	2,400	–	2,400	–
Basement & finished	1,200	1,200	–	1,200	–	1,200	–
rooms below grade	800	800	–	800	–	800	–
Functional utility	Average	Average	–	Average	–	Average	–
Energy-efficient items	Standard	Equal	–	Equal	–	Equal	–
Heating and cooling	GFA/cent. AC	GFA/cent. AC	–	GFA/cent. AC	–	GFA/cent. AC	–
Garage/carport	2-car/att./gar.	2-car/att./gar.	–	2-car/att./gar.	–	2-car/att./gar.	–
	Scr. porch	Scr. porch	–	Scr. porch	–	Scr. porch	–
	1 fireplace	1 fireplace	–	1 fireplace	–	1 fireplace	–
Net adjustment		☐+ ☐–	0	☐+ ☐–	-5,000	☐+ ☐–	0
Adjusted sale price of comparable			$315,000		$315,800		$315,000

Design (Style)

One-story versus two-story homes can be a significant factor in the analysis of some residential markets. Ranch homes, bungalows, Southern colonials, English Tudors, and New England salt boxes–when compared to each other–also present valuation issues in other markets.

Does a two-story home sell for more than a one-story home *of the same size*? If a comparison is made on a reproduction cost new basis, the one-story home should sell for more because it costs more, with all other things being equal. However, in many markets, two-story homes are larger (because they cost less to build), and some buyers think that they are better because they are bigger. Despite logic, the market may consider a two-story home to be the superior design because it is usually larger than a one-story design. Appraisers must perform market extractions on the value difference between designs, or at least talk to area brokers to help formulate an opinion on this issue.

Wall height can also be a significant design issue in some markets. The taller the home, the more impressive it is considered to be. A one-story home with a steep roof pitch may appear to be much larger than a two-story home with a lower roof pitch. Many buyers are impressed by the height of the improvement.

Methods of Extracting and Supporting Adjustments for Design

Cost Approach

The cost approach could be used to develop and support an adjustment for design if the more valuable design is also the most expensive. In some cases, the more popular design does not cost more, it just sells for more. If this is the case, the cost approach is useless for developing this adjustment amount.

Sales Comparison Approach

The sales comparison approach is the only objective way to develop and support an adjustment for design. It involves finding sales of one design and comparing them to sales that are identical except for differences in design. This paired data analysis technique is very difficult to achieve, even though it sounds appealing. An appraiser who finds that the subject is selling for a premium compared to the other sales may develop an opinion on the value of a design because of the higher sale price.

Other

In many markets, appraisers develop an opinion of the design adjustment amount based on input from brokers. This method is probably the easiest and most accurate to use for this very subjective amenity.

Quality of Construction

Construction quality is a rating used to describe the cost, durability, and craftsmanship of the design, details, and materials of a building.

Case in Point

A house with a 12/12 pitch roof, slate or clay roof shingles, copper gutters, hardwood floors, numerous windows, and durable exterior siding or veneer is considered to be of higher quality than a similar-sized improvement with a 3/12 pitch roof, mopped asphalt roof covering, plastic gutters, vinyl square floors, fewer windows, and a low-cost, short-lived exterior veneer. The underlying principle is that buildings of better quality cost more to construct and last longer than structures of poorer quality.

Novice practitioners and the public are often confused by the terms "quality" and "condition." It is possible to have a very high quality home that is in fair to poor condition. Most appraisers and lenders still ask for a comparison with the competing properties.

Case in Point

The subject real estate is a five-acre tract in a rural area improved with a manufactured home. The construction is of typical manufactured quality: a low-pitch roof, few windows, and vinyl trim. The plumbing and electric fixtures are inexpensive as are the interior finishes.

Is this home considered to be of fair quality construction? It is if the appraiser compares it to all housing in its market. However, the home is of average quality for the $100,000 to $110,000 price range in Smallburg.

Page **2** of 6

There are comparable properties currently offered for s

There are comparable sales in the subject neighborhoo

FEATURE	SUBJECT	COMP
Address		
Proximity to Subject		
Sale Price	$	
Sale Price/Gross Liv. Area	$ sq. ft.	$
Data Source(s)		
Verification Source(s)		
VALUE ADJUSTMENTS	DESCRIPTION	DESCRIPTI
Sale or Financing Concessions		
Date of Sale/Time		
Location		
Leasehold/Fee Simple		
Site		
View		
Design (Style)		
Quality of Construction		
Actual Age		
Condition		
Above Grade Room Count	Total / Bdrms. / Baths	Total / Bdrms
Gross Living Area	sq. ft.	
Basement & Finished Rooms Below Grade		
Functional Utility		
Heating/Cooling		
Energy Efficient Items		
Garage/Carport		
Porch/Patio/Deck		
Net Adjustment (Total)		☐ + ☐
Adjusted Sale Price of Comparables		Net Adj. Gross Adj.

SALES COMPARISON APPROACH

I ☐ did ☐ did not research the sale or transfer history of the

My research ☐ did ☐ did not reveal any prior sales or tr

The answer that most appraisers would give is that the property is of average construction quality for its market, thus comparing it with only the properties with which it competes.

Conversely, if another subject property is valued at $1,500,000 and the home has the best finishes, construction details, workmanship, materials, and design, most appraisers will consider it to be of average quality for its market.

Appraisers who consider the manufactured home to be of average quality must also consider the second home to be of average quality for its market. If the subject is of better quality than most of the homes with which it competes, it would be considered good quality. If the property is an overimprovement, the appraiser must provide explanation and be able to support it. Any classification of a property as poor, fair, good, or even excellent requires much explanation. Keep in mind that "average" means standard, typical, or normal; the other classifications mean that the subject is not average, standard, or typical.

Methods of Extracting and Supporting Adjustments for Quality of Construction

Cost Approach

The cost approach is an excellent way to support an adjustment for quality. Appraisers can compare the cost of construction of the subject building with the cost of construction of the comparables. The difference must then be adjusted for the depreciation applicable to the property. This process is time-consuming but effective.

Sales Comparison Approach

Paired data analysis is also an appropriate means of extracting and supporting adjustments for quality of construction. This approach can be difficult when the data is poor and sometimes even when the data is good. Sales data on the various grades of construction must be available in order for the appraiser to isolate this issue.

Other

Compiling brokers' opinions on the construction quality can be ineffective because brokers may be biased and may not understand the questions being asked.

Actual Age

For most appraisers, actual age is an easy feature to adjust for. Some appraisers believe that the age and condition of the improvements are essentially the same thing, but newer homes usually sell for more than older ones in a matched pair analysis. Age is an attribute that can be isolated in a paired data analysis by comparing a property with a five-year-old building on it and a property with a 10-year-old building on it.

Condition is not the same as age. Some appraisers use the effective age in place of actual age, but this constitutes adding another condition adjustment line to the grid. Some appraisers correctly use effective age as a numerical condition rating on the condition line. Instead of using the descriptions "good," "average," "fair," and "poor" to rate condition, these appraisers list effective age as an actual number of years. While using effective age as a numerical condition rating is logical and may make more sense in some appraisals than indicating "fair," "average," or "good," it is not logical to use it to replace actual age because it adds another line to the sales comparison grid for condition.

Some appraisers who value old homes that have been substantially remodeled use the effective age to compare them to much newer homes. It is illogical to say that a remodeled 55-year-old home that has a 55-year-old design and floor plan and is surrounded by other 55-year-old homes is effectively the same as a three-year-old home and can be compared to three-year-old homes in three- to eight-year-old neighborhoods. The remodeled 55-year-old home will probably lack appeal to a buyer attracted to a three-year-old home. This does not necessarily mean that the remodeled home will not sell for more, but only that it is dangerous to ignore the design and locational differences between the three-year-old home and the 55-year-old home.

Methods of Extracting and Supporting Adjustments for Actual Age

Cost Approach

An appraiser cannot directly convert the overall depreciation amount in the cost approach to the actual age adjustment, even if it is annualized or converted to a percentage. The overall depreciation in the cost approach includes depreciation for the main structure as well as depreciation for all the other improvements such as porches, patios, pools, garages, basements, and any other buildings. Since the other components (porches, patios, garages, and basements) are added to the sales comparison analysis on a depreciated basis, the adjustment for age cannot reflect the amount in the cost approach without double-counting depreciation.

The depreciation amount in dollars can be reduced to a percentage, which can then be applied to the cost of the main structure. However, this method has possible flaws. The depreciation costs for the main structure are complicated by including both short- and long-lived items with significantly different rates of depreciation.

It is possible to extract the depreciation amount attributed to the main building structure from the market, but this process is complicated and involves breaking down the cost approach into short- and long-lived items. Most appraisers will not expend that much effort for something that bears so little fruit.

Income Capitalization Approach

An adjustment for age may be developed by comparing rental rates for properties with old buildings to rental rates for properties with new ones, but this is difficult and the data is not usually sound enough to provide adequate support.

Sales Comparison Approach

The sales comparison approach is actually the best tool for extracting and supporting an adjustment for actual age. Several techniques are available for extracting and applying adjustments, but most are done by paired sales analysis.

Page 2 of 6

There are comparable properties currently offered f...
There are comparable sales in the subject neighborho...

FEATURE	SUBJECT	COMP...
Address		
Proximity to Subject		
Sale Price	$	
Sale Price/Gross Liv. Area	$ sq. ft.	$
Data Source(s)		
Verification Source(s)		
VALUE ADJUSTMENTS	DESCRIPTION	DESCRIPTI...
Sale or Financing Concessions		
Date of Sale/Time		
Location		
Leasehold/Fee Simple		
Site		
View		
Design (Style)		
Quality of Construction		
Actual Age		
Condition		
Above Grade Room Count	Total Bdrms. Baths	Total Bdrms
Gross Living Area	sq. ft.	
Basement & Finished Rooms Below Grade		
Functional Utility		
Heating/Cooling		
Energy Efficient Items		
Garage/Carport		
Porch/Patio/Deck		
Net Adjustment (Total)		☐ + ☐
Adjusted Sale Price of Comparables		Net Adj. Gross Adj.

SALES COMPARISON APPROACH

I ☐ did ☐ did not research the sale or transfer history of the...

My research ☐ did ☐ did not reveal any prior sales or tra...

Condition

It is common to make an adjustment for condition for older properties–especially properties that have been rented or have fallen into foreclosure. It is difficult to accept large adjustments in condition when comparing properties with newer improvements. Adjustments in condition should be at least discussed and explained. Most users of appraisal reports are skeptical of large one-line adjustments on any line of the report but especially on the line for condition. Although it is common for some properties to have large adjustments for condition, the astute appraiser always provides some rationale for the adjustment and in some cases gives numeric estimates of the cost to cure.

Methods of Extracting and Supporting Adjustments for Condition

Cost Approach

The cost approach to supporting an adjustment for condition is best described as the cost to cure. It is based on the logic that a typical buyer would adjust for a better or worse condition equal to the cost of making the repairs or updating the property. For properties that need considerable work, an adjustment must include compensation for entrepreneurial incentive. This adjustment recognizes that for many properties, the buyer needs more than just the cost to cure to be enticed to purchase the subject. In other words, a property in fair-to-poor condition will not sell for the same price as one in average or good condition after subtracting the cost of repairs; it will more likely sell for an amount that will enable the investor-buyer to make the repairs and realize a profit. This brings in the discussion of retail versus wholesale buyers for real estate.

This also raises the question of whether a retail buyer of residential real estate will buy a residential property that needs substantial work and updating. The answer to this question is usually no. The actions of a retail buyer may not represent the actions of a typical buyer for a property in fair-to-poor condition. A retail buyer may buy a property in fair condition and factor in the cost of repairs but probably will not do this when the repairs are so substantial as to become "a project," which would be the case if the property were in poor condition. For each appraisal, the appraiser must determine who the buyer will be and what he or she will pay. Sometimes it is a retail buyer, and sometimes it is a wholesale (investor) buyer.

Income Capitalization Approach

Although it is possible to base an adjustment on the difference in rental rates for a property in fair condition versus one that is in average condition and then capitalize the difference, this is not always practical. Properties that need extensive repairs will not rent at all, which means that a gross rent multiplier (GRM) analysis is not possible–especially for extracting an adjustment. Comparing a rental property in average condition to one in poor condition is not possible in many markets because the property in poor condition will not be rentable. Condition issues are different for buyers than they are for tenants; this is evidenced in the age of a roof. The tenant of the building only cares about the roof if it leaks, while the buyer considers the roof's age as well as the likelihood and timing of its replacement.

Sales Comparison Approach

Sales comparison analysis (paired data) is usually difficult to use for extracting and supporting adjustments for condition. Again, the logic of finding sales with and without a particular feature and comparing the prices is a sound practice that is easily understood, but the problem lies in finding the data to fit the situation. Most appraisers cannot find this adjustment in a paired data analysis because too many variables in condition exist.

Consider the following example:

- Property 1 sells for $440,000 and needs nine items of repair or replacement as well as six items that are in fair condition and do not warrant replacement.
- Property 2 sells for $456,000 and needs only three items replaced. Four items are in fair condition and do not warrant replacement. The items that need replacement are not the same ones that need to be replaced in the first property.
- The subject needs eight items replaced and has four items in fair condition. The items that need to be replaced and the items in fair condition are not the same as those in Property 1 or Property 2.

The sales comparison approach should work well in theory, but finding data with quantifiable differences in condition is a challenge.

Above Grade Room Count

Some appraisers believe that adjusting for room count and GLA is duplicative. Those who do not make these room count adjustments assume that the adjustment for room count is not needed because more room implies a larger house. For example, one home has 4,000 square feet of GLA partitioned into 12 rooms, including four bedrooms and three bathrooms. Another home with 4,000 square feet of GLA is divided into only seven rooms that include three bedrooms and three bathrooms. If both types of homes were salable to a viable market segment (a big assumption), then no adjustment would be needed for room count and GLA. However, if only one of the floor plans was marketable, an adjustment for room count could be appropriate. An adjustment can also be made for an unmarketable floor plan on a "functional utility" adjustment line.

The number of bedrooms greatly affects value in some markets. If a home is located in a market where the typical buyer would be a large family or where students or families "double up" or "triple up," extra bedrooms could be the largest issue. If the home is located in a market where the typical buyer is a small family, a home with four bedrooms and small common areas could be unmarketable. It is possible to have a 10-room, 2,000-sq.-ft. home with four bedrooms and three bathrooms, but it is also possible to have 2,000 square feet of GLA with only seven rooms in all, including two bedrooms and three bathrooms. The house with more partitioning would have to

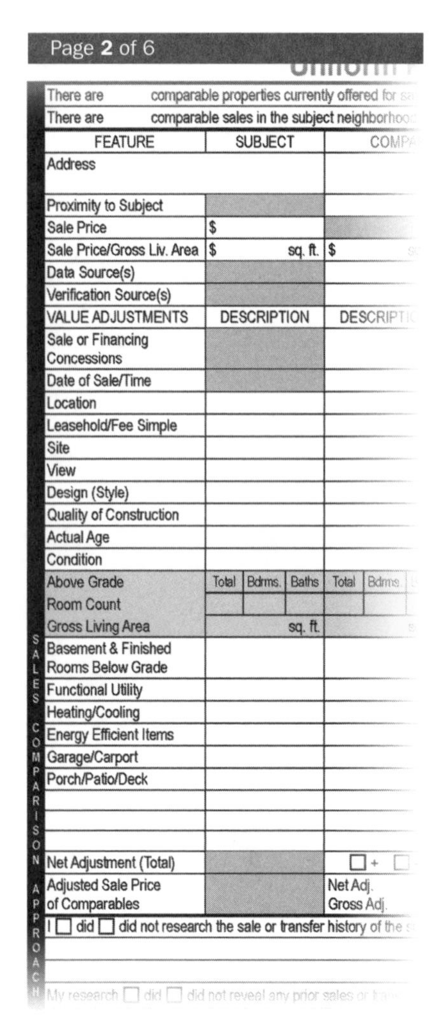
Page 2 of 6

There are comparable properties currently offered for s

There are comparable sales in the subject neighborhoo

FEATURE	SUBJECT			COMP
Address				
Proximity to Subject				
Sale Price	$			
Sale Price/Gross Liv. Area	$		sq. ft.	$
Data Source(s)				
Verification Source(s)				
VALUE ADJUSTMENTS	DESCRIPTION			DESCRIPTI
Sale or Financing Concessions				
Date of Sale/Time				
Location				
Leasehold/Fee Simple				
Site				
View				
Design (Style)				
Quality of Construction				
Actual Age				
Condition				
Above Grade	Total	Bdrms.	Baths	Total Bdrms.
Room Count				
Gross Living Area			sq. ft.	
Basement & Finished Rooms Below Grade				
Functional Utility				
Heating/Cooling				
Energy Efficient Items				
Garage/Carport				
Porch/Patio/Deck				
Net Adjustment (Total)				☐ + ☐
Adjusted Sale Price of Comparables				Net Adj. Gross Adj.

SALES COMPARISON APPROACH

I ☐ did ☐ did not research the sale or transfer history of the

My research ☐ did ☐ did not reveal any prior sales or

have much smaller rooms. A discussion in the appraisal report of the number of persons living in a residence or the typical family size in a market could violate federal fair lending rules. Nonetheless, if an appraiser researches the market and finds a difference in the marketplace for 10-room homes as opposed to eight-room homes, making an adjustment for room count and GLA would be appropriate as long as the inhabitants were not discussed.

It is important to note that floor plans are significant to many if not all buyers and appraisers need to focus on configuration issues as well as room counts. The size and location of specific rooms can also be an issue. Consider the following example.

Case in Point

The subject improvement has 3,000 square feet of GLA and is divided into seven rooms, with two bedrooms and three bathrooms. The appraiser immediately focuses on the two bedrooms and decides that this would be adequate because two-person families make up much of the market. However, the appraiser missed the issue of the lack of a formal dining room. This home appeals to a market in which the typical buyer has owned many houses before and probably has formal dining room furniture, as was evidenced by the comparables that *all* had formal dining rooms. The appraiser should have adjusted for this floor plan deficiency but missed it. An adjustment for configuration can be made here but is more likely made on the functional utility line.

Methods of Extracting and Supporting Adjustments for Above-Grade Room Count

Cost Approach

The cost approach can be used to support an adjustment for room configuration. This works if both of the configurations are supported in the market. If a house with more partitioning sells for more than a house with less, the adjustment could simply be the difference in the cost of the two structures less any applicable depreciation.

Sales Comparison Approach

The sales comparison or "paired data analysis" approach can be used to extract and support an adjustment rate for above-grade room count. Finding the data is always the problem for this type of analysis, however. In this case, the amount is typically small and may be confused with an adjustment for the seller's motivations or some other hard-to-find adjustment.

Other

Some appraisers have been able to support adjustments by interviewing several buyers on this issue. If the buyers indicate that they paid more or less for a feature, it supports the adjustment for that feature.

Gross Living Area

The size of a residence can be the largest single-line adjustment for many appraisals. The methodology for extracting this adjustment can be based on the same premise used for the other adjustments, which allows the appraiser to use home sales that are not exactly the same size as the subject for comparisons. A common problem in many markets is that if the comparables are widely different from the subject, the sales may be attractive to a different market segment and may not be indicative of value in the subject's market.

Methods of Extracting and Supporting Adjustments for Gross Living Area

Cost Approach

Some appraisers prepare one cost estimate to build the subject house and another to build the comparable's improvement and then depreciate the difference between the two estimates to develop an adjustment amount. Although this is a logical approach, it is labor intensive. It might be prudent, however, for an appraiser to perform this step on occasion to validate other methods that are used more commonly.

Income Capitalization Approach

It is possible to develop a rental rate for a smaller building versus a larger one and then capitalize the difference using a GRM. However, this would be difficult to do because of the lack of data.

Sales Comparison Approach

The paired data analysis method works well for GLA, but obtaining the data is difficult. The paired data analysis most commonly used by residential appraisers is the sensitivity analysis method, in which the appraiser enters the attributes of the subject and the comparables on an adjustment grid and then tries various rates of adjustment until the range in indicated values narrows. An example of a sensitivity analysis follows.

Sensitivity Analysis Example

The first grid, Exhibit 15, reflects an adjustment rate of $5 per square foot of GLA. With this rate, the range in indicated value is from $167,000 to $180,000, reflecting a 7.8% difference from low to high.

Exhibit 16 shows the impact when the adjustment for GLA is increased from $5 per square foot to $50 per square foot. The range is now $166,500 to $180,500. The former low sale is now the high one, and vice versa. The range from low to high is now 8.4%.

The third grid, Exhibit 17, shows the analysis with $27.50 per square foot of GLA. This seems "just right," and it tightens the range in adjusted values to only 0.5% (1/2 of 1%).

A common criticism of this analysis is that it is "backing into the number." However, this is not true; rather, this analysis is actually paired data analysis in its basic terms. If Sales 1 and 2 are compared, the difference in gross price is $16,000 and the difference in area is 600 square feet. By dividing $16,000 by 600, the indicated extracted adjustment is $26.67 per square foot of GLA. If Comparables 1 and 3 are compared, the difference in price and GLA is $9,500 / 335 = $28.36. If Comparables 2 and 3 are compared, the extracted adjustment is $6,500 / 265 = $24.53. The $27.50 used in the third grid seems to be reflective of the extracted rate. The logic of paired data analysis

Exhibit 15. Adjustment at $5 per Square Foot

	Adjustment Rate	Subject	Comparable 1		Comparable 2		Comparable 3	
Sale price				$181,500		$165,500		$172,000
Sale price/GLA				$75.63		$91.94		$83.29
Value Adjustments		**Description**	**Description**	**+(–) $ Adj.**	**Description**	**+(–) $ Adj.**	**Description**	**+(–) $ Adj.**
Concessions			No concessions	–	No concessions	–	No concessions	–
Date of sale/time	0.0%	Now	1 month ago	–	2 months ago	–	2 months ago	–
Location		Green Acres	Green Acres	–	Green Acres	–	Green Acres	–
Site (size)/view	$-	0.56 acre/residential	0.54 acre/residential	–	0.58 acre/residential	–	0.55 acre/residential	–
Design (style)		2-story/colonial	2-story/Queen Anne	–	2-story/Cape Cod	–	2-story/contemp.	–
Quality of const.		Brick/frame/avg.	Brick/frame/avg.	–	Brick/frame/avg.	–	Brick/frame/avg.	–
Actual age	$-	39	39	–	39	–	39	–
Condition		Average	Average	–	Average	–	Average	–
Above grade room count		Total 8 | Bdrms. 4 | Baths 2.5	Total 8 | Bdrms. 4 | Baths 2.5	–	Total 8 | Bdrms. 4 | Baths 2.5	–	Total 8 | Bdrms. 4 | Baths 2.5	–
Gross living area	$5	2,100	2,400	-1,500	1,800	1,500	2,065	200
Basement-finishing	$-	0	0	–	0	–	0	–
Garage/carport		2-car/att./gar.	2-car/att./gar.	–	2-car/att./gar.	–	2-car/att./gar.	–
Porch/patio/deck		Porch/deck	Porch/deck	–	Porch/deck	–	Porch/deck	–
Net adjustment				(1,500)		1,500		200
Adjusted sale price of comparable				$180,000		$167,000		$172,200

Exhibit 16. Adjustment at $50 per Square Foot

	Adjustment Rate	Subject	Comparable 1		Comparable 2		Comparable 3	
Sale price				$181,500		$165,500		$172,000
Sale price/GLA				$75.63		$91.94		$83.29
Value Adjustments		**Description**	**Description**	**+(–) $ Adj.**	**Description**	**+(–) $ Adj.**	**Description**	**+(–) $ Adj.**
Concessions			No concessions	–	No concessions	–	No concessions	–
Date of sale/time	0.0%	Now	1 month ago	–	2 months ago	–	2 months ago	–
Location		Green Acres	Green Acres	–	Green Acres	–	Green Acres	–
Site (size)/view	$-	0.56 acre/residential	0.54 acre/residential	–	0.58 acre/residential	–	0.55 acre/residential	–
Design (style)		2-story/Colonial	2-story/Queen Anne	–	2-story/Cape Cod	–	2-story/contemp.	–
Quality of const.		Brick/frame/avg.	Brick/frame/avg.	–	Brick/frame/avg.	–	Brick/frame/avg.	–
Actual age	$-	39	39	–	39	–	39	–
Condition		Average	Average	–	Average	–	Average	–
Above grade room count		Total 8 | Bdrms. 4 | Baths 2.5	Total 8 | Bdrms. 4 | Baths 2.5	–	Total 8 | Bdrms. 4 | Baths 2.5	–	Total 8 | Bdrms. 4 | Baths 2.5	–
Gross living area	$50	2,100	2,400	-15,000	1,800	15,000	2,065	1,800
Basement-finishing	$-	0	0	–	0	–	0	–
Garage/carport		2-car/att./gar.	2-car/att./gar.	–	2-car/att./gar.	–	2-car/att./gar.	–
Porch/patio/deck		Porch/deck	Porch/deck	–	Porch/deck	–	Porch/deck	–
Net adjustment				(15,000)		15,000		1,800
Adjusted sale price of comparable				$166,500		$180,500		$173,800

Exhibit 17. Adjustment at $27.50 per Square Foot

	Adjustment Rate	Subject	Comparable 1		Comparable 2		Comparable 3	
Sale price				$181,500		$165,500		$172,000
Sale price/GLA				$75.63		$91.94		$83.29
Value Adjustments		**Description**	**Description**	**+(–) $ Adj.**	**Description**	**+(–) $ Adj.**	**Description**	**+(–) $ Adj.**
Concessions			No concessions	–	No concessions	–	No concessions	–
Date of sale/time	0.0%	Now	1 month ago	–	2 months ago	–	2 months ago	–
Location		Green Acres	Green Acres	–	Green Acres	–	Green Acres	–
Site (size)/view	$-	0.56 acre/residential	0.54 acre/residential	–	0.58 acre/residential	–	0.55 acre/residential	–
Design (style)		2-story/colonial	2-story/Queen Anne	–	2-story/Cape Cod	–	2-story/ contemp.	–
Quality of const.		Brick/frame/avg.	Brick/frame/avg.	–	Brick/frame/avg.	–	Brick/frame/avg.	–
Actual age	$-	39	39	–	39	–	39	–
Condition		Average	Average	–	Average	–	Average	–
Above grade room count		Total 8 / Bdrms. 4 / Baths 2.5	Total 8 / Bdrms. 4 / Baths 2.5	–	Total 8 / Bdrms. 4 / Baths 2.5	–	Total 8 / Bdrms. 4 / Baths 2.5	–
Gross living area	$27.50	2,100	2,400	-8,300	1,800	8,300	2,065	1,000
Basement-finishing	$-	0	0	–	0	–	0	–
Garage/carport		2-car/att./gar.	2-car/att./gar.	–	2-car/att./gar.	–	2-car/att./gar.	–
Porch/patio/deck		Porch/deck	Porch/deck	–	Porch/deck	–	Porch/deck	–
Net adjustment				(8,300)		8,300		1,000
Adjusted sale price of comparable				$173,200		$173,800		$173,000

Page **2** of 6

There are comparable properties currently offered for s...
There are comparable sales in the subject neighborhoo...

FEATURE	SUBJECT	COMP...
Address		
Proximity to Subject		
Sale Price	$	
Sale Price/Gross Liv. Area	$ sq. ft.	$
Data Source(s)		
Verification Source(s)		
VALUE ADJUSTMENTS	DESCRIPTION	DESCRIPTI...
Sale or Financing Concessions		
Date of Sale/Time		
Location		
Leasehold/Fee Simple		
Site		
View		
Design (Style)		
Quality of Construction		
Actual Age		
Condition		
Above Grade	Total Bdrms. Baths	Total Bdrms.
Room Count		
Gross Living Area	sq. ft.	
Basement & Finished Rooms Below Grade		
Functional Utility		
Heating/Cooling		
Energy Efficient Items		
Garage/Carport		
Porch/Patio/Deck		
Net Adjustment (Total)		☐ + ☐
Adjusted Sale Price of Comparables		Net Adj. Gross Adj.

SALES COMPARISON APPROACH

I ☐ did ☐ did not research the sale or transfer history of the s...

My research ☐ did ☐ did not reveal any prior sales or tra...

will result in nearly identical indicated values. This is not an accident; it is the process. When the appraiser measures the difference in the property to explain the difference in price, the indicated values are narrowed.

In some cases, the subject or comparables might be overimprovements, which confounds the adjustment line. If the subject is an overimprovement, the common or standard adjustment rate in that market may give a false indication of value because of the overimprovement. If the appraiser believes that the subject or comparable sale is an overimprovement, the adjustment rate may need to be lowered to compensate or a different adjustment rate may be required for one comparable as opposed to another. If a property has an overimprovement, it means that the property would have suffered some loss and would not have sold proportionally for as much as it should have. It the subject is an overimprovement, the appraiser would have to compensate for this problem in both the sales and cost approaches to value. If the overimprovement is a comparable sale, the appraiser must consider how the market discount affected the sale price and then adjust accordingly, as illustrated in the following example.

Case in Point

The analysis shown in Exhibit 18 is perfect except for Sale 3. The data from Sale 3 is inconsistent with the other data. It is possible that this sale is an overimprovement because it sold at a discount even though it is a much larger home. It could be that the data lacks support for a home of this size. It is also possible that the home has other problems related to its floor plan or may have termite damage or some other significant deficiency that may not be related to its size. A call to the listing agent would be needed to clear up this inconsistency. Most listing brokers make follow-up calls after each showing to get a potential buyer's opinion of the property. As a result, most agents are aware of listings that have problems associated with them. Although such phone calls can be an annoyance to real estate brokers, they show diligence on the appraiser's part. When recommending a competent appraiser, the real estate broker will remember those who were diligent in their research. Because real estate brokers can influence homeowners when choosing an appraiser for relocation purposes, performing this step may have a hidden benefit.

In the "other" category, some appraisers use a percentage of the average dollar price-per-square foot of gross building area, including land as a baseline of adjustment. For example, many appraisers would use 30% to 40% of the average of these sale price ratios listed in the adjustment grid in Exhibit 18.

Sale price/GLA	$119.73	$115.95	$79.57	$112.41

The average of these prices per square foot is $106.92, and 35% of that number would be $37 per square foot. The previously listed adjustment is $35 per square foot. Many appraisers swear by this method, but it is effective only if it represents market behavior. The technique need not replicate the behavior, but it allows the appraiser to find the correct ratios. This technique can be verified by using superior and inferior comparables. The correct adjustment brings the indicated values together.

Exhibit 18. Extracting Adjustments for an Overimprovement

	Adjustment Rate	Subject	Comparable 1		Comparable 2		Comparable 3		Comparable 4	
Address		656 E. Anderson St. Smallburg	159 Long Creek Drive Smallburg		959 Geen Pasture Smallburg		858 Green Pasture Smallburg		1124 South Creek Drive Smallburg	
Proximity to subject			0.1 mile		0.5 mile		0.5 mile		0.85 mile	
Sale price				$358,000		$389,000		$366,000		$366,000
Sale price/GLA				$119.73		$115.95		$79.57		$112.41
Data source(s)		Inspection	MLS 448324		MLS 439249		MLS 419223		MLS 459223	
Verification source(s)										
Value Adjustment		**Description**	**Description**	**+(–) $ Adj.**	**Description**	**+(–) $ Adj.**	**Description**	**+(–) $ Adj.**	**Description**	**+(–) $ Adj.**
Sales or financing concessions			New mortgage no concessions	–	New mortgage no concessions	–	New mortgage no concessions	–	New mortgage no concessions	–
Date of sale/time		Now	2 months ago	–	3 months ago	–	9 months ago	–	14 months ago	–
Location		Long Creek	Long Creek	–	Long Creek	–	Long Creek	–	Long Creek	–
Leasehold/ fee simple		Fee simple	Fee simple	–	Fee simple	–	Fee simple	–	Fee simple	–
Site		0.45 acre	0.39 acre	–	0.49 acre	–	0.41 acre	–	0.45 acre	–
View		Residential	Residential	–	Residential	–	Residential	–	Residential	–
Design (style)		2-story/Garrison	2-story/chalet	–	2-story/Cape Cod	–	2-story/contemp.	–	2-story/contemp.	–
Quality of const.		Brick/frame/avg.	Brick/frame/avg.	–	Brick/frame/avg.	–	Brick/frame/avg.	–	Brick/frame/avg.	–
Actual age		8	9	–	9	–	7	–	9	–
Condition		Average	Average	–	Average	–	Average	–	Average	–
Above grade room count		Total | Bdrms. | Baths 8 | 4 | 3.5	Total | Bdrms. | Baths 8 | 4 | 3.5	–	Total | Bdrms. | Baths 9 | 4 | 3.5	–	Total | Bdrms. | Baths 9 | 4 | 3.5	–	Total | Bdrms. | Baths 9 | 4 | 3.5	–
Gross living area	35	3,300	2,990	10,900	3,355	-1,900	4,600	-45,500	3,256	1,500
Basement & finished	15	1,000	1,000	0	1,800	-12,000	900	1,500	900	1,500
rooms below grade	10	900	800	1,000	1,400	-5,000	600	3,000	600	3,000
Functional utility		Average	Average	–	Average	–	Average	–	Average	–
Energy-efficient items		Standard	Equal	–	Equal	–	Equal	–	Equal	–
Heating and cooling		GFA/cent. AC	GFA/cent. AC	–	GFA/cent. AC	–	GFA/cent. AC	–	GFA/cent. AC	–
Garage/carport		3-car/att./gar.	3-car/att./gar.	–	3-car/att./gar.	–	3-car/att./gar.	–	3-car/att./gar.	–
Porches/patio/deck		Scr. porch	Deck	3,500	Scr. porch	–	Deck	3,500	Scr. porch	–
		1 fireplace	1 fireplace	–	1 fireplace	–	1 fireplace	–	1 fireplace	–
Net adjustment			☐ + ☐ –	15,400	☐ + ☐ –	(18,900)	☐ + ☐ –	(37,500)	☐ + ☐ –	6,000
Adjusted sale price of comparable				$373,400		$370,100		$328,500		$372,000
			Net adj. %	4.30%	Net adj. %	-4.86%	Net adj. %	-10.25%	Net adj. %	1.64%
			Gross adj. %	4.3%	Gross adj. %	4.9%	Gross adj. %	14.6%	Gross adj. %	1.6%

Page 2 of 6

There are	comparable properties currently offered for s	
There are	comparable sales in the subject neighborho	
FEATURE	SUBJECT	COMP
Address		
Proximity to Subject		
Sale Price	$	
Sale Price/Gross Liv. Area	$ sq. ft.	$
Data Source(s)		
Verification Source(s)		
VALUE ADJUSTMENTS	DESCRIPTION	DESCRIPT
Sale or Financing Concessions		
Date of Sale/Time		
Location		
Leasehold/Fee Simple		
Site		
View		
Design (Style)		
Quality of Construction		
Actual Age		
Condition		
Above Grade Room Count	Total / Bdrms. / Baths	Total / Bdrms
Gross Living Area	sq. ft.	
Basement & Finished Rooms Below Grade		
Functional Utility		
Heating/Cooling		
Energy Efficient Items		
Garage/Carport		
Porch/Patio/Deck		
Net Adjustment (Total)		☐ + ☐
Adjusted Sale Price of Comparables		Net Adj. Gross Adj.

SALES COMPARISON APPROACH

I ☐ did ☐ did not research the sale or transfer history of the

My research ☐ did ☐ did not reveal any prior sales o

Basement & Finished Rooms Below Grade

The next section is used for adjusting the basement (below-grade) areas. The most significant concern about this line lies in geographic areas where it is common to have homes with and without basements in the same market. In some northern markets, nearly all homes have basements and adjustments for basement space would not be needed. In many southern markets, homes are seldom built with basements and no adjustments would be needed either. In the middle sections of the United States where some properties have basements and others do not, this line causes many problems for the inexperienced appraiser and underwriter.

Methods of Extracting and Supporting Adjustments for Basements

Cost Approach

Most appraisers make the basement adjustment by comparing the unit cost of this feature with the unit cost of that for the comparables. After adjusting for depreciation, this is often called the adjustment rate based on cost. Brokers prefer that appraisers include the basement area as living area because they believe the space is as valuable as the above-grade area. As a rule, however, the basement area is not as valuable as the above-grade area, although it is more valuable than some appraisers rate it in their analysis.

Sales Comparison Approach

The paired data analysis method works well for the basement adjustment but, again, obtaining the data is the problem. The paired data analysis used most commonly by residential appraisers is the sensitivity analysis method in which the appraiser enters the attributes of the subject and the comparables on an adjustment grid and then tests various rates of adjustment until the range in indicated values narrows.

Rationale of Cost-Based Extraction

The underlying foundation of the cost approach is that real estate is worth what it costs to construct less any losses from physical, functional, or external depreciation. Cost equals value, unless the appraiser reports losses. If an item is not worth what it costs, then some depreciation is present. If a basement costs $100,000, the appraiser judges the basement as an overimprovement, there is 10% obsolescence, and the value would be $90,000 if no other losses existed. The 10% obsolescence is an opinion, but the remainder is a calculation. Exhibit 19 illustrates the cost analysis used in adjusting for a basement via the cost approach. It is not unusual for an appraiser to base this adjustment on the depreciated cost new.

Case in Point

In the analysis shown in Exhibits 19 and 20, the cost of the basement is $50 per square foot (including finishing). There was 10% physical, 2% functional, and 2% external depreciation listed in the cost approach, for a total of slightly less than 13.6% depreciation overall. These dollar amounts of depreciation are calculated after subtotaling each depreciation item. If the same percentages are used, the math is $50,000 × 0.864 = $43,200, but in this example only $39,600 was allocated to that amenity (see Comparable 3). Although the total depreciation is estimated at 13.6% overall, it would not have to be assigned to the components on the same percentage basis. The depreciation percentages in the cost approach are not segregated into long-lived and short-lived items, nor is the basement composed of all long-lived or all short-lived cost. As a result, it would not necessarily be wrong to use a slightly different percentage than the aggregate number in the cost approach because the basement includes both long- and short-lived items that are not included in the same percentages as the remainder of the structure. This does not mean that the numbers can have no correlation whatsoever, but rather that they do not have to match up exactly.

Exhibit 19. Adjusting for a Basement Using the Cost Approach

Cost Approach					
Estimated site value					$75,000
Estimated reproduction cost new of improvements					
Dwelling	2,800	sq. ft. @	$90.00	= $252,000	
Basement	1,000	sq. ft. @	$50.00	= $50,000	
Fireplace, porches, patio, pool				= $7,400	
Garage/carport	750	sq. ft. @	$25.00	= $18,750	
Total estimated cost new				$328,150	
Less	Physical	Functional	External		
	10%	2%	2%		
Depreciation	$32,815	$5,907	$5,789	= $44,511	
Depreciated value of improvements				$283,639	$283,639
"As is" value of the site improvements					$4,500
Indicated value of cost approach					$363,139

Exhibit 20. Sales Comparison Analysis with Basement Adjustments Based on Depreciated Cost

	Adjustment Rate	Subject	Comparable 1		Comparable 2		Comparable 3	
Sale price				$320,000		$345,800		$315,800
Sale price/GLA				$120.75		$128.07		$112.79
Value Adjustments		**Description**	**Description**	**Adj.**	**Description**	**Adj.**	**Description**	**Adj.**
Sales or financing concessions			New mortgage no concessions	–	New mortgage no concessions	–	New mortgage no concessions	–
Date of sale/time	-2.0%	Now	1 month ago	(500)	5 months ago	(2,900)	9 months ago	(4,700)
Location		Thorp Acres	Keller Green	–	Keller Green	–	Keller Green	–
Leasehold/fee simple		Fee simple	Fee simple	–	Fee simple	–	Fee simple	–
Site		0.25 acre	0.25 acre	0	0.25 acre	0	0.45 acre	(5,000)
View		Residential	Residential	–	Residential	–	Residential	–
Design (style)		2-story/colonial	2-story/colonial	–	2-story/colonial	–	2-story/colonial	–
Actual age	3,000	10 years	9 years	(3,000)	9 years	(3,000)	12 years	6,000
Condition		Average	Average	–	Average	–	Average	–
Above Grade room count		Total | Bdrms. | Baths 10 | 4 | 2.5	Total | Bdrms. | Baths 10 | 4 | 2.5	–	Total | Bdrms. | Baths 10 | 4 | 2.5	–	Total | Bdrms. | Baths 10 | 4 | 2.5	–
Gross living area	$46	2,800	2,650	6,900	2,700	4,600	2,800	0
Basement & finished	$22	1,000	650	7,700	800	4,400	0	22,000
rooms below grade	$22	800	0	17,600	700	2,200	0	17,600
Functional utility		Average	Average	–	Average	–	Average	–
Heating and cooling		GFA/cent. AC	GFA/cent. AC	–	GFA/cent. AC	–	GFA/cent. AC	–
Garage/carport		2-car/d.t./gar.	2-car/att./gar.	–	2-car/att./gar.	–	2-car/att./gar.	–
Porch, patio, deck		Scr. porch	Scr. porch	–	Scr. porch	–	Scr. porch	–
Net adjustment				28,700		5,300		35,900
Adjusted sale price of comparable				$348,700		$351,100		$351,700

Functional Utility

The functional utility section is for various issues that may require adjustments. Most appraisers use this line for functional inadequacies such as unmarketable floor plans, unappealing decorating, or lack of a required feature such as a second bathroom. Sometimes appraisers adjust for these problems on other lines. For example, the lack of a second bathroom could be adjusted for on the bathroom line instead of this line. Superadequacies are usually adjusted for by not adding value for the item. For example, a house with a six-car garage in a market where two- or three-car garages are marketable but do not return value equal to cost are compensated for by adjusting upward for extra space but at a reduced rate.

A superadequacy can be adjusted for on this line, but most appraisers refrain from doing this. For example, a $45,000 in-ground swimming pool on a lot with a $75,000 home in a very cold climate will most likely fail to return value equal to cost. However, this is easily compensated for by adding zero for the item rather than adding a figure and then subtracting it because it is superadequate. Appraisers must be careful not to count the same feature twice while accounting for a superadequacy.

Methods of Extracting and Supporting Adjustments for Functional Utility

Cost Approach

The line for functional utility nearly always addresses some deficiency, so the cost to cure the problem is usually an option that may represent the market behavior. If the item is incurable, the cost approach may not be viable.

Income Capitalization Approach

The difference in rents for a property that has deficiencies and one that does not can be capitalized by using a GRM analysis. This approach is tedious but logical.

Sales Comparison Approach

As always, paired sales data analysis is effective for extracting and supporting adjustments for deficiencies and features. Finding nearly identical sales that have the deficiencies and others that lack them is sometimes possible and other times impossible.

A discussion with brokers on the impact of a particular feature on the market can often reveal an adjustment. For example, an appraiser may think that the lack of a second bath may be a problem, but the brokers indicate that it is not a problem because the market for the subject has shifted from family-oriented buyers to singles for whom one bath is adequate. Real estate brokers are on the cutting edge of the market, while real estate appraisers are on the trailing edge and must research continually to learn market expectations. Keep in mind that discussion of who the typical buyer is in an appraisal report could cause some problems from a fair lending standpoint.

Page **2** of 6

There are comparable properties currently offered for s

There are comparable sales in the subject neighborho

FEATURE	SUBJECT			COMP
Address				
Proximity to Subject				
Sale Price	$			
Sale Price/Gross Liv. Area	$		sq. ft.	$
Data Source(s)				
Verification Source(s)				
VALUE ADJUSTMENTS	DESCRIPTION			DESCRIPTI
Sale or Financing Concessions				
Date of Sale/Time				
Location				
Leasehold/Fee Simple				
Site				
View				
Design (Style)				
Quality of Construction				
Actual Age				
Condition				
Above Grade	Total	Bdrms.	Baths	Total Bdrms
Room Count				
Gross Living Area			sq. ft.	
Basement & Finished Rooms Below Grade				
Functional Utility				
Heating/Cooling				
Energy Efficient Items				
Garage/Carport				
Porch/Patio/Deck				
Net Adjustment (Total)				☐ + ☐
Adjusted Sale Price of Comparables				Net Adj. Gross Adj.

SALES COMPARISON APPROACH

I ☐ did ☐ did not research the sale or transfer history of the s

My research ☐ did ☐ did not reveal any prior sales or

Heating/Cooling

The line for heating and cooling accommodates adjustments for differences in HVAC systems. These adjustments can be a small issue in some markets and a larger one in others. The efficiency of one heating or cooling system over another may be a reason for a large adjustment. The total life of the unit may also be an issue. For example, heat pumps may be much less expensive to operate in a market, but the life of a compressor is shorter than a gas forced-air unit with an air-to-air, Freon-based air conditioner. As a result, the overall cost of operation including maintenance and replacements may still be higher for heat pumps.

In markets where energy costs are the largest expense of homeownership, the design efficiency may mean more than any other single issue. It is also possible to adjust for energy efficiency on the next line in the grid. Again, appraisers must be careful to not adjust twice for the same item.

Methods of Extracting and Supporting Adjustments for Heating and Cooling

Cost Approach

The cost approach can be used to extract and support a heating and cooling adjustment. It would be based on the difference in the cost of the subject's unit versus the cost of the comparable's unit. Some adjustment for accrued depreciation would also be applied against the cost difference. This approach is a favorite for many appraisers.

Income Capitalization Approach

The income capitalization approach could be the best way to support a heating and cooling adjustment overall. If one unit is more efficient than another, the annual savings could be divided by a capitalization rate to convert the annual savings to a lump sum amount. Effectively, the buyers would pay an amount based on the annual savings. This presupposes that buyers know the annual expense of one system compared to the other, which may or may not be true. In some markets, real estate agents publish utility costs on sales brochures.

Sales Comparison Approach

As always, paired sales data analysis works for extracting and supporting the heating and cooling adjustment. In many markets, finding nearly identical sales of properties equipped with and without a particular HVAC system could pose a problem.

Other

Contacting local brokers for their opinions may be invaluable when it comes to heating and cooling. Brokers may have discussed heating and cooling issues with buyers during the buying process and are able to give some insight into buyers' actions.

Energy Efficient Items

The next line is for recording superior energy-efficient designs that return increased market value to the owner. While many energy-efficient items may be included in a residence, some are so insignificant that they do not warrant adjustments. Other items may be significant, but the market does not desire them. Consider the following examples:

- In many markets, solar panels installed on roofs increase energy efficiency, but buyers feel that they detract from the property's appearance. Some buyers will not buy such houses if they have a viable alternative.
- A high-efficiency $200 setback thermostat does not add significant value to a $500,000, single-unit property. Such a feature will not likely be remembered by a buyer who has viewed several other homes and must decide which one to make an offer on.
- A single-unit property that has been built with 2 × 6 wood frame walls instead of the standard 2 × 4 frame walls that allow for more sidewall insulation will not likely be noticed by the typical buyer in a 15-minute inspection.

Methods of Extracting and Supporting Adjustments for Energy-Efficient Items

Cost Approach

The cost approach is based on the difference in the cost of the subject improvements with and without the feature in question. Some adjustment for accrued depreciation would also be applied against the cost difference.

Income Capitalization Approach

The income capitalization approach could be the best way to support an energy-efficient items adjustment overall if the feature in question generates savings that can be capitalized into a lump sum present value. If an item was perceived by a buyer to save a property owner $500 per year, that savings could be divided by a capitalization rate to get an adjustment of $500/0.10 = $5,000.

Sales Comparison Approach

The paired sales data analysis works in extracting and supporting adjustments for energy-efficient items. Again, finding nearly identical sales that are equipped with a particular energy-efficient feature and those that lack such a feature is a challenge for appraisers.

Garage/Carport

Appraisers use this next line to adjust for the amount of garage or carport space, which can be a big concern in some areas. In markets where buyers seek workshop areas, it may also be an issue. In markets where automobile theft is a problem, this feature could be a major reason for adjustment.

Page 2 of 6

There are comparable properties currently offered for s

There are comparable sales in the subject neighborhoo

FEATURE	SUBJECT	COMPA
Address		
Proximity to Subject		
Sale Price	$	
Sale Price/Gross Liv. Area	$ sq. ft.	$
Data Source(s)		
Verification Source(s)		
VALUE ADJUSTMENTS	DESCRIPTION	DESCRIPTI
Sale or Financing Concessions		
Date of Sale/Time		
Location		
Leasehold/Fee Simple		
Site		
View		
Design (Style)		
Quality of Construction		
Actual Age		
Condition		
Above Grade Room Count	Total / Bdrms. / Baths	Total / Bdrms
Gross Living Area	sq. ft.	
Basement & Finished Rooms Below Grade		
Functional Utility		
Heating/Cooling		
Energy Efficient Items		
Garage/Carport		
Porch/Patio/Deck		
Net Adjustment (Total)		☐ + ☐
Adjusted Sale Price of Comparables		Net Adj. Gross Adj.

SALES COMPARISON APPROACH

I ☐ did ☐ did not research the sale or transfer history of the s

My research ☐ did ☐ did not reveal any prior sales or tra

There is no line on either form for on-site, nonsheltered parking. Having a designated place for the owner's exclusive parking use can be an asset. In those markets, this line can be used to indicate on-site parking. Some appraisers also use this line to adjust for the owner's ability to park a car on site. These adjustments are not common in suburban and rural areas where lot sizes are larger, but they are common in urbanized areas where on-street parking is a problem.

Methods of Extracting and Supporting Adjustments for Garages or Carports

Cost Approach

The cost approach would be a common method of extracting and supporting an adjustment for garage or carport area.

Income Capitalization Approach

An extraction using gross rent comparison is possible, and the amenity is large enough for an appraiser to quantify the difference in rent for a property that has a two-car garage as opposed to a three-car garage.

Sales Comparison Approach

Obviously, a paired sales data analysis is a great way to extract and support a garage adjustment.

Porch/Patio/Deck

Typically, the porch/patio/deck line is used to list and adjust for exterior features of a property that add value. For some properties, these features can be of significant value.

Methods of Extracting and Supporting Adjustments for Porches, Patios, or Decks

Cost Approach

The cost approach is a common method for extracting and supporting an adjustment for porches, patios, and decks. A buyer of a home that lacks a deck could consider adding one after purchase as an alternative to buying a property that already has the feature.

Income Capitalization Approach

An extraction using the gross rent comparison is possible, but usually these features are not significant enough to enable the appraiser to isolate the difference in rents between properties that have porches and those that lack them.

Sales Comparison Approach

A paired sales data analysis is an effective way to extract and support a porch/patio/deck adjustment. If comparable properties that have the feature and those that lack it have been sold, the difference in price between them is attributable to the feature.

Blank Lines

Three blank lines are provided for the appraiser to add adjustments for any factors that he or she considers worthy of adjustment. The space can also be used to adjust for significant items such as swimming pools, large barns, country club memberships, personal property of all kinds, or features that are not included in the previous categories. It is important for appraisers to be aware of the USPAP Standards Rules regarding including personal property in real estate appraisals.

Net Adjustment (Total)

The net adjustment is the sum of all adjustments entered on the sales comparison grid. This line is mathematical and can be easily completed using a computer. The net adjustment percentage and gross adjustment percentage are also required. These percentages are quality ratings for the analysis. Fannie Mae has guidelines for how much net and gross adjustments should be, and appraisers must explain why they are exceeded. If an appraiser has adjusted a comparable sale more than 15% in one direction, it may not be comparable and its use may be invalid. If an appraiser has adjusted a comparable more than 25% on an absolute (overall) basis, the sale itself may not be comparable. Excessive adjustments should be explained for all appraisals in which they occur.

Appraisers may wonder what choices they have when they exceed Fannie Mae's guidelines. If the appraiser is working in a market where data is hard to find or nonexistent, exceeding these guidelines is often the rule rather than the exception. When an appraiser finds low property turnover rates that result in a lack of data, the appraiser needs to explain the reasons for the poor quality of data and most clients will accept it. An appraiser who uses data that is not very comparable but does not explain why will receive complaints and may lose clients.

The location and zoning map may be the appraiser's best friend when it comes to justifying the lack of good comparables in rural areas. If the subject is in a low-density area and the comparables are few and far between, the maps will show the low density. If the problem lies in the design, improvement size, or property use, the appraiser must find another means to support the lack of better comparables.

Adjusted Sale Price of Comparables

The adjusted sale price of comparables line represents the gross reported sale price of the comparable, plus or minus the adjustments arrived at on the previous line. It shows the reader the logic and support for the value estimate arrived at. It is common thinking in the appraisal profession that if the range in indicated values exceeds a certain percentage, which differs from market to market, the appraiser must perform more research or try to provide an explanation. When performing a sales comparison analysis, it is not unusual for an appraiser to find a significant variance in the amount that each comparable sale indicates the subject is worth. When this happens, it is most commonly a situation in which the appraiser lacks some important fact about the details of the sale or sales. As a result, it is necessary for the appraiser to investigate to learn these details. A spread of more than 5% in indicated values from comparable sales is unacceptable in some markets. In some areas of low population density, a 10% spread in the indicated values may be considered an outstanding analysis. Typically, the spread is much greater when the number of buyers and sellers are limited because of the lack of market refinement. Keep in mind that a wide range in indicated values could lead to client dissatisfaction and the belief that the appraiser does not really know the market.

Sales Comparison Approach Section: Additional Information

P R O A C H

I ☐ did ☐ did not research the sale or transfer history of the subject property and comparable sales. If not, explain

My research ☐ did ☐ did not reveal any prior sales or transfers of the subject property for the three years prior to the effective date of this appraisal.

Data source(s)

My research ☐ did ☐ did not reveal any prior sales or transfers of the comparable sales for the year prior to the date of sale of the comparable sale.

Data source(s)

Report the results of the research and analysis of the prior sale or transfer history of the subject property and comparable sales (report additional prior sales on page 3).

ITEM	SUBJECT	COMPARABLE SALE # 1	COMPARABLE SALE # 2	COMPARABLE SALE # 3
Date of Prior Sale/Transfer				
Price of Prior Sale/Transfer				
Data Source(s)				
Effective Date of Data Source(s)				

Analysis of prior sale or transfer history of the subject property and comparable sales

Summary of Sales Comparison Approach

Indicated Value by Sales Comparison Approach $

I ☐ did ☐ did not research the sale or transfer history of the subject property and comparable sales. If not, explain.

In the next section of the form, check boxes accompany the two and one-half lines allowed for narrative description. The appraiser has only two options. The appraiser who indicates that the history has been researched will be held accountable for the report's accuracy. If the appraiser indicates that the history has not been researched, it will raise red flags for nearly all investors, lenders, and underwriters. This section of the report requires the appraiser to research the history of the subject and comparable sales and meet the following criteria:

- Comply with USPAP Standard Rule 1-5, which requires a three-year search for the subject's market history.
- Ensure that the appraiser is familiar with the subject's market history and its significance.
- Ensure that the appraiser knows whether the current comparable sale is an arm's-length sale–i.e., a transaction between unrelated parties under no duress.[2]

2. *The Dictionary of Real Estate Appraisal*, 4th ed. (Chicago: Appraisal Institute, 2002), 18.

For example, if a property reportedly sells for $190,000 but sold only two weeks before for $100,000, this would suggest that something unusual has occurred. The previous sale may not have been arm's length, but it could also mean that the current sale is not arm's length either. A property could be upgraded in only two weeks, but this is doubtful. Regardless of the reason, inconsistency in sale prices is a red flag that suggests the need for more research.

- Research the previous sales of comparable properties. Researching previous sales of comparable properties allows the appraiser and the recipient of the report to establish a trend in property values. In some markets, this data can be so sparse that no trend can be gleaned from the sales and resales of the comparables. In others, it may be primary evidence of a change in the market. Forcing appraisers to research this information is a good way to show trends in real estate prices in various markets.

The question then arises of whether USPAP (2008-2009) requires appraisers to research the history of the comparable sales. The answer to this is "maybe." USPAP requires an appraiser to research and then report the market history for the subject for three years, but it does not mention the sales history of the comparables. Standards Rule 1-5 states the following:

> When the value opinion to be developed is market value, an appraiser must, if such information is available to the appraiser in the normal course of business:
>
> (a) Analyze all agreements of sale, options, and listings of the subject property current as of the effective date of the appraisal; and
>
> (b) Analyze all sales of the subject property that occurred within the three (3) years prior to the effective date of the appraisal.
>
> Comment: See the Comments to Standards Rules 2-2 (a) (viii), 2- 2 (b) (viii), and 2-2 (c) (viii) for corresponding reporting requirements relating to the availability and relevance of information.[3]

This rule requires appraisers to research and analyze the history of the subject for three years, and the comments referring to Standards Rule 2-2 require the appraiser to report the results of that analysis. Advisory Opinion 1 (AO-1) also focuses on this issue, but nothing implies that appraisers must research the history of the comparable sales.

Because Fannie Mae designs these forms to be used for its loans and they have the power to stipulate what rules should be followed by lenders that sell loans to them, they have the ability to increase the appraisal and reporting requirements above the USPAP minimums. For an appraisal prepared for the State Bank of Smallburg in which the appraiser did not agree to follow Fannie Mae's rules (i.e., a portfolio loan), Standards Rule 1-5 need not necessarily apply. It could be ruled at some state boards, however, that the use of a Fannie Mae form necessitates following Fannie Mae's rules. This interpretation may or may not be widely accepted, which implies that it would be best practice for appraisers to ask each client if the assign-

3. *Uniform Standards of Professional Appraisal Practice (USPAP)* (Washington, D.C.: The Appraisal Foundation, 2008), U-19.

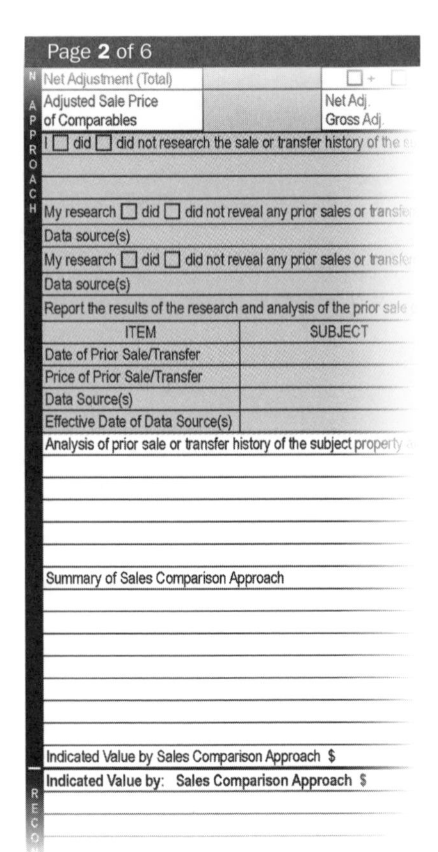

Page 2 of 6

Net Adjustment (Total)

Adjusted Sale Price of Comparables		Net Adj. Gross Adj.

I ☐ did ☐ did not research the sale or transfer history of the

My research ☐ did ☐ did not reveal any prior sales or

Data source(s)

My research ☐ did ☐ did not reveal any prior sales or

Data source(s)

Report the results of the research and analysis of the prior

ITEM	SUBJECT
Date of Prior Sale/Transfer	
Price of Prior Sale/Transfer	
Data Source(s)	
Effective Date of Data Source(s)	

Analysis of prior sale or transfer history of the subject property

Summary of Sales Comparison Approach

Indicated Value by Sales Comparison Approach $

Indicated Value by: Sales Comparison Approach $

ment at hand is for a mortgage loan that will eventually be sold to Fannie Mae. If so, researching the sales history of comparable sales is a requirement. If not, the State Appraisers Board or a court may interpret "recognized methods and techniques" to include researching the sales history of comparable sales.

Recognized Methods and Techniques

A case could be made that the standard to research the prior sales of the comparables becomes more and more part of recognized methods and techniques with each passing day and as a result would be required by USPAP Standards Rule 1-1 as follows:

> In developing a real property appraisal, an appraiser must:
>
> (a) be aware of, understand, and correctly employ those recognized methods and techniques that are necessary to produce a credible appraisal[4]

This rule leaves it up to the individual to decide what is currently part of the appraisal industry's "recognized methods." If it is decided that researching prior sales of comparables is a recognized method, then the appraiser must do so. If it is decided that this is not a recognized method, then the intended use constitutes the defining rule.

My research ☐ did ☐ did not reveal any prior sales or transfers of the subject property for the three years prior to the effective date of this appraisal.

Data source(s)

USPAP requires the appraiser to state whether the historical research revealed any sales of the subject property for the three years prior to the effective date of appraisal. The previous statement refers only to whether the appraiser has researched this issue. This statement requires that the appraiser state whether the research revealed any activity. If the appraiser's research did not reveal prior sales or transfers, the appraiser can move on. If the research did reveal such information, more questions will follow. In responding to this statement, appraisers should indicate the sources they used. If these data sources do not match those used to obtain the comparables presented, red flags will be raised.

My research ☐ did ☐ did not reveal any prior sales or transfers of the comparable sales for the year prior to the date of sale of the comparable sale.

Data source(s)

If the appraiser's research revealed no other activity prior to the sale reported on the grid, the appraiser can check the box and move on. If the research did reveal prior market activity for the comparables, the appraiser must be prepared to provide an explanation. In any case, appraisers should indicate the sources they used to answer this question.

4. *USPAP*, U-15.

Report the results of the research and analysis of the prior sale or transfer history of the subject property and comparable sales (report additional prior sales on page 3).

The next section inquires about the most recent prior sales of the subject and comparables that have occurred in the last three years for the subject and in the last year for the comparables. The information about the listing history of the subject is on page 1 in the subject section, and the information about the current sale of the subject is on page 1 in the contract section. This provides the appraiser with space in which to list market activity.

Date of Prior Sale/Transfer

The appraiser should not include data from the current sale of the subject or the sales reported on the grid in this section. These lines are for data on prior sales of the subject and comparables. This line should also include non-sale transfers such as quitclaim deeds, deeds in lieu of foreclosure, corporate deeds, and deeds of trust. It requires the appraiser to report any known transfer history about the property. This information is usually not readily accessible within the appraiser's normal course of business.

The standard of practice in this case is similar to that for many other areas–i.e., the standard as set by one's peers. It would seem that if a review appraiser could obtain data that the first appraiser was not able to, then the initial appraiser would be culpable. If an appraiser's peers or the State Certification Board would expect an appraiser to obtain the information for an appraisal, then the standard would be to do so. Furthermore, it would appear that in states where easily accessible county records document the transfer history, reporting this data is not difficult and as a result will be expected in each appraisal report. In markets where the data is not compiled, not freely accessible, or highly unreliable, the standard of practice would be to explain why the transfer history is not reported. If the review appraiser can get the data and the initial appraiser did not include it, this may suggest that the initial appraiser intentionally omitted it.

Price of Prior Sale/Transfer

Next, the forms ask for the sale price of the subject's prior sales. Researching this data is also intended to make the appraiser recognize a non-arm's-length sale when it comes up in the data source. For example, if a comparable sale was reported in the MLS as having sold at a price of $422,000 but was also found to have sold three months earlier for $209,000, the appraiser would know there had to be some extenuating circumstances that required additional research. This data may also be used by the underwriter to show a trend in the market that can be applied to the appraisal at hand or other appraisals. The report can show the reader of the appraisal report consistency in the marketplace as well as consistency in the subject's value over time. If the subject is currently for sale and there is a history of two previous sales for analysis, the underwriter can glean much information from the data.

Page 2 of 6

Net Adjustment (Total)		☐ +
Adjusted Sale Price of Comparables		Net Adj. Gross Adj.

I ☐ did ☐ did not research the sale or transfer history of the

My research ☐ did ☐ did not reveal any prior sales or trans

Data source(s)

My research ☐ did ☐ did not reveal any prior sales or trans

Data source(s)

Report the results of the research and analysis of the prior sal

ITEM	SUBJECT
Date of Prior Sale/Transfer	
Price of Prior Sale/Transfer	
Data Source(s)	
Effective Date of Data Source(s)	

Analysis of prior sale or transfer history of the subject property

Summary of Sales Comparison Approach

Indicated Value by Sales Comparison Approach $

Indicated Value by: Sales Comparison Approach $

Case in Point

The subject sold 36 months ago for $200,000 and sold again 24 months ago for $206,000, for a change in value of 3.0% over that year ($\Delta\% = 3.0\%$). The same property is now selling for $214,000, which means that the difference between Sale 2 and Sale 3 is 3.88% ($\Delta\% = 3.88\%$). However, the sales (2 and 3) occurred over two years, which means that the annual rate is 1.94% per year. The rate of change overall between Sale 1 and Sale 3 is 7.0%, but it represents a period of three years, which equals 2.333% per year.

This data does not show a tightly defined rate of appreciation, but it does show that the rate of appreciation is not 5% or 0%. This is commonly the type of result an appraiser finds when researching sales and resales of the same property. If the market in this area has been characterized by these rates of appreciation, the underwriter should feel good about this deal at $214,000 but would be very uncomfortable if the current reported price was $235,000. If the price was currently $235,000, it would reflect a 17.5% increase overall or a 5.83% increase per year, which is much higher than the difference between Sale 1 and Sale 2. If the appraiser reports these levels of appreciation rates but the subject shows an increase in value of 6% per year due to comparison of the subject's prior sales with the current one, the underwriter will likely become suspicious. In some markets, the appraiser must provide much explanation to show the user why the value is so much higher than the historical sale price including appreciation.

Data Source(s)

Appraisers should indicate where they obtained their data so that the review appraiser can confirm it and determine its adequacy. It is always painful when review appraisers say that they could not find the data and so assumed it was fabricated or that they found relevant data that was not reported and ignored when in fact it was obtained from a source that was unavailable to the appraiser at the time.

Effective Date of Data Source(s)

In some databases, data is downloaded from its source on a weekly or monthly basis. As a result, the appraiser could exercise due diligence in obtaining up-to-date sales information but still may miss some data that would appear to be readily available to review appraisers after the fact. If the "data dump" is not frequent, the appraiser may be very limited in obtaining recent sales.

Analysis of prior sale or transfer history of the subject property and comparable sales

The appraiser shows the results of the analysis in the next section, indicating in narrative form what the sales history shows. Listing the data is not enough; this space on the form gives the appraiser the opportunity to explain why historical sales are or are not truly indications of market value. The report reader will assume that all sales listed are arm's length, but that may not necessarily be true. *Market value* is defined on page 4 of both forms as

> The most probable price which a property should bring in a competitive and open market under all conditions requisite to a fair sale, the buyer and seller, each acting prudently, knowledgeably and assuming the price

is not affected by undue stimulus. Implicit in this definition is the consummation of a sale as of a specified date and the passing of title from seller to buyer under conditions whereby:

(1) Buyer and seller are typically motivated;

(2) Both parties are well informed or well advised, and each acting in what he or she considers his or her own best interest;

(3) A reasonable time is allowed for exposure in the open market;

(4) Payment is made in terms of cash in U. S. dollars or in terms of financial arrangements comparable thereto; and

(5) The price represents the normal consideration for the property sold unaffected by special or creative financing or sales concessions granted by anyone associated with the sale.

The following examples illustrate problems that the appraiser would need to discuss, analyze, and report in this section of the appraisal report.

Case in Point

1 Sale 1 is a property improved with a 2,000-sq.-ft. home located in Smallburg. It is listed on the grid as having sold for $205,000 three months ago. It sold two years and three months before that for $204,000. This sale and resale seem to imply that no appreciation occurred. The home was listed for sale at $196,000 and had been on the market for 99 days at that price when the offer of $204,000 with a 95% mortgage in "as is" condition with an $8,000 allowance for seller-paid financing was received. If the $8,000 is subtracted from the $204,000 price, the appreciation rate is 4.59% overall, which equals 2.2959% per year. With this explanation, the underwriter would assume that a reasonable amount of appreciation had occurred. Without it, there might be concern about a flat real estate market.

2 The subject is located in a market where 3% appreciation is common. The previous sale of the subject or comparable sale was a foreclosure sale at $183,000 one year ago, and the appraiser believes that the property is now worth $235,000 after substantial repairs. This situation is believable. If the appraiser reports that the property sold for $183,000 one year ago and indicates that it is worth $235,000 now but does not report the conditions of sale then and the repairs now, it would not be believable in most markets. This explanation would only be acceptable to most investors if details on the prior sale and changes in the property conditions between the sale and appraisal dates were provided.

3 The subject is located in a market where 2% appreciation is common. The subject is a single-unit residential property that was tenant occupied five years ago. At that time, it was listed for sale in the MLS at $325,900. The listing agent reported that it sold then for $303,000. The appraiser believes it is worth about $385,000 today. A phone call to the listing agent is needed to explain a 5% (compounded) increase in a market that typically only brings 2% appreciation. The listing agent responded that during the listing period, the tenants would take off the lock box every time she put it on the door. When agents would come to show the listing, they would not have access to the building. Eventually the lease ran out, but the tenants would not leave. They stayed even though the power and water supply were turned off. After six months, an entrepreneur made a low offer, and the owners took it. The sellers were highly motivated.

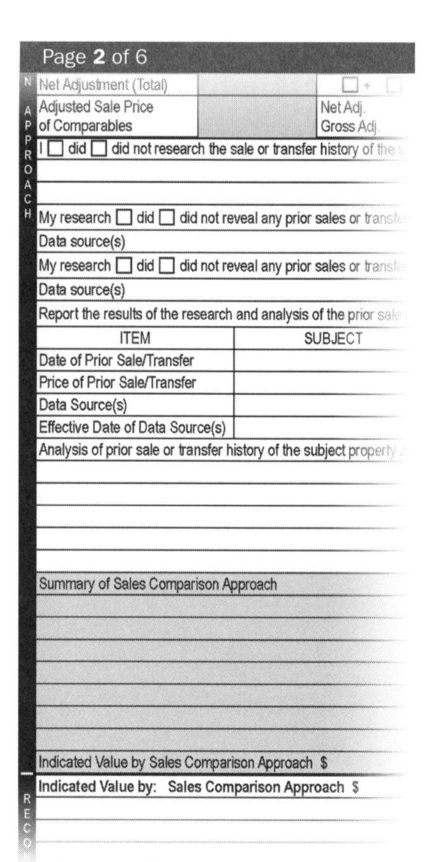
Page 2 of 6

Net Adjustment (Total)

Adjusted Sale Price of Comparables		Net Adj. Gross Adj.

I ☐ did ☐ did not research the sale or transfer history of the

My research ☐ did ☐ did not reveal any prior sales or transf

Data source(s)

My research ☐ did ☐ did not reveal any prior sales or transf

Data source(s)

Report the results of the research and analysis of the prior sale

ITEM	SUBJECT
Date of Prior Sale/Transfer	
Price of Prior Sale/Transfer	
Data Source(s)	
Effective Date of Data Source(s)	

Analysis of prior sale or transfer history of the subject property

Summary of Sales Comparison Approach

Indicated Value by Sales Comparison Approach $

Indicated Value by: Sales Comparison Approach $

Summary of Sales Comparison Approach

Several blank lines are provided under the sales comparison approach summary section to give the appraiser space to discuss unusual terms, support the rates of adjustment and the rationale for the selection of comparables, and perhaps give directions for another sales comparison grid for three more comparable sales. For most lenders, this area is reserved for the appraiser to explain why the analysis does not comply with generally accepted or specific guidelines or rules. Unfortunately, some appraisers fill in this space with pre-written "canned" comments. If an appraiser's analysis is limited because of the lack of available data, this is the place to make that statement and provide support for it.

Indicated Value by Sales Comparison Approach $

The last line of this section of the report contains the results for the sales comparison phase of the appraisal assignment. The indicated value is a reconciled number. Appraisers often try to round the answer to imply a level of precision. For example, if the subject of an appraisal is a parcel containing a 2,500-sq.-ft., two-story home located in a tract development surrounded by homes of almost identical design, and six comparable sales were used that ranged from $217,000 to $219,000 after adjustments, the appraiser might choose to indicate the value to be $218,000. This amount implies precision to a $1,000 level. If, on the other hand, the subject of the appraisal is improved with a two-year-old, 4,500-sq.-ft. home located in an area of 30- to 40-year-old, 2,000- to 3,000-sq.-ft. homes and the indicated values of the comparables range from $305,000 to $329,000, the appraiser might want to reconcile the value opinion at $325,000 to imply a precision of only $25,000.

> Fannie Mae discusses the sales comparison approach section of the appraisal report in depth in their single-family *Selling Guide*, Section B4-1.4, Appraisal Report Assessment. The *Selling Guide* is available on Fannie Mae's Web site at *www.efanniemae.com.*
>
> To access the guide, type "Selling Guide" in the search box that appears in the top right corner of the home page. The *Selling Guide* can also be accessed by first clicking on "Appraisers" under the "Industry Specialists" heading. Next, click on "Single-Family Guides for free online" under the heading "AllRegs Online." A list of documents will then appear. If pop-ups are blocked, click on "View Support Tips and AllRegs Contact Info" under the "AllRegs Online" heading to access directions for changing the browser settings to allow pop-ups.

Reconciliation Section of the URAR

RECONCILIATION

Indicated Value by: Sales Comparison Approach $	Cost Approach (if developed) $	Income Approach (if developed) $
This appraisal is made ☐ "as is", ☐ subject to completion per plans and specifications on the basis of a hypothetical condition that the improvements have been completed, ☐ subject to the following repairs or alterations on the basis of a hypothetical condition that the repairs or alterations have been completed, or ☐ subject to the following required inspection based on the extraordinary assumption that the condition or deficiency does not require alteration or repair:		
Based on a complete visual inspection of the interior and exterior areas of the subject property, defined scope of work, statement of assumptions and limiting conditions, and appraiser's certification, my (our) opinion of the market value, as defined, of the real property that is the subject of this report is $, as of , which is the date of inspection and the effective date of this appraisal.		

Freddie Mac Form 70 March 2005 Page 2 of 6 Fannie Mae Form 1004 March 2005

The reconciliation section of the URAR is slightly different from that of Form 2055, so this section of each form will be discussed separately. The difference pertains to the extent of the visual inspection of the property. The URAR will be discussed first.

Indicated Value by: Sales Comparison Approach $______ Cost Approach (if developed) $______ Income Approach (if developed) $______

The first line of the reconciliation section of the URAR pulls together in one place all three approaches to value: the sales comparison approach, the cost approach, and the income capitalization approach. It brings focus to the other approaches to value, which may or may not be the goal of many lenders that want appraisers to focus only on sales and listings.

The three blank lines that follow are open to whatever discussion is considered necessary to reconcile the approaches to value or to explain why the other approaches were not used in the analysis. In this section, the appraiser justifies the value opinion as listed. The section should be used by appraisers to explain the process, not to provide standard statements that do not support the opinion. The appraiser can explain why the cost approach was omitted or why the income capitalization approach is or is not typically applicable in the market.

This appraisal is made ☐ "as is," ☐ subject to completion per plans and specifications on the basis of a hypothetical condition that the improvements have been completed, ☐ subject to the following repairs or alterations on the basis of a hypothetical condition that the repairs or alterations have been completed, or ☐ subject to the following required inspection based on the extraordinary assumption that the condition or deficiency does not require alteration or repair:

In the next part of the URAR's reconciliation section, the appraiser stipulates the special conditions of the appraisal. These may include such conditions as "subject to completion of construction per plans and specifications," "subject to repairs being completed," or, most recently, to stipulate that something does not need repair. The last

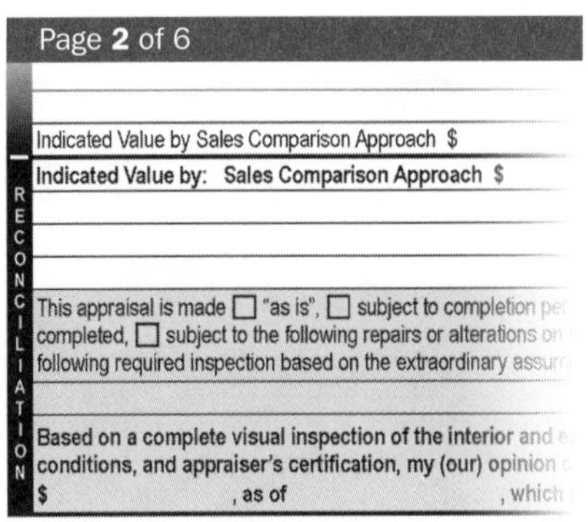
Page 2 of 6

Indicated Value by Sales Comparison Approach $

Indicated Value by: Sales Comparison Approach $

RECONCILIATION

This appraisal is made ☐ "as is", ☐ subject to completion pe
completed, ☐ subject to the following repairs or alterations o
following required inspection based on the extraordinary assu

Based on a complete visual inspection of the interior and e
conditions, and appraiser's certification, my (our) opinion
$, as of , which

Freddie Mac Form 70 March 2005

condition is most significant for appraisers who are concerned about liability when performing mortgage appraisals. Under this condition, the appraiser can stipulate that the value opinion is subject to a favorable roof, termite, well, septic, crawl space, attic, or electrical or plumbing system inspection. The way this section of the form reads, the appraiser assumes that the possible problem does not exist and the value opinion is made "as if the problem was actually not a problem."

Appraisers should never use this part of the form as a template. Those who do use a template can forget to stipulate the repairs needed or neglect to make the value subject to construction completion. If this section is left blank on a template, the underwriter will likely call the appraiser. If this section is completed erroneously, it can create problems that may lead to litigation.

Based on a complete visual inspection of the interior and exterior areas of the subject property, defined scope of work, statement of assumptions and limiting conditions, and appraiser's certification, my (our) opinion of the market value, as defined, of the real property that is the subject of this report is $________, as of ______, which is the date of inspection and the effective date of this appraisal.

On this last line, the appraiser indicates the amount of the final value opinion and the effective date of the appraisal, which is the same as the date of inspection. This is the "bottom line" of the appraisal report for most readers. Appraisal reports that are back-dated to settle estates or divorces are going to be inconsistent because of this statement.

Reconciliation Section of Form 2055

RECONCILIATION

Indicated Value by: Sales Comparison Approach $ Cost Approach (if developed) $ Income Approach (if developed) $

This appraisal is made ☐ "as is", ☐ subject to completion per plans and specifications on the basis of a hypothetical condition that the improvements have been completed, ☐ subject to the following repairs or alterations on the basis of a hypothetical condition that the repairs or alterations have been completed, or ☐ subject to the following required inspection based on the extraordinary assumption that the condition or deficiency does not require alteration or repair:

Based on a visual inspection of the exterior areas of the subject property from at least the street, defined scope of work, statement of assumptions and limiting conditions, and appraiser's certification, my (our) opinion of the market value, as defined, of the real property that is the subject of this report is $, as of , which is the date of the inspection and the effective date of this appraisal.

The last part of the reconciliation section of Form 2055 is worded differently than that of the URAR.

Based on a visual inspection of the exterior areas of the subject property from at least the street, defined scope of work, statement of assumptions and limiting conditions, and appraiser's certification, my (our) opinion of the market value, as defined, of the real property that is the subject of this report is $________, as of______, which is the date of the inspection and the effective date of this appraisal.

This last part of the reconciliation section of Form 2055 has been adjusted to exclude the reference to an interior inspection. Here, the appraiser should indicate the amount of the value opinion and the effective date of the appraisal, which is the same as the date of inspection.

Uniform Residential Appraisal Report

File #

ADDITIONAL COMMENTS

COST APPROACH

COST APPROACH TO VALUE (not required by Fannie Mae)

Provide adequate information for the lender/client to replicate the below cost figures and calculations.

Support for the opinion of site value (summary of comparable land sales or other methods for estimating site value)

ESTIMATED ☐ REPRODUCTION OR ☐ REPLACEMENT COST NEW	OPINION OF SITE VALUE ... = $
Source of cost data	Dwelling Sq. Ft. @ $ ... =$
Quality rating from cost service Effective date of cost data	Sq. Ft. @ $ ... =$
Comments on Cost Approach (gross living area calculations, depreciation, etc.)	
	Garage/Carport Sq. Ft. @ $ ... =$
	Total Estimate of Cost-New ... = $
	Less Physical | Functional | External
	Depreciation =$( )
	Depreciated Cost of Improvements ... =$
	"As-is" Value of Site Improvements ... =$
Estimated Remaining Economic Life (HUD and VA only) Years	Indicated Value By Cost Approach ... =$

INCOME

INCOME APPROACH TO VALUE (not required by Fannie Mae)

Estimated Monthly Market Rent $ X Gross Rent Multiplier = $ Indicated Value by Income Approach

Summary of Income Approach (including support for market rent and GRM)

PUD INFORMATION

PROJECT INFORMATION FOR PUDs (if applicable)

Is the developer/builder in control of the Homeowners' Association (HOA)? ☐ Yes ☐ No Unit type(s) ☐ Detached ☐ Attached

Provide the following information for PUDs ONLY if the developer/builder is in control of the HOA and the subject property is an attached dwelling unit.

Legal name of project

Total number of phases Total number of units Total number of units sold

Total number of units rented Total number of units for sale Data source(s)

Was the project created by the conversion of an existing building(s) into a PUD? ☐ Yes ☐ No If Yes, date of conversion

Does the project contain any multi-dwelling units? ☐ Yes ☐ No Data source(s)

Are the units, common elements, and recreation facilities complete? ☐ Yes ☐ No If No, describe the status of completion.

Are the common elements leased to or by the Homeowners' Association? ☐ Yes ☐ No If Yes, describe the rental terms and options.

Describe common elements and recreational facilities

Freddie Mac Form 70 March 2005 Page 3 of 6 Fannie Mae Form 1004 March 2005

Additional Comments, Cost Approach, Income Capitalization Approach, and PUD Information

Page 3 is exactly the same on the URAR and Form 2055.

Additional Comments Section

The additional comments section of the URAR and Form 2055 is designed for the practitioner's input. It is an open space with 38 blank lines, which could accommodate a considerable amount of narrative detail if small print is used. In this area, appraisers can discuss all the issues that did not fit within the confines of pages 1 and 2 of the form. This is a welcome change from the earlier version of the URAR, in which the attached pages were separate from the form itself. This modification makes it more difficult for the appraisal report form to be separated from the annotated comments.

This section of the form could be used to accommodate the expansion of the scope of work. A common complaint about residential appraisal reports is that appraisers only make standard statements and neglect to provide explanations for significant factors that affect the property because discussing them takes too long or takes up too much space. Keep in mind that many clients only know what the appraiser tells them about the property. If an appraiser makes a mistake because he or she cloned an old report or did not proofread the work well, the client will be led to think the appraiser is incompetent. Appraisers are often judged by what they write.

Cost Approach Section

COST APPROACH	COST APPROACH TO VALUE (not required by Fannie Mae)	
	Provide adequate information for the lender/client to replicate the below cost figures and calculations.	
	Support for the opinion of site value (summary of comparable land sales or other methods for estimating site value)	
	ESTIMATED ☐ REPRODUCTION OR ☐ REPLACEMENT COST NEW	OPINION OF SITE VALUE = $
	Source of cost data	Dwelling Sq. Ft. @ $ =$
	Quality rating from cost service Effective date of cost data	Sq. Ft. @ $ =$
	Comments on Cost Approach (gross living area calculations, depreciation, etc.)	
		Garage/Carport Sq. Ft. @ $ =$
		Total Estimate of Cost-New = $
		Less Physical | Functional | External
		Depreciation =$( )
		Depreciated Cost of Improvements =$
		"As-is" Value of Site Improvements =$
	Estimated Remaining Economic Life (HUD and VA only) Years	Indicated Value By Cost Approach =$

The current cost approach grid used on the forms is similar to the one used in older versions of the appraisal report forms. Even in its abbreviated format, history has shown that this grid is probably all

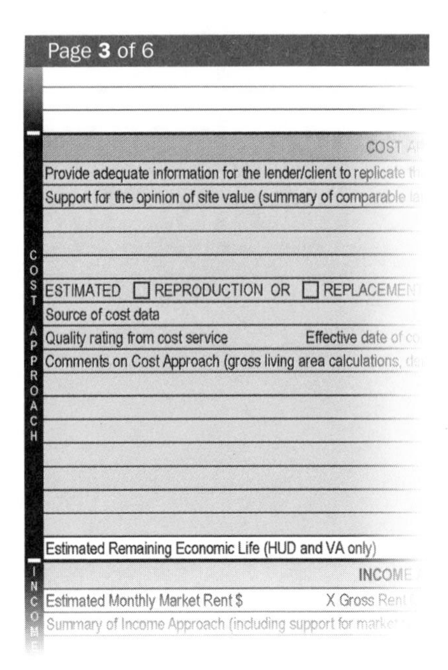
Page 3 of 6

COST A

Provide adequate information for the lender/client to replicate

Support for the opinion of site value (summary of comparable

ESTIMATED ☐ REPRODUCTION OR ☐ REPLACEME

Source of cost data

Quality rating from cost service | Effective date of

Comments on Cost Approach (gross living area calculations,

Estimated Remaining Economic Life (HUD and VA only)

INCOME

Estimated Monthly Market Rent $ | X Gross Rent

Summary of Income Approach (including support for mark

that is needed for most single-unit residences. The grid has been modified to include an extra line for other "as is" items, which may include swimming pools, well and septic systems, or other site improvements that are not included on the preceding line.

The cost approach to value is not required by Fannie Mae for the appraisal of residential properties. This approach can be an excellent tool for valuing residential real estate because it works in most markets. Moreover, it is an excellent check against the sales comparison approach, which can be tainted in markets where data is questionable. In appraising newer homes, the cost approach can function as a supporting approach. For lenders who seek confirmable data, it is usually based too heavily on opinion and is of little use.

Other lenders use this section to confirm the appropriate amount of fire insurance for the improvement. Appraisers must exercise caution in completing this section. In particular, they should be careful about the numbers used. For instance, it could be disastrous if the appraiser underestimates the cost of construction and if the lender discounts the amount of insurance required based on an understated cost new estimate. If a loss did occur, the property would be underinsured.

COST APPROACH TO VALUE (not required by Fannie Mae) Provide adequate information for the lender/client to replicate the below cost figures and calculations.

The first line of the cost approach section requires the appraiser to provide references for the cost numbers and calculations used. To comply, the Marshall & Swift *Residential Cost Handbook* pages and designated sections can be referenced or a computerized cost new calculation can be attached. If local cost comparables are used as a basis for the new construction cost, it would necessitate providing a summary listing of the data.

Support for the opinion of site value (summary of comparable land sales or other methods for estimating site value)

The next line requires the appraiser to support the land value (V_L) opinion. Such support has always been a part of the cost approach. This would not necessarily include a land sales comparison grid or even the details of the sales but would include the addresses, dates, and sale prices. This requirement may significantly increase the amount of required work for appraisers who are used to not researching sales to support land values. A significant reason for doing the research to develop a land value opinion is to ensure that it does not exceed the value of the property as improved. If the land value does exceed the improved property value, the appraisal becomes a vacant land value rather than an improved property value.

ESTIMATED ☐ REPRODUCTION OR ☐ REPLACEMENT COST NEW

Source of cost data

Quality rating from cost service

Effective date of cost data

Comments on Cost Approach (gross living area calculations, depreciation, etc.)

In the next part of the cost approach section, the appraiser must list the sources and references for the cost estimate. This should be fairly easy for appraisers who use cost services regularly, while those who use local cost comparables may have some difficulty. Appraisers who do not use cost-estimating services may not satisfy loan underwriters who expect a cost manual title, book, and page. In addition to these requirements, several lines are available for the appraiser to record general comments on the cost approach.

All earlier versions of the URAR and Form 2055 provided for only "reproduction cost new." The new forms allow the appraiser to indicate whether the cost estimate is based on reproduction or replacement cost. *Reproduction cost* is the estimated cost to construct, at current prices as of the effective date of the appraisal, an exact duplicate or replica of the building being appraised, using the same materials, construction standards, design, layout, and quality of workmanship and embodying all the deficiencies, superadequacies, and obsolescence of the subject building.[1]

Reproduction cost represents the cost of the improvement at today's prices; it can be easy to estimate if the improvement is relatively new. If the improvement is older, the materials and designs may no longer be available or may not even be legal to use or reproduce, as is the case with asbestos shingles, lead-based paint, or 60-amp service on knob-and-tube wiring. As a result, reproduction cost is not realistic for many assignments. An alternative cost estimate to fit these situations is *replacement cost*, which is defined as the estimated cost to construct, at current prices as of the effective appraisal date, a building with utility equivalent to the building being appraised, using modern materials and current standards, design, and layout.[2]

Replacement cost represents an estimate of the cost of constructing the existing building using modern materials and techniques but in some cases without some of the functional problems associated with the original design and materials. Appraisers apply this cost estimate when the buildings appraised are older and the materials or techniques are obsolete or no longer available.

The option chosen by the appraiser depends on the way in which depreciation is extracted. If depreciation was extracted using reproduction cost new, then reproduction cost should also be used when estimating the cost new and vice versa. In most appraisals of properties with newer improvements, this is not a major issue because reproduction and replacement cost are not much different. When

---

1. *The Dictionary of Real Estate Appraisal*, 4th ed. (Chicago: Appraisal Institute, 2002), 244.
2. Ibid., 244.

Page 3 of 6

COST A

Provide adequate information for the lender/client to replicate

Support for the opinion of site value (summary of comparable

ESTIMATED ☐ REPRODUCTION OR ☐ REPLACEMEN

Source of cost data

Quality rating from cost service Effective date of

Comments on Cost Approach (gross living area calculations,

Estimated Remaining Economic Life (HUD and VA only)

INCOME

Estimated Monthly Market Rent $ X Gross Rent

Summary of Income Approach (including support for market

appraising properties with older improvements, however, this does become an issue. If the appraiser feels obligated to perform the cost approach on an older improvement, he or she should use either reproduction or replacement cost and then use the same method for the depreciation estimate.

Estimated Remaining Economic Life (HUD and VA only) _____ Years

Economic life is defined as the period over which improvements to real property contribute to property value.[3]

Some appraisers have been applying the overall age/life concept to estimate depreciation using a fixed total economic life estimate. This method assumes that a building will stop adding value on a particular day in the future or the life of the building can be extended by maintenance. The problem with this concept is that many appraisers never extend the life of the building. Instead, they shorten its effective age, but this is not consistent with the definition of effective age.

Effective age was defined by the 2002 edition of USPAP as the age of a property that is based on the amount of observed deterioration and obsolescence it has sustained. Effective age may be different from chronological age.

When a building was more than 50 years old, appraisers would often bend this definition to make the effective age shorter instead of the economic life longer; this allowed the appraiser to use a fixed term as the total economic life.

Using a 65-year life estimate for a building is probably close to being mathematically accurate when the building is nearly new, but it loses credibility when the improvements are 40 years old or older. If a building has a total economic life of 65 years, the percent deprecation per year is calculated as 1/65 = 0.015385, or 1.5385% per year. Many studies have shown this calculation to be reasonably close to reality when improvements are less than 15 years old. When an improvement is more than 15 years old, the amount of depreciation found in the market begins to diminish as the improvements get replaced; this generally shows rates of depreciation of less than 1.5% per year. In the case of a 75-year-old home located in an older but still viable neighborhood, the overall depreciation may only be 40%, which equals 0.005333 or 0.5333% (less than 1%), for a total economic life of 187.5 years. For appraisers, the depreciation percentage is the necessary number rather than the fraction.

When completing this part of the form, it is important for appraisers to remember what they indicated on pages 1 and 2. If an appraiser indicates that there were no repairs needed and no recent updates or remodeling done, then the effective age would be the same as the actual age. If an appraiser indicates that the effective age is much lower than the actual age, the condition is good. If the actual and effective ages are the same, the condition is average.

Most appraisers know that the economic life of a building is more a function of its location rather than how well it was built. If a build-

3. Ibid., 92.

ing was constructed with low-cost materials, it is not expected to last as long as one that was built with more expensive materials. However, the location was still more of a determinant of the level of maintenance overall, and the level of maintenance determined the structure's life. Conversely, an improvement on a property located in a good neighborhood with very high levels of maintenance stands a better chance of being maintained well and living longer. After a property falls into disrepair, its economic life is diminished. As a result, a "one-size-fits-all" method of estimating depreciation by dividing the effective age by the arbitrary estimate of total economic life is often inaccurate.

The problem for appraisers who estimate remaining economic life arises when underwriters believe that the appraiser is expressing the opinion that buildings only last a certain number of years. While appraisers use estimated remaining economic life to support depreciation, some underwriters use the data to determine how long the loan term should be.

> Fannie Mae's position on estimated remaining economic life is quite telling as stated in their single-family *Selling Guide*, Section B4-1.4-10, Appraisal Report Review: Improvements Analysis Overview. The *Selling Guide* is available at *www.efanniemae.com.*
>
> To access the guide, type "Selling Guide" in the search box that appears in the top right corner of the home page. The *Selling Guide* can also be accessed by first clicking on "Appraisers" under the "Industry Specialists" heading. Next, click on "Single-Family Guides for free online" under the heading "AllRegs Online." A list of documents will then appear. If pop-ups are blocked, click on "View Support Tips and AllRegs Contact Info" under the "AllRegs Online" heading to access directions for changing the browser settings to allow pop-ups.

Improvements Analysis Requirements

The appraisal must provide a clear, detailed, and accurate description of the improvements consistent with the level of fieldwork required in connection with the appraisal assignment. It must be as specific as possible, including comments on such items as needed repairs, additional features, and modernization, and should provide supporting addenda if necessary. If the subject property has an accessory apartment, the appraisal should describe it.

Remaining Economic Life

Fannie Mae does not require the mortgage term to have any correlation to the remaining economic life of the property. However, related property deficiencies must be discussed in the sections of the appraisal report that address the improvement analysis and property condition.

Fannie Mae's appraisal report forms are designed to meet the needs of several different user groups. Consequently, the forms address the remaining economic life for the property being appraised, but appraisers are not required to report this.

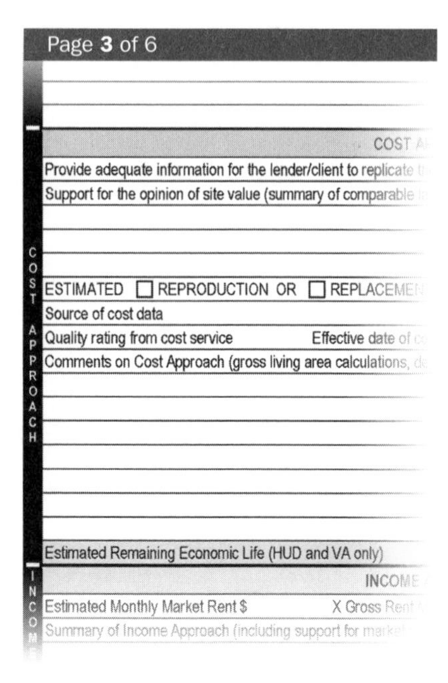
Page 3 of 6

COST APPROACH

COST A

Provide adequate information for the lender/client to replicate

Support for the opinion of site value (summary of comparable

ESTIMATED ☐ REPRODUCTION OR ☐ REPLACEME

Source of cost data

Quality rating from cost service Effective date of c

Comments on Cost Approach (gross living area calculations, d

Estimated Remaining Economic Life (HUD and VA only)

INCOM

INCOME

Estimated Monthly Market Rent $ X Gross Ren

Summary of Income Approach (including support for mar

If appraisers report the remaining economic life, lenders do not need to consider it because any related property deficiencies will be discussed in the sections of the appraisal report that address the improvement analysis and property condition.

The relationship between the actual and effective ages of the property is a good indication of its condition. A property that has been well maintained generally has an effective age somewhat lower than its actual age. On the other hand, a property that has an effective age higher than its actual age probably has not been well maintained or may have a particular physical problem. In such cases, the lender should pay particular attention to the condition of the subject property in its review of any appraisal report that requires the appraiser to address the actual and effective ages of a property.

Estimating depreciation by dividing the effective age by an arbitrary estimate of total economic life is discouraged because it can be misused by underwriters and other parties. Appraisers who are asked to estimate economic life or remaining economic life by a lender or insurer (FHA/VA) should be aware that this estimate may be used for a different reason than the appraiser may expect. More comments on this issue will follow.

Market (Sales) Extraction Method of Estimating Depreciation

The market extraction method for estimating depreciation reduces the opportunities for misusing an appraiser's opinion because the appraiser never provides the user with an arbitrary estimate of the length of time a building will stand. The market extraction method of estimating depreciation is as follows:

1. Determine sale prices for several comparable sales
2. Determine adjustment for rights conveyed
3. Determine adjustment for seller concessions
4. Determine adjustment for conditions of sale
5. Equals net sale price
6. Less estimated land value (V_L)
7. Less site improvement value
8. Equals depreciated value of buildings (V_B)
9. Estimate reproduction cost
10. Less building value (previously calculated)
11. Equals total depreciation
12. $ Depreciation / $ Reproduction Cost New = % Depreciation
13. % Depreciation / Actual Age = % Depreciation/Year

Notice that the appraiser does not need to estimate total life or economic life. The only number needed in the cost approach is the percentage depreciation, not the age or life of the improvements. This does not necessarily mean that the age/life calculation for depreciation is unusable, only that it is not supported unless the appraiser has support for the denominator used in the equation.

An example of using the market extraction technique follows. Notice that there is no subject because the method is used to extract depreciation for a specific property type in a specific market with improvements of a similar age from comparable sales.

Case in Point

The sales listed in Exhibit 21 show depreciation of about 1% per year. This rate of depreciation is specific to the particular property type and market, and this amount of depreciation includes losses from all causes. If external depreciation existed in this market, each of these sales would include it as well. If one sale has functional problems but the others do not, it may show up as a higher rate of depreciation. Although it is irrelevant, the calculation in Exhibit 21 shows an economic life of 100 years because a depreciation of 1% per year equals a 100-year life.

Exhibit 21. Using the Market Extraction Technique to Determine Depreciation

	Sale 1	Sale 2	Sale 3
	1430 Goldenleaf Way	1317 Jeanine Dr.	8317 N. 39th St.
Sale price of each comparable (V_O)	$296,900	$285,000	$327,900
Adjustment for rights conveyed	$0	$0	$0
Adjustment for seller concessions	$0	$0	($5,000)
Adjustment for conditions of sale	$0	$0	$0
Net sale price of each comparable sale	$296,900	$285,000	$322,900
Estimated land value (V_L)	($59,000)	($65,000)	($73,000)
Site improvement value	($8,000)	($6,000)	($8,000)
Dep. value buildings (V_B)	$229,900	$214,000	$241,900
Reproduction cost new	$369,800	$396,800	$426,800
Less bldg. value	($229,900)	($214,000)	($241,900)
Total depreciation	$139,900	$182,800	$184,900
Depreciation %	37.83%	46.07%	43.32%
Actual age	39	48	42
Depreciation %/year	0.97%	0.96%	1.03%

An astute appraiser recognizes that the overall depreciation stabilizes as the improvements on the property age and the calculation yields an even longer economic life. If a property has 50% depreciation but its actual age is 100 years, the rate of depreciation is only 1/2 of 1% per year (0.005), which equals an economic life of 200 years and a remaining life of 100 years. For properties in good locations, the remaining life extends as the building ages but the percentage of depreciation stays the same. If Fannie Mae does not need or want an estimate of the remaining economic life of the entire structure, why should an appraiser provide it? Appraisers never needed this number anyway. They need the percentage depreciation for application in the cost approach, not the remaining life of the building. This age/life tool is invaluable for estimating depreciation for the building components (such as roofs, furnaces, and garage doors) but has limited use for the entire structure.

The age/life calculation does not appear on the form and would need to be performed as a side calculation to support the deprecia-

Page 3 of 6

COST A

Provide adequate information for the lender/client to replicate

Support for the opinion of site value (summary of comparable

ESTIMATED ☐ REPRODUCTION OR ☐ REPLACEMEN

Source of cost data

Quality rating from cost service   Effective date of

Comments on Cost Approach (gross living area calculations,

Estimated Remaining Economic Life (HUD and VA only)

INCOME

Estimated Monthly Market Rent $ X Gross Rent

Summary of Income Approach (including support for market

tion estimate. Because unknown issues that may affect the sale price but are not reported can skew the results, this calculation should not be done with only one or two sales. It is also inadvisable to perform this analysis in one market and then apply the results to another market. The rate of depreciation varies from place to place because of maintenance levels, external issues, and even higher or lower land-to-property value ratios. Nonetheless, this tool is effective and can be used often. Depreciation that is extracted on a percentage basis is most logically applied on a percentage basis. If it is extracted in a dollar amount, the comparables should be similar in price to the subject.

The Veterans Administration's Position on Estimating Depreciation

The Veterans Administration's (VA's) position on estimating depreciation is outlined as follows in Chapter 11 of their *Pamphlet 26-7, Revised*:

> **Remaining Economic Life of Improvements**
>
> **Change Date**
> October 1, 2008, Change 8
> This section has been updated for minor grammatical edits.
>
> **a. Definition**
> Remaining economic life is the estimated period of time until the improvements lose their ability to serve their intended purpose as a home.
>
> **b. Basic Requirements**
> For VA Loan Guaranty purposes, the remaining economic life of the security must be at least as long as the loan repayment term, typically 30 years.
>
> A remaining economic life estimate of less than 30 years must be adequately explained and not arbitrarily established. This is to avoid depriving veterans of the home of their choice in an area where they can afford to live.
>
> **c. What the Appraiser Must Consider**
> In estimating remaining economic life, the appraiser must consider:
>
> - The relationship between the property and the economic stability of the block, neighborhood, and community;
> - Comparisons with homes in the same or similar areas;
> - The need for a home of the particular type being appraised;
> - The architectural design, style, and utility from a functional point of view;
> - The workmanship and durability of the construction, its physical condition, and probable cost of maintenance and/or repair;
> - The extent to which other homes in the area are kept in repair; and
> - In areas where rehabilitation and code enforcement are operating or under consideration, their expected results in improving the neighborhood for residential use.
>
> **d. What the Appraiser Must Report**
> If the estimate of remaining economic life is less than 30 years, the appraiser must provide a supporting explanation, based on either known economic factors or observed physical condition.
>
> If the estimate of remaining economic life is 30 years or more, the appraiser must state the estimate at its maximum (for example, 40 years).
>
> For condominium units, the estimate of remaining economic life must be reported in the "Reconciliation" section of Fannie Mae Form 1073, Individual Condominium Unit Appraisal Report.[4]

This position is evidence of the lending community's thoughts on the issue of remaining economic life. Notice that the VA does not state that the appraiser should base this estimate on the depreciation

4. U.S. Department of Veterans Affairs, *Pamphlet 26-7, Revised*, p. 11-18–11-19. Available at the VA Web site, *www.va.gov*. Direct link: *warms.vba.va.gov/pam26_7.html*.

percentages presented in the cost approach. Instead, the VA states that the appraiser should not arbitrarily establish the remaining economic life, which implies that the lending community is looking for a 30- to 40-year number unless the appraiser can provide supporting data for a different number.

HUD's Position on Estimating Depreciation—Recommended Methodologies

Generally, the Marshall & Swift square-foot method is the most applicable method for estimating replacement cost new. It is a simplified procedure, and all appraisers must have the knowledge and skills needed to apply this methodology. This methodology may not be used for custom-built homes or unique buildings that require the segregated cost method.

Typical residential construction with which the U.S. Department of Housing and Urban Development (HUD) is involved should be rated "fair," "average," or "good" quality. Mass produced, tract-built homes are rated either "fair" or "average," meeting only the minimum construction requirements of lending institutions, mortgage insurance agencies, and building codes. Appraisers must review the basic description to determine the correct construction type.

The appraiser should

- Complete the cost approach for each proposed construction case based on the construction type and quality rating of the property as shown in the Marshall & Swift *Residential Cost Handbook*
- Reference on the form the page numbers that the figures were obtained from (usually two pages) and the revision date
- Include a marketing expense with the replacement cost of improvements and an applicable current multiplier

Remaining economic life is discussed in Chapter 3 of HUD's *Handbook 4150.2: Valuation Analysis for Single-Family One- to Four-Unit Dwellings*:

> **Remaining Economic Life of Building Improvements**
> Because a building is subject to physical deterioration and obsolescence, its period of usefulness is limited. As a building deteriorates or becomes obsolete, its ability to serve useful purposes decreases and eventually ends. This may occur gradually or rapidly.
>
> **A. Economic Life Vs. Physical Life**
>
> - The *total physical life* of a building is the period from the time of completion until it is no longer fit or safe for use or when maintaining the building in a safe, usable manner is no longer practicable.
> - The *total economic life* of a building is the period of time from its completion until it can no longer produce services or net returns over and above a return on the land value.
>
> Economic life can never be longer than the physical life, but may be and frequently is shorter. A structure that is sound and in good physical condition with many years of physical life remaining may have reached the end of its economic life - if its remaining years of physical usefulness will not be profitable.
>
> **B. Estimation of Remaining Economic Life**
> In predicting the remaining economic life of a building, consider these factors:
>
> - The economic background of the community or region and the need for accommodations of the type represented

Page **3** of 6			
OPINION OF SITE VALUE			
Dwelling	Sq. Ft. @ $		
	Sq. Ft. @ $		
Garage/Carport	Sq. Ft. @ $		
Total Estimate of Cost-New			
Less	Physical	Functional	External
Depreciation			
Depreciated Cost of Improvements			
"As-is" Value of Site Improvements			
Indicated Value By Cost Approach			
(not required by Fannie Mae)			
Indicated Value by Income Approach			

- The relationship between the property and the immediate environment, the architectural design, style, and utility from a functional point of view, and the likelihood of obsolescence attributable to new inventions, new materials, and changes in tastes
- The trends and rate of change of characteristics of the neighborhood and their effect on land values
- Workmanship, durability of construction, and the rate with which natural forces cause physical deterioration
- The physical condition and probable cost of maintenance and repair, the maintenance policy of owners and occupants, and the use or abuse to which structures are subjected

C. End of Useful Life of Building Improvements

The useful life of a building has come to an end:

- When the building can no longer produce annual income or services sufficient to offset maintenance expense, insurance, and taxes to produce returns on the value of the land

  and

- When rehabilitation is not feasible

The improvements on the lot at the time have no more value than the amount obtainable from a purchaser who will buy them and remove them from the site.[5]

Indicated Value By Cost Approach

The actual format of the cost approach is very similar to that found on previous forms.

1. The cost of the dwelling is estimated by a reliable source based on a cost per square foot of GLA. The most common way to estimate this is by using a cost estimating service.
2. The cost of construction for garages, basements, and porches is also added.
3. The sum of all of the estimated costs of construction will be the cost of construction of all building improvements.
4. The depreciation is listed in three sections: physical, functional, and external.

   If an appraiser estimates depreciation at 35% using the age/life or market extraction method, the depreciation amount will usually represent all forms of depreciation. As a result, classifying it as physical depreciation is often wrong. If a property is in a market with external obsolescence, the measured loss will include this deduction by the market and should not be labeled as physical depreciation on the form. It is also common for many improvements to have functional losses that are typical in the market and do not require adjustment but are nevertheless functional rather than physical. With the exception of the partitioning of external losses, these are for the most part just labels, so it is not a big problem if they are labeled incorrectly.

   As discussed before, the preferred method for estimating this amount is the market extraction method. Age/life depreciation estimates are very difficult to adequately support and their use is discouraged.

---

5. U.S. Department of Housing and Urban Development, *Handbook 4150.2: Valuation Analysis for Home Mortgage Insurance for Single-Family One- to Four-Unit Dwellings* (July 1, 1999), Section 3-4. Available on the HUD Web site at *www.hud.gov*. Direct link: *www.hud.gov/offices/adm/hudclips/handbooks/hsgh/4150.2/index.cfm*.

5. The "as is" value of the site improvements are added to the building improvement's depreciated value and the land value to obtain a fee simple indication of market value.
6. If the subject is the leasehold interest, an additional adjustment would have to be made to the value estimate in the cost approach to compensate for that interest appraised.

Income Section

INCOME APPROACH TO VALUE (not required by Fannie Mae)			
Estimated Monthly Market Rent $	X Gross Rent Multiplier	= $	Indicated Value by Income Approach
Summary of Income Approach (including support for market rent and GRM)			

In most cases, Fannie Mae does not require the use of the income capitalization approach to value, and the scope of work would not include it unless the appraiser has decided that it was relevant or necessary. Because most single-unit homes are not purchased for their income potential, this approach is not widely used. However, it is a viable option in markets where properties are bought for the rent they generate.

INCOME APPROACH TO VALUE (not required by Fannie Mae)
Estimated Monthly Market Rent $____ × Gross Rent Multiplier _____ = $ ______ Indicated Value by Income Approach
Summary of Income Approach (including support for market rent and GRM)

The income capitalization approach to value on the URAR and Form 2055 is limited to the use of gross rent multiplier (GRM) analysis. In this ratio analysis, the appraiser finds comparable sales that were bought for their rental potential and then divides the sale price by the proposed gross monthly rent. This calculation yields a ratio of sale price to the monthly rental rate, which can be used to capitalize the subject's monthly rent into a lump sum capital amount or value opinion.

This analysis should be made using the gross sale prices of similar properties divided by the gross monthly income expectancy of the buyer. The buyer's income estimate is used because the gross rent used on the subject side of the analysis is nearly always based on the potential rents. To maintain an "apples to apples" analysis, the ratio extracted from the sales and applied to the subject should be based on gross potential monthly rents. Using tomorrow's rents for the subject and yesterday's rents for the comparables can yield an erroneous result.

If the income capitalization approach to value is used, the appraiser should be aware that the GRM does not give consideration to higher or lower expense ratios. If an older house is compared to a newer one, the maintenance levels will be different and the GRM should also be different. Although this fact may not be reflected in the rents, it will be reflected in the sale prices. Because they pay few of the expenses in most residential properties, tenants are as a rule not as concerned as the owners are about maintenance costs.

PUD Information Section

PUD INFORMATION	PROJECT INFORMATION FOR PUDs (if applicable)		
	Is the developer/builder in control of the Homeowners' Association (HOA)? ☐ Yes ☐ No Unit type(s) ☐ Detached ☐ Attached		
	Provide the following information for PUDs ONLY if the developer/builder is in control of the HOA and the subject property is an attached dwelling unit.		
	Legal name of project		
	Total number of phases	Total number of units	Total number of units sold
	Total number of units rented	Total number of units for sale	Data source(s)
	Was the project created by the conversion of an existing building(s) into a PUD? ☐ Yes ☐ No If Yes, date of conversion		
	Does the project contain any multi-dwelling units? ☐ Yes ☐ No Data source(s)		
	Are the units, common elements, and recreation facilities complete? ☐ Yes ☐ No If No, describe the status of completion.		
	Are the common elements leased to or by the Homeowners' Association? ☐ Yes ☐ No If Yes, describe the rental terms and options.		
	Describe common elements and recreational facilities		

Fannie Mae defines a planned unit development (PUD) as a project or subdivision that includes common property and improvements that are owned and maintained by an owners' association for the benefit and use of the individual units within the project. For a project to qualify as a PUD, the owners' association must require automatic, nonseverable membership for each individual unit owner and provide for mandatory assessments.

Zoning should not be the basis for classifying a project as a PUD. Instead, "PUD" is a Fannie Mae term to describe properties that are not condominiums but are located in projects that have mandatory dues and common elements. They can be attached or detached homes or part of small or large projects. This definition is not the same as that used by some zoning authorities for which a PUD is a master-planned project with a variety of land uses all platted at one time. Such a PUD is usually a project in which the developer takes the underlying zoning and makes a new master plan for the land equal to the size of the project being developed. Developers write their own bylaws based on the city, town, or county ordinances with amendments to fit the property. When appraising this type of property, the appraiser should ignore any reference to a PUD as defined by zoning authorities. Exhibit 22 is an example of a PUD determined by zoning and modified according to a developer's master plan.

In the plan shown in Exhibit 22, the developer included many different types of land uses but has restricted commercial uses to the perimeter of the development. The existing homes on the north are located next to the highest-priced homes, and the existing homes on the east are located near the high- and medium-priced homes, the condominiums, and a church site. The commercial land uses are located along the highways and are not near the existing housing. This configuration may or may not meet Fannie Mae's definition of a PUD.

A PUD usually has common areas that are owned by the association rather than the individuals, whereas a condominium usually has common areas that are deeded to each owner as a tenant in common. Such an arrangement allows the owners to be taxed for the common areas and often deduct the taxes paid. In a PUD, the

Exhibit 22. Developer's Master-Planned PUD

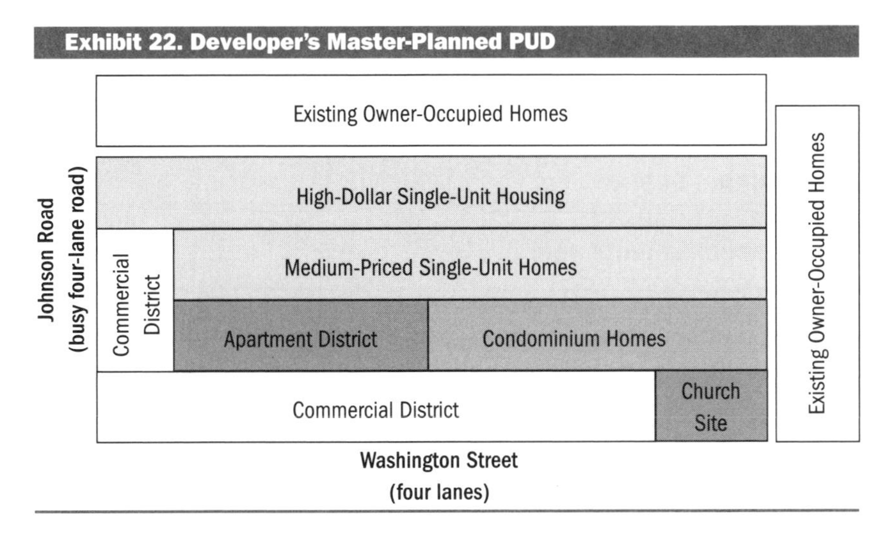

association typically owns the common areas and the individuals cannot deduct the expenses paid to maintain them. Condominiums are defined in each state's laws. To determine what constitutes a condominium, the appraiser should check with the title insurance company or their attorney. Defining a condominium is not possible by just looking at the structure. Each state has specific laws about what constitutes a condominium property, and appraisers must research the legal definition for the areas in which they are working.

PROJECT INFORMATION FOR PUDs (if applicable)

Is the developer/builder in control of the Homeowners' Association (HOA)?

☐ Yes ☐ No Unit type(s) ☐ Detached ☐ Attached

The first question in the PUD section asks if the developer or builder is in control of the homeowners association. A little research may be required to answer this question, although it is easy to answer if the information can be obtained by the property owner. The appraiser may have to research this information for every appraisal assignment in a project that he or she has not appraised before. This part of the form is important because it leads to other requirements depending on how it is answered.

Provide the following information for PUDs ONLY if the developer/builder is in control of the HOA and the subject property is an attached dwelling unit.

If the subject is located in a development in which the management association has been released to the owners or the unit is detached, the appraiser's work is finished and he or she need not go any further. The following data is needed if the project will be perceived in the market as condominiums, for which the value of most units is predicated on the success of the project overall. There have been large losses to lenders in some projects because the developer could not finish the project or the promise of specific amenities was not fulfilled.

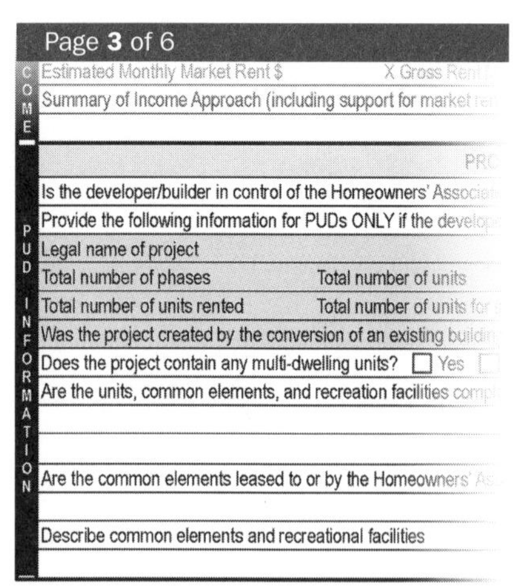
Page 3 of 6

COME
Estimated Monthly Market Rent $ X Gross Rent
Summary of Income Approach (including support for market re

PRO

PUD INFORMATION
Is the developer/builder in control of the Homeowners' Associ
Provide the following information for PUDs ONLY if the develo
Legal name of project
Total number of phases Total number of units
Total number of units rented Total number of units fo
Was the project created by the conversion of an existing build
Does the project contain any multi-dwelling units? ☐ Yes ☐
Are the units, common elements, and recreation facilities comp
Are the common elements leased to or by the Homeowners' A
Describe common elements and recreational facilities

Freddie Mac Form 70 March 2005

Legal name of project

All PUDs have a legal name, and it is usually not difficult for the appraiser to determine this.

Total number of phases
Total number of units
Total number of units sold

The next part of the PUD section requires the appraiser to indicate the total number of phases, units, and sold units. This information is needed for loan underwriting purposes because the project requirements are based on the number of units that are proposed, built, and sold. The appraiser must research this information carefully to ensure that the lender is not misled, but it generally can be verified easily. Developments that are difficult to categorize may require explanation, since it is common for appraisers to consider sections of a subdivision to be phases of a development when actually they are not. This section is to be completed only if the developer is no longer in control of the homeowners association.

Total number of units rented
Total number of units for sale
Data source(s)

The number of units for sale should be easy to obtain; however, the number rented may require a little more work. The management company can usually be contacted for the number of rented units. Also, county assessor's data is accessible via the Internet or the MLS system in some markets. A quick search using the legal description and the owners' names can reveal whether one person or company owns many properties. If one person owns several units, this usually indicates that the property is a rental. An excessive number of rented units can present big problems for the solvency of the project and the individual units, as illustrated in the following example.

Case in Point

The subject is an individual attached home in a project of attached homes. The homeowners association is responsible for exterior and site maintenance. The project has 79 units, 48 of which are owned by four investors. The 48 rental units are nearly equally distributed among the four individuals. The other 31 units are owner occupied. At homeowners association meetings, the landlords control 48 votes out of the total 79, and they vote repeatedly in favor of repairs and against replacements. They vote continually for improvements that are absolutely required to maintain rental income only and never for aesthetic improvements or items that improve resale value. For instance, they install new shingles on roofs only when the roofer cannot repair the old ones. The parking lot has huge potholes. The paint is peeling off the exterior siding. The project is not maintained well, and the property values are falling. The rents are average, but the resales are dismal.

This example shows why mortgage investors are concerned about the high level of rental units in a development, and it should also be a concern to all appraisers who value these types of properties.

When a client asks an appraiser to value more than four units in one project, a completely different set of rules applies. In other words, an appraiser can appraise up to four units on a retail basis, and these units can be entered on the residential forms and mortgaged like any other property. However, if the subject includes more than four units, the lenders can be required to make a wholesale project loan, depending on the loan amount. Such appraisals are sometimes called bulk sale value, wholesale valuation, or discounted cash flow analysis. Regardless of the name given the appraisal, the appraiser must consider doing an analysis that includes an absorption study, cash flows per quarter or year, and an expense analysis if the subject includes more than four units. If the lender insists that the appraiser complete individual appraisal reports on more than four units in the same project and the loan amount is above the de minimus level, the appraiser should be wary of that assignment.

Was the project created by the conversion of an existing building(s) into a PUD?

☐ Yes ☐ No   If Yes, date of conversion

The conversion of existing buildings into PUDs is not as common as the conversion of apartments or industrial buildings into condominiums, but it does happen. If the subject is an old retail building that was converted into dwelling units or an attached two-unit home that was converted to individual units (with a party wall agreement), it should be indicated as such on the appraisal form. If the project has not sold out, it can pose a problem for unit resales. In project conversions, it is important for appraisers to use comparables from the same project that are not part of the developer's initial sales effort. The resales of units in the project that are reported by a diverse number of brokers are the best comparable sales.

Apartment or multiunit conversions are notorious for noncompliance with the current market and will not sell for as much as the original buyer paid on a resale basis. In some markets, the biggest problem with the two- to four-unit conversions is that they do not have garages or some other amenity that the market requires. While tenants will rent an apartment in a two-unit building, buyers may not want the property if it lacks a private garage. The appraiser must know the market.

There is a difference in the marketing effort between a conversion and a resale. In a conversion, the sales agent is paid to sell only the units in that project. When a broker who is not tied to the project markets the property, he or she relies on other agents to sell the property and those selling agents do not care what they sell as long as they get a sale. As a result, resale buyers will shop around for other projects that may or may not be priced better. Buyers involved in the conversion project often do not encounter many competitors because the agent representing the property usually will not encourage them to look at competitors' properties. There are often big differences between the sale prices of properties sold by the developer's

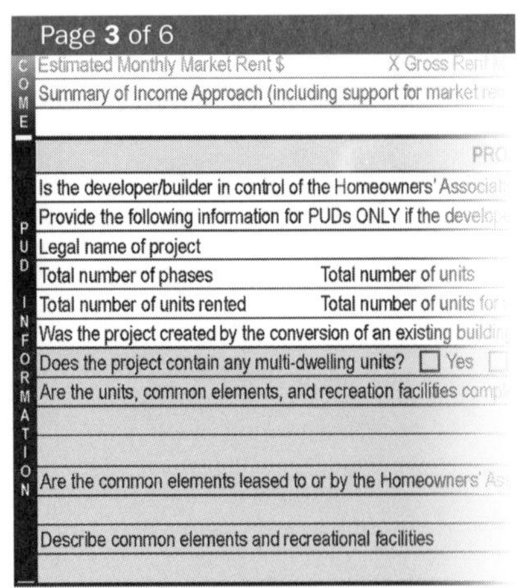
Page 3 of 6

INCOME
Estimated Monthly Market Rent $ X Gross Ren
Summary of Income Approach (including support for market re

PUD INFORMATION
PR
Is the developer/builder in control of the Homeowners' Associa
Provide the following information for PUDs ONLY if the develo
Legal name of project
Total number of phases Total number of units
Total number of units rented Total number of units fo
Was the project created by the conversion of an existing buildi
Does the project contain any multi-dwelling units? ☐ Yes ☐
Are the units, common elements, and recreation facilities com
Are the common elements leased to or by the Homeowners' As
Describe common elements and recreational facilities

Freddie Mac Form 70 March 2005

agents and the resales sold by the local broker in cases when buyers shop around more.

Does the project contain any multi-dwelling units?

☐ Yes ☐ No Data source(s)

The next question requires the appraiser to indicate if the property contains any multi-dwelling units. For example, a developer built 95 single-unit homes (attached or detached) along with at least a dozen four-unit buildings designed for sale to a single owner. If a project features many of these units, the appraiser should investigate to find out who controls the homeowners association and the percentage of the project dedicated to units that are not owner-occupied.

Are the units, common elements, and recreation facilities complete?

☐ Yes ☐ No If No, describe the status of completion.

Loan underwriting depends on whether common elements are completed. In some projects, common areas and recreational facilities were promised but never built. In PUD projects as well as condominiums, the health of the project is significant to the value of the individual units. If the project fails, it will be very difficult to sell the units to a retail buyer. Care should be taken to ensure that lenders are protected from these kinds of issues, as shown in the following example.

Case in Point

A new project is planned to include 112 units. They are to be single-unit, attached ("townhouse type") homes. The developer has promised all the buyers that the streets will be publicly maintained and that there will be a common pool, pool house, tennis court, and park in the center of the development. The assignment is to prepare an appraisal report on one of the units in this project.

The appraiser contacted the developer to get the plans and specifications for a proposed unit in the development. The developer reported that the common areas were completed and 75 units were sold. A drive-by review of the project revealed that only 13 units had curtains on the windows and the clubhouse, pool, and tennis court could not be found. The developer was contacted again and he apologized, saying that the common elements were not built yet because he was having trouble getting the permit. Furthermore, 13 units were sold, but 62 units were under contract and would close when the construction was completed. The appraiser reported the information as it was reported to him, including the fact that he was initially given misinformation. The mortgage lender rejected the appraisal report and ordered another one from another appraiser who was less diligent in performing the research. The project failed, and the construction lender was forced to take over the project.

Are the common elements leased to or by the Homeowners' Association?

☐ Yes ☐ No If Yes, describe the rental terms and options.

Answering this next question requires a bit of research, but it is very important. In some condominium and PUD projects, the developers have leased the pool, clubhouse, and even the streets from another partnership. The lease runs for a set period of time, such as 25 years, with annual payments from the homeowners association. At the end of the lease, the payments are negotiable and the rates increase significantly.

There have been instances in which developers lease a project's parking lot from an adjacent owner and then stop making the lease payments upon completion of the project. The buyers assumed the extra parking was automatically included with the property and were surprised to find that it actually was not. Nobody thought to ask whether the parking was owned or leased, and there was no place for the residents to park their cars once the lease payments stopped. This is an important issue for the appraiser to address. Because so many projects do not experience problems in this area, many appraisers have become complacent and stop checking this information. The real estate appraiser is the one person in the process who is supposed to be aware of these technical issues pertaining to property ownership. It is the responsibility of the appraiser to research, analyze, and report the facts when these issues come into play. The typical buyer may or may not recognize them as being important, but appraisers are charged with the responsibility of investigating them.

Describe common elements and recreational facilities

The last two lines of the PUD section require the appraiser to describe common elements and recreational facilities in summary. The appraiser should inquire about the streets, sidewalks, green areas, pool, clubhouse, and tennis courts. Streets that are privately owned can be burdensome for the association and may explain why the monthly homeowners association fees are high, since the association is likely to be responsible for maintaining them.

> Fannie Mae discusses the PUD information section of the appraisal report in depth in their single-family *Selling Guide*, Section B4-2.3, PUD Requirements and Cooperative Project Eligibility. The *Selling Guide* is available at *www.efanniemae.com.*
>
> To access the guide, type "Selling Guide" in the search box that appears in the top right corner of the home page. The *Selling Guide* can also be accessed by first clicking on "Appraisers" under the "Industry Specialists" heading. Next, click on "Single-Family Guides for free online" under the heading "AllRegs Online." A list of documents will then appear. If pop-ups are blocked, click on "View Support Tips and AllRegs Contact Info" under the "AllRegs Online" heading to access directions for changing the browser settings to allow pop-ups.

Uniform Residential Appraisal Report

File #

This report form is designed to report an appraisal of a one-unit property or a one-unit property with an accessory unit; including a unit in a planned unit development (PUD). This report form is not designed to report an appraisal of a manufactured home or a unit in a condominium or cooperative project.

This appraisal report is subject to the following scope of work, intended use, intended user, definition of market value, statement of assumptions and limiting conditions, and certifications. Modifications, additions, or deletions to the intended use, intended user, definition of market value, or assumptions and limiting conditions are not permitted. The appraiser may expand the scope of work to include any additional research or analysis necessary based on the complexity of this appraisal assignment. Modifications or deletions to the certifications are also not permitted. However, additional certifications that do not constitute material alterations to this appraisal report, such as those required by law or those related to the appraiser's continuing education or membership in an appraisal organization, are permitted.

SCOPE OF WORK: The scope of work for this appraisal is defined by the complexity of this appraisal assignment and the reporting requirements of this appraisal report form, including the following definition of market value, statement of assumptions and limiting conditions, and certifications. The appraiser must, at a minimum: (1) perform a complete visual inspection of the interior and exterior areas of the subject property, (2) inspect the neighborhood, (3) inspect each of the comparable sales from at least the street, (4) research, verify, and analyze data from reliable public and/or private sources, and (5) report his or her analysis, opinions, and conclusions in this appraisal report.

INTENDED USE: The intended use of this appraisal report is for the lender/client to evaluate the property that is the subject of this appraisal for a mortgage finance transaction.

INTENDED USER: The intended user of this appraisal report is the lender/client.

DEFINITION OF MARKET VALUE: The most probable price which a property should bring in a competitive and open market under all conditions requisite to a fair sale, the buyer and seller, each acting prudently, knowledgeably and assuming the price is not affected by undue stimulus. Implicit in this definition is the consummation of a sale as of a specified date and the passing of title from seller to buyer under conditions whereby: (1) buyer and seller are typically motivated; (2) both parties are well informed or well advised, and each acting in what he or she considers his or her own best interest; (3) a reasonable time is allowed for exposure in the open market; (4) payment is made in terms of cash in U. S. dollars or in terms of financial arrangements comparable thereto; and (5) the price represents the normal consideration for the property sold unaffected by special or creative financing or sales concessions* granted by anyone associated with the sale.

*Adjustments to the comparables must be made for special or creative financing or sales concessions. No adjustments are necessary for those costs which are normally paid by sellers as a result of tradition or law in a market area; these costs are readily identifiable since the seller pays these costs in virtually all sales transactions. Special or creative financing adjustments can be made to the comparable property by comparisons to financing terms offered by a third party institutional lender that is not already involved in the property or transaction. Any adjustment should not be calculated on a mechanical dollar for dollar cost of the financing or concession but the dollar amount of any adjustment should approximate the market's reaction to the financing or concessions based on the appraiser's judgment.

STATEMENT OF ASSUMPTIONS AND LIMITING CONDITIONS: The appraiser's certification in this report is subject to the following assumptions and limiting conditions:

1. The appraiser will not be responsible for matters of a legal nature that affect either the property being appraised or the title to it, except for information that he or she became aware of during the research involved in performing this appraisal. The appraiser assumes that the title is good and marketable and will not render any opinions about the title.

2. The appraiser has provided a sketch in this appraisal report to show the approximate dimensions of the improvements. The sketch is included only to assist the reader in visualizing the property and understanding the appraiser's determination of its size.

3. The appraiser has examined the available flood maps that are provided by the Federal Emergency Management Agency (or other data sources) and has noted in this appraisal report whether any portion of the subject site is located in an identified Special Flood Hazard Area. Because the appraiser is not a surveyor, he or she makes no guarantees, express or implied, regarding this determination.

4. The appraiser will not give testimony or appear in court because he or she made an appraisal of the property in question, unless specific arrangements to do so have been made beforehand, or as otherwise required by law.

5. The appraiser has noted in this appraisal report any adverse conditions (such as needed repairs, deterioration, the presence of hazardous wastes, toxic substances, etc.) observed during the inspection of the subject property or that he or she became aware of during the research involved in performing this appraisal. Unless otherwise stated in this appraisal report, the appraiser has no knowledge of any hidden or unapparent physical deficiencies or adverse conditions of the property (such as, but not limited to, needed repairs, deterioration, the presence of hazardous wastes, toxic substances, adverse environmental conditions, etc.) that would make the property less valuable, and has assumed that there are no such conditions and makes no guarantees or warranties, express or implied. The appraiser will not be responsible for any such conditions that do exist or for any engineering or testing that might be required to discover whether such conditions exist. Because the appraiser is not an expert in the field of environmental hazards, this appraisal report must not be considered as an environmental assessment of the property.

6. The appraiser has based his or her appraisal report and valuation conclusion for an appraisal that is subject to satisfactory completion, repairs, or alterations on the assumption that the completion, repairs, or alterations of the subject property will be performed in a professional manner.

Freddie Mac Form 70 March 2005 Page 4 of 6 Fannie Mae Form 1004 March 2005

Scope of Work, Intended Use and User, Market Value, and Statement of Assumptions and Limiting Conditions

Page 4 is nearly identical on the URAR and Form 2055. The forms differ only in the scope of work section and in the statement of assumptions and limiting conditions.

Paragraph 1 of page 4 details the purpose of the report as well as what it is *not* designed for. This statement is significant because it removes any doubt as to how the report can be used.

Paragraph 2 provides directions for interpreting the report and prohibits the form from being changed. This prohibition includes changes to adapt the form's use for Fannie Mae appraisals. The appraiser can add certifications on a separate page or form but cannot amend the report in any way. Any additional certifications and limiting conditions are not to conflict with those shown in the report. This paragraph stipulates that the appraiser agree to and certify compliance with the requirements, ethics, and statements set forth. Some appraisers are uncomfortable about the liability associated with these very rigid certifications.

Most appraisers already know that the scope of work section for appraisal reports has long been mandated by USPAP (see USPAP Standards Rule 2-2(a)vii or (b)vii). Because the former reporting forms did not include this section, it had to be added. Many appraisers may conclude that this section of the report is inadequate and add comments to complete the job.

There may be changes to USPAP in the future that cause the certification on these forms to be inadequate. If this happens, the appraiser must decide to follow either the form or USPAP. In most states, all appraisals must follow USPAP, so following the form alone would not be an option.

Scope of Work

The scope of work informs the user of the report of the level of detail that was included in the subject property analysis. Designed for use with single-unit improved properties, the scope of work for the URAR certifies that the appraiser inspected the interior and exterior of the subject property and the scope of work for Form 2055 certifies that the appraiser inspected the exterior only of the subject property. The scope also certifies that the neighborhood was inspected and comparable sales were obtained from the adjacent street. The appraiser indicates that the market has been researched and the data confirmed. Conclusions must also be included in the scope of work section.

Page 4 of 6

Uniform

This report form is designed to report an appr
including a unit in a planned unit developme
manufactured home or a unit in a condominiu

This appraisal report is subject to the followin
statement of assumptions and limiting conditi
use, intended user, definition of market value,
expand the scope of work to include any addi
assignment. Modifications or deletions to the
not constitute material alterations to this appr
continuing education or membership in an ap

SCOPE OF WORK: The scope of work for
reporting requirements of this appraisal report
assumptions and limiting conditions, and cert
inspection of the interior and exterior areas of
comparable sales from at least the street, (4)
and (5) report his or her analysis, opinions, a

INTENDED USE: The intended use of this
subject of this appraisal for a mortgage financ

INTENDED USER: The intended user of th

DEFINITION OF MARKET VALUE: The
market under all conditions requisite to a fair
the price is not affected by undue stimulus. Im
the passing of title from seller to buyer under
parties are well informed or well advised, and
reasonable time is allowed for exposure in the
of financial arrangements comparable thereto
unaffected by special or creative financing or

*Adjustments to the comparables must be ma
necessary for those costs which are normally
readily identifiable since the seller pays these
adjustments can be made to the comparable
lender that is not already involved in the prop
dollar for dollar cost of the financing or conce
reaction to the financing or concessions base

STATEMENT OF ASSUMPTIONS AND
subject to the following assumptions and lim

Many appraisers are concerned about the following statement that appears in the scope of work section of the URAR: "The appraiser must, at a minimum: (1) perform a complete visual inspection of the interior and exterior areas of the subject property." The word *complete* can increase an appraiser's liability if it is interpreted to mean that the appraiser did more work than was actually done. Appraisers must be aware of this scope of work requirement.

The significant difference between the scope of work for the URAR and Form 2055 lies in the thoroughness of the property inspection. For an appraisal reported on Form 2055, Fannie Mae requires only an exterior inspection as set forth in the following directive:

> The appraiser must, at a minimum: (1) perform a visual inspection of the exterior areas of the subject property from at least the street...The appraiser must be able to obtain adequate information about the physical characteristics (including, but not limited to, condition, room count, gross living area, etc.) of the subject property from the exterior-only inspection and reliable public and/or private sources to perform this appraisal. The appraiser should use the same type of data sources that he or she uses for comparable sales such as, but not limited to, multiple listing services, tax and assessment records, prior inspections, appraisal files, information provided by the property owner, etc.

When reviewing the scope of work, it should be remembered that by signing his or her name to the form, the appraiser is stating that he or she drove past the comparables.

In this vein, it is not believable that an appraiser would use MLS photos for all the comparables if he or she actually drove past them. It is common for some appraisers to sign their name to the form, stating that they drove past the comparables (indicated as number 3 in the scope of work discussion on the forms) when in reality they did not. This is the reason why many reviewers are critical of the use of MLS photos.

Intended Use and User

Intended Use

The intended use paragraph is required by USPAP. It states that the purpose of the appraisal is for a mortgage finance transaction. Most appraisers believe that this precludes the appraisal's use for divorces, estate settlements, and court litigation. The Appraisal Institute has developed a single-unit residential form that is intended to be used for nonlender assignments.

Intended User

The intended user requirement is included in all USPAP appraisals and states that the report is for the lender/client only, which does not include the property owner.

Definition of Market Value

To understand the definition of *market value* and the value opinion associated with it, it must first be established that the definition's parameters must be applied to the comparable sales and adjusted for in the income and cost approaches to produce an estimate that fits within this definition. Any sale used to estimate market value must meet or be adjusted for these conditions. This would include any needed adjustments to bring the sale in line with the stipulated financing. The pertinent details of this definition follow.

Most Probable Price

The market value definition is intended to preclude appraisers from using or at least requiring an adjustment for non-arm's-length sales or sales with uniform or ill-advised buyers or sellers. Most appraisers have little difficulty comprehending and adjusting for these items. Appraisers can quote the first line of the definition of market value when they are asked why they cannot use a non-arm's-length sale or a sale in which the buyer had few or no choices.

Typically Motivated Buyer and Seller

A sale of the property must be assumed, which means that appraisers estimate the amount that the property would sell for on the open market as of the effective date–a reiteration of the "arm's-length" sale requirement. If a comparable sale does not meet these requirements, it cannot provide an indication of market value, as illustrated by the following example.

Case in Point

In September of last year, a young family bought a home after moving to Bigville from Smallburg. They shopped around and visited 22 homes in the Bigville market with their broker. They made second visits to three houses and then chose the one they liked best. They were happy with their decision to buy the home for $209,000. The day after the purchase agreement was signed, the couple enrolled their 10-year-old in a new elementary school located only one mile away from their new home.

The home inspection report came back indicating that the roof on the eight-year-old home had only two years left on it. Roof shingles on such houses typically last 20 to 25 years, but the builder did not vent the attic, causing rapid deterioration. The buyers were unhappy and tried to negotiate with the sellers for a new roof. The sellers insisted that the home inspector was wrong, but they could not produce anyone to support the claim. The roof was clearly deficient, but the sellers would not compensate the buyers. The buyers were tempted to walk away from the deal, but they did not want to move their child from one school to another after only two weeks. They decided to overpay for the property rather than displace their child. The listing agent insisted the property sold at a fair price, but the selling agent tells a different story.

The sale price reflects a house with a defective roof selling for an amount equal to a house with a sound roof. If the appraiser is using this sale as a comparable and knows this background information, it can be compensated for. However, if the appraiser does not know this information, an error will result. A number of these kinds of issues surface in comparable sales used in appraisals every day, which supports the need for appraisers to use more than the minimum number of comparable sales to ensure the reliability of their results.

Page **4** of 6

INTENDED USER: The intended user of th

DEFINITION OF MARKET VALUE: The m
market under all conditions requisite to a fair s
the price is not affected by undue stimulus. Im
the passing of title from seller to buyer under c
parties are well informed or well advised, and
reasonable time is allowed for exposure in the
of financial arrangements comparable thereto
unaffected by special or creative financing or s

*Adjustments to the comparables must be ma
necessary for those costs which are normally
readily identifiable since the seller pays these
adjustments can be made to the comparable p
lender that is not already involved in the prope
dollar for dollar cost of the financing or conces
reaction to the financing or concessions base

STATEMENT OF ASSUMPTIONS AND L
subject to the following assumptions and limit

1. The appraiser will not be responsible for ma
to it, except for information that he or she bec
appraiser assumes that the title is good and m

2. The appraiser has provided a sketch in this
The sketch is included only to assist the read

Sales that do not have a typically motivated buyer or seller may include sales to family members and sales involving buyers or sellers who are not acting on their own behalf. An example of such a case could be a sale in which the seller does not get the highest price possible or a sale in which the decision maker is not the actual seller or buyer and may or may not care if the buyer pays too much. This could include sales in trust, sales or purchases by corporations, and sales via court order. Some sale prices of real estate are negotiated more aggressively if there is pressure to consummate a quick sale to get fees in the door. Others may be the result of stonewalling or may not have been negotiated well for other reasons. These types of problems are not difficult to comprehend or to adjust for.

Well-Informed or Well-Advised Parties

The part of the market value definition that specifies well-informed or well-advised parties pertains to adjusting for any poorly informed buyers or sellers. In some sales, the buyer or seller may not have known their options and paid too much or too little.

Reasonable Time for Exposure in the Open Market

For a sale to be fair, it must have a reasonable amount of exposure time on the market. This would also lead to the elimination of or at least an adjustment to compensate for a sale in which the seller required a quick sale. For example, if a property had to be sold in fewer than 30 days, it is reasonable to expect that the price would be discounted to attract a larger number of potential buyers. This would render it as less than a fair comparable and would lead many appraisers to assume that if a shorter marketing time (exposure time) nets a lower price, a longer time would net a higher price. In most areas, the longer a residential property is on the market, the less it tends to sell for because of the higher motivation of the seller.

Payment in Terms of Cash in U.S. Dollars

Standardization of payment terms eliminates the need for appraisers to convert dollars to pesos or Canadian dollars.

Special or Creative Financing or Sales Concessions

The value opinion must be based on normal financing that does not include any special or creative financing. As described earlier, there is no limit to how high a property's value could rise if special financing is not accounted for in the value opinion.

Adjustments to the Comparables

The sale price of the comparable (which translates to a value estimate for the subject) should not be affected by special or creative financing or sales concessions granted by anyone associated with the sale. Market value would require an adjustment for any special or creative financing included in the sale of a comparable property. The problem lies in classifying a sales concession. To assist in this classification, the definition addresses seller-paid expenses that are typically associated with each sale, some of which are concessions and some of which are only "typical seller expenses." These expenses could be any or all of the following:

- Real estate broker's commissions
- Title insurance expense
- Home inspections, surveys, fees for recording deeds, and closing fees

Expenses that would not normally be paid by the seller include

- Decorating allowances
- Repair allowances that are negotiated in the price but that do not reflect needed items
- Seller-paid financing costs

Exceptions to what is paid by whom exist in many different markets, but in most markets buyers and sellers generally seek to minimize their outlay.

The best way to identify a sales or financing concession is to compare the seller-paid expense with what a seller would have to pay in a cash deal. If the seller did not have to pay this expense on a sale where the buyer is paying cash, then it is a sales or financing concession and should be adjusted out of the comparable sale.

Adjustments for Special or Creative Financing

A clear sense of the intent of this next part of the market value definition is understood when an appraiser compares the financing in question to what a third-party institution not involved in the sale would provide. This statement is significant for those who insist that if it is common practice for a builder to pay several thousand dollars to buy down an interest rate, it is acceptable to reflect it in the sales prices of the comparables. The question then becomes whether a third-party institutional lender would offer this financing incentive if it were not involved in the deal.

Statement of Assumptions and Limiting Conditions for the URAR

The statement of assumptions and limiting conditions for the URAR is slightly different from that for Form 2055, so this part of each form will be discussed separately. These statements and conditions are not required in an appraisal report, but they are certainly needed. They amplify the discussion of scope of work and protect the appraiser (albeit minimally) from misinterpreting his or her role in the real estate transaction.

Appraiser's Accountability and Responsibility (1)

The appraiser cannot be held accountable for clouds on the title, surveying errors, or legal issues that may affect the value of the

Page 4 of 6

to it, except for information that he or she
appraiser assumes that the title is good and

2. The appraiser has provided a sketch in this
The sketch is included only to assist the read
of its size.

3. The appraiser has examined the available
(or other data sources) and has noted in this
identified Special Flood Hazard Area. Becaus
implied, regarding this determination.

4. The appraiser will not give testimony or ap
unless specific arrangements to do so have b

5. The appraiser has noted in this appraisal re
presence of hazardous wastes, toxic substan
she became aware of during the research inv
report, the appraiser has no knowledge of an
property (such as, but not limited to, needed r
adverse environmental conditions, etc.) that w
conditions and makes no guarantees or warr
conditions that do exist or for any engineerin
Because the appraiser is not an expert in the
an environmental assessment of the propert

6. The appraiser has based his or her apprai
completion, repairs, or alterations on the assu
be performed in a professional manner.

Freddie Mac Form 70 March 2005

property being appraised. The appraiser is expected to be aware of title issues but should not be held to the same level of accountability as the title insurance agency or the lawyer who prepares the abstract. Appraisers who are aware of clouds on the title, easements, encroachments, or other legal problems should state this.

Sketch of Approximate Dimensions of Improvement (2)

A sketch is used to help determine the residence size. Some clients require a floor plan sketch. Different lenders have different requirements. Some lenders require detailed floor plans with interior walls, doors, and even window locations. These sketches should not be used as building plans or for construction details.

Flood Maps (3)

Discussion of flood hazards has long been a part of residential appraisal forms. This section certifies that the appraiser has reviewed the flood maps to determine whether the subject is prone to this additional risk. Most lenders are very reluctant to lend money on improved properties that are subject to flooding unless the properties have flood insurance. Reporting on the location of flood hazard zones has historically been an area of high risk and liability for appraisers. Sometimes appraisers have not researched this area when they claim they have, or at other times they make errors in the research. In many appraisals, this section is tied to the highest and best use portion of the report and requires reconciliation with that part of the appraisal process if the property is in a flood area.

Testimony and Court Appearances (4)

It is always a nasty surprise when an appraiser receives a subpoena to appear in court to testify for a divorce proceeding when the appraisal was done for mortgage financing purposes. Some divorce attorneys actually order mortgage appraisals through a lender just so they can attest to the fact that they were ordered by a third party. In these instances, appraisers may or may not be paid for their time in the courtroom. A subpoena will most likely trump this statement in the appraisal report.

Adverse Conditions (5)

The next part of the statement helps to define the scope of work for an appraiser. It may not protect the appraiser from liability because the clients–i.e., the lenders– usually will not have agreed to these terms and conditions. An appraiser may not be an environmental engineer, but he or she can often know when to call one. Appraisers should seek the advice of a competent attorney about limiting liability for these issues.

Satisfactory Completion, Repairs, or Alterations (6)

If the appraiser has based the property value on repairs or completion of construction, the work must be done in a professional manner. It is always a big surprise as well as a problem when the appraiser assumes that quality work will be performed, but the applicant or owner decides to do the work instead. The quality of the work affects value, and the appraiser cannot know ahead of time whether the quality will be as envisioned. This statement helps the appraiser to make the value subject to the quality of the construction work.

Statement of Assumptions and Limiting Conditions for Form 2055

The statement of assumptions and limiting conditions for Form 2055 differs from the URAR only in that Section 2 was deleted and the remaining sections were renumbered. Section 2 was deleted because of the difficulty associated with completing a sketch without being able to go on site.

In exterior-only appraisals, appraisers usually use the square footage as listed on the assessor's or auditor's records. In some areas these figures are notoriously incorrect, but data from the same source is usually used for the comparable sales as well because appraisers believe that this would still constitute an "apples to apples" comparison. A significant error in one direction cannot be offset by a significant error in the opposite direction unless the magnitude of the errors is known.

APPRAISER'S CERTIFICATION: The Appraiser certifies and agrees that:

1. I have, at a minimum, developed and reported this appraisal in accordance with the scope of work requirements stated in this appraisal report.

2. I performed a complete visual inspection of the interior and exterior areas of the subject property. I reported the condition of the improvements in factual, specific terms. I identified and reported the physical deficiencies that could affect the livability, soundness, or structural integrity of the property.

3. I performed this appraisal in accordance with the requirements of the Uniform Standards of Professional Appraisal Practice that were adopted and promulgated by the Appraisal Standards Board of The Appraisal Foundation and that were in place at the time this appraisal report was prepared.

4. I developed my opinion of the market value of the real property that is the subject of this report based on the sales comparison approach to value. I have adequate comparable market data to develop a reliable sales comparison approach for this appraisal assignment. I further certify that I considered the cost and income approaches to value but did not develop them, unless otherwise indicated in this report.

5. I researched, verified, analyzed, and reported on any current agreement for sale for the subject property, any offering for sale of the subject property in the twelve months prior to the effective date of this appraisal, and the prior sales of the subject property for a minimum of three years prior to the effective date of this appraisal, unless otherwise indicated in this report.

6. I researched, verified, analyzed, and reported on the prior sales of the comparable sales for a minimum of one year prior to the date of sale of the comparable sale, unless otherwise indicated in this report.

7. I selected and used comparable sales that are locationally, physically, and functionally the most similar to the subject property.

8. I have not used comparable sales that were the result of combining a land sale with the contract purchase price of a home that has been built or will be built on the land.

9. I have reported adjustments to the comparable sales that reflect the market's reaction to the differences between the subject property and the comparable sales.

10. I verified, from a disinterested source, all information in this report that was provided by parties who have a financial interest in the sale or financing of the subject property.

11. I have knowledge and experience in appraising this type of property in this market area.

12. I am aware of, and have access to, the necessary and appropriate public and private data sources, such as multiple listing services, tax assessment records, public land records and other such data sources for the area in which the property is located.

13. I obtained the information, estimates, and opinions furnished by other parties and expressed in this appraisal report from reliable sources that I believe to be true and correct.

14. I have taken into consideration the factors that have an impact on value with respect to the subject neighborhood, subject property, and the proximity of the subject property to adverse influences in the development of my opinion of market value. I have noted in this appraisal report any adverse conditions (such as, but not limited to, needed repairs, deterioration, the presence of hazardous wastes, toxic substances, adverse environmental conditions, etc.) observed during the inspection of the subject property or that I became aware of during the research involved in performing this appraisal. I have considered these adverse conditions in my analysis of the property value, and have reported on the effect of the conditions on the value and marketability of the subject property.

15. I have not knowingly withheld any significant information from this appraisal report and, to the best of my knowledge, all statements and information in this appraisal report are true and correct.

16. I stated in this appraisal report my own personal, unbiased, and professional analysis, opinions, and conclusions, which are subject only to the assumptions and limiting conditions in this appraisal report.

17. I have no present or prospective interest in the property that is the subject of this report, and I have no present or prospective personal interest or bias with respect to the participants in the transaction. I did not base, either partially or completely, my analysis and/or opinion of market value in this appraisal report on the race, color, religion, sex, age, marital status, handicap, familial status, or national origin of either the prospective owners or occupants of the subject property or of the present owners or occupants of the properties in the vicinity of the subject property or on any other basis prohibited by law.

18. My employment and/or compensation for performing this appraisal or any future or anticipated appraisals was not conditioned on any agreement or understanding, written or otherwise, that I would report (or present analysis supporting) a predetermined specific value, a predetermined minimum value, a range or direction in value, a value that favors the cause of any party, or the attainment of a specific result or occurrence of a specific subsequent event (such as approval of a pending mortgage loan application).

19. I personally prepared all conclusions and opinions about the real estate that were set forth in this appraisal report. If I relied on significant real property appraisal assistance from any individual or individuals in the performance of this appraisal or the preparation of this appraisal report, I have named such individual(s) and disclosed the specific tasks performed in this appraisal report. I certify that any individual so named is qualified to perform the tasks. I have not authorized anyone to make a change to any item in this appraisal report; therefore, any change made to this appraisal is unauthorized and I will take no responsibility for it.

20. I identified the lender/client in this appraisal report who is the individual, organization, or agent for the organization that ordered and will receive this appraisal report.

Appraiser's Certification

Page 5 of the URAR and Form 2055 are identical with one exception that will be discussed here.

Appraiser's Certification

The appraiser's certification section of the report is not designed to limit the appraiser's liability. Most of its content is required by USPAP and is intended for appraisers to attest that they have complied with the professional and ethical requirements mandated by USPAP. The certification is required in all appraisal reports, and each appraiser should carefully read the attestation to which they are signing their name. A lawsuit against an appraiser can bring these signed certifications into the courtroom for use against the appraiser.

Scope of Work (1)

The appraiser first certifies that the preprinted scope of work has been followed. If desired, the appraiser can expand the definition of the scope of work.

Visual Inspection (2)

Next, the appraiser states that he or she has inspected the property. This certification is important for the cases in which an appraiser does not inspect the property personally but signs the report anyway. It is also important for ensuring that the appraiser has observed, analyzed, and reported any problems and instances of deferred maintenance for the subject property.

On the URAR, this certification states that the appraiser has performed a "complete visual inspection of the interior and exterior areas of the subject property," while this certification on Form 2055 states that the appraiser has performed a "visual inspection of the exterior areas of the subject property from at least the street."

Adherence to USPAP (3)

The appraiser then attests that USPAP has been followed and its rules and regulations have been adhered to throughout the course of the assignment.

Market Value Opinion by Sales Comparison (4)

Next, the appraiser certifies that the sales comparison approach was used to value the property and the cost and income capitalization approaches to value were not required to obtain a credible value opinion on the appraisal of the subject single-unit residence.

The appraiser also states that adequate market data was used to develop a reliable sales comparison analysis. Appraisers in all markets are aware that only inadequate data may be available for some

Page **5** of 6

Practice that were adopted and promulgated
place at the time this appraisal report was pre

4. I developed my opinion of the market value
comparison approach to value. I have adequa
for this appraisal assignment. I further certify t
them, unless otherwise indicated in this repor

5. I researched, verified, analyzed, and report
sale of the subject property in the twelve mon
property for a minimum of three years prior to

6. I researched, verified, analyzed, and report
to the date of sale of the comparable sale, un

7. I selected and used comparable sales that ar

8. I have not used comparable sales that were t
has been built or will be built on the land.

9. I have reported adjustments to the comparab
property and the comparable sales.

10. I verified, from a disinterested source, all inf
the sale or financing of the subject property.

11. I have knowledge and experience in apprai

12. I am aware of, and have access to, the n

appraisals and may not want to go on record to say that they provided the client a reliable conclusion for these appraisals. Rather, they might choose to state that the subject is a difficult property and the final opinion is not as reliable as what might have been expected.

Case in Point

The subject property is being appraised for a first mortgage lender. The subject real estate is a single-unit home located on a two-acre parcel just outside of Bigville. The improvement is unique for the area because its design is a triple geodesic dome. The living room, dining room, and kitchen are in dome 1. Three bedrooms are located in dome 2, and the garage and workshop are located in dome 3. All are connected by tunnels that are similar to igloos. There is a basement under the residence area and a loft-den section over the master bedroom that is accessible by a spiral staircase. The home has 4,500 square feet of GLA and 1,000 square feet of garage area. The home has an in-ground pool in the backyard with a 20-ft. diving board and a hot tub that is 12 feet in diameter. The site is located next to an interstate highway, and there is a landfill within view of the front porch. There are no comparable sales for this type of home or comparable homes of this size near the interstate or landfill.

The appraiser accepted the assignment without knowledge of these issues and is forced to use standard, colonial, two-story home sales as comparables. Nearly every line of the report has adjustments. The gross adjustment percentages are 79%, 89%, 76%, 81%, and 45%. The net adjustment ratios are 10%, 18%, 22%, 18%, and 12%. The only similarity that the appraiser could note was that the comparables were located in the same school system. His comments in the report were: "These comparisons are like comparing a Chevrolet to a toaster; they have little in common except that they are both metal. These are terrible comparisons, but they are the best comparables available at this time. The comparables are fine but the subject improvement is the problem, and this cannot be changed."

An appraiser who accepts such an assignment would not likely want to say that adequate comparable market data with which to develop a reliable sales comparison analysis was available in the subject market area. Instead, he or she would likely report that a value opinion was developed but confidence in its reliability is lacking. An appraiser of such a property may decide to develop a narrative appraisal report that includes a more appropriate certification, use an appraisal form that lacks such a certification, or decline the assignment.

Research on Current Sale Agreements for the Subject Property (5)

Certification 5 makes it clear that nondisclosure of significant historical data about the subject property is unacceptable, and the appraiser is required to disclose all relevant data.

Research on Prior Sales of Comparable Sales (6)

The appraiser then certifies that the minimum amount of research on comparable sales has been done in compliance with Fannie Mae Supplemental Standards. Appraisers who sign this form but do not perform the minimum amount of work are misleading the user.

The appraiser, in making this certification, is stating that he or she performed the research for one year prior to the comparable's sale, not one year before the effective date of the appraisal. For a sale dated one year ago, the appraiser would be required to conduct research for the prior two years.

Similarity of Comparable Sales to the Subject Property (7)

Next, the appraiser attests that the most similar comparable sales available were used to develop the value opinion. Because USPAP does not address this issue, lenders now require that appraisers include this statement in their reports. Using the best comparables available is the only acceptable appraisal practice. Appraisers who do not use the best comparables available expose themselves to liability.

Comparable Sales Resulting from Combining a Land Sale with a Contract Purchase (8)

This next certification represents an all-new consideration for some appraisers. It evolved from manufactured home guidelines, which have eliminated the practice of using comparable sales that result from combining a land sale with a contract purchase. This issue remains significant for appraisers who perform new home construction appraisals. Appraisers cannot use comparable sales that were developed by adding the land value to the "contract to build a new home" amount. It is common appraisal thinking that to achieve a market value opinion, all the comparable sales must have been exposed to the market. This type of sale, along with others that have not been exposed to the market, should be excluded from the comparable sales.

In some markets, resales of new homes may show a 15% loss due to overbuilding. However, an appraiser can show that cost equals value by using "contract to build" comparable sales, which do not reflect external obsolescence. Using these comparable sales has never been considered good appraisal practice because it is effectively employing another cost approach. This issue is significant for appraisers who value a considerable number of newly constructed homes. It is a big step forward for appraisal guidelines, which have been silent on this subject until now, and will make it more difficult for some less legitimate builders to "hide" seller-paid closing costs, allowances, kickbacks, and other incentives that appraisers were previously unable to detect in their prices.

Adjustments to Comparable Sales (9)

In past appraisal practices, appraisers made inappropriate adjustments to comparable sales to provide a misleading indication of the subject's value. The appraiser is certifying that this practice is unacceptable in certification 9.

Verification of Information from Financially Interested Parties (10)

The appraiser then acknowledges that it is unacceptable appraisal practice to obtain comparable sales data from the builders, sellers, or brokers involved in the sale of the subject without independent verification by parties who have no financial interest in the sale. This issue is important for appraisers who use sales provided by the subject's builder and have no independent means of verifying this interest. It is

Page 5 of 6

9. I have reported adjustments to the compara... property and the comparable sales.

10. I verified, from a disinterested source, all inf... the sale or financing of the subject property.

11. I have knowledge and experience in apprai...

12. I am aware of, and have access to, the nec... services, tax assessment records, public land r...

13. I obtained the information, estimates, and ... reliable sources that I believe to be true and c...

14. I have taken into consideration the factors ... property, and the proximity of the subject prop... have noted in this appraisal report any advers... presence of hazardous wastes, toxic substanc... subject property or that I became aware of dur... adverse conditions in my analysis of the prope... marketability of the subject property.

15. I have not knowingly withheld any signific... statements and information in this appraisal r...

16. I stated in this appraisal report my own pe... are subject only to the assumptions and limiti...

17. I have no present or prospective interest in... prospective personal interest or bias with respe... completely, my analysis and/or opinion of mark... status, handicap, familial status, or national ori... present owners or occupants of the properties ...

18. My employment and/or compensation for ... conditioned on any agreement or understandi... predetermined specific value, a predetermine... any party, or the attainment of a specific resul... mortgage loan application).

19. I personally prepared all conclusions and ... relied on significant real property appraisal as... or the preparation of this appraisal report, I ha... appraisal report. I certify that any individual so... a change to any item in this appraisal report; I... responsibility for it.

20. I identified the lender/client in this apprais... ordered and will receive this appraisal report...

Freddie Mac Form 70 March 2005

common in some markets for appraisers to get a HUD-1 closing statement for a comparable sale and consider it to be verification. With computers, it would be possible for a builder or broker to create and print out their own HUD-1 forms. In some markets, the builders or brokers also own the title insurance companies and close their own sales. As a result, it is possible for a person with a financial interest in the sale to create a sales disclosure form that has incorrect prices on it. Using sales reported to the MLS by a broker who is also an employee or who a builder uses regularly is not good appraisal practice either because the broker has an interest in the appraisal's outcome.

If an appraiser uses a sale from the builder of the subject or from a broker that is representing the seller of the subject, they must recognize the possibility of erroneous data being presented. If such data is used, the appraiser must supplement these sales with additional sales from sources that are considered reliable.

Clearly, appraisers who use tainted data are not following best appraisal practice. They must either reliably verify data or use so much data that a single erroneous piece cannot have a significant impact on the conclusion. If the appraiser uses only three comparable sales, each must be verified and confirmed to be correct. If an appraiser uses six comparable sales from diverse sources, the verification process need not be as stringent because of the diversity of the data. Of course, using six comparable sales from the same broker or builder should also be avoided. With computers, color printers, and scanners, almost any document can be fabricated and it is hard to know the source of the fraudulent documents. If any doubt about the authenticity of the data exists, the data either should not be used or should be minimized through the use of more verifiable data.

Keep in mind that a price associated with a contract to build a new home that has never been exposed to the market because it is meant for a specific buyer (contract for construction) is not a comparable sale but a cost of construction comparable. This price does not show what a buyer will pay for a completed product, only what the cost of the various components add up to. For example, a buyer designed and built an 8,000-sq.-ft. residence with one bedroom and the cost was $600,000 (plus the $100,000 lot). If the cost is added up, the indication of value for a one-bedroom home is $700,000. Adding up the cost of construction ignores any external or functional obsolescence and should not be done in the sales comparison analysis.

Knowledge and Experience of the Appraiser (11)

Next, the appraiser certifies and agrees that he or she has the experience to do the job. This certification merely restates the competency requirements from USPAP.

Access to Necessary and Appropriate Public and Private Data Sources (12)

Lack of access to necessary data has been used as a defense for poor appraisals in the past. Certification 12 removes this defense when appraisers sign their name to verify that they have access to the necessary data.

Reliability of Sources (13)

Certification 13 is a limiting condition in which the appraiser states that the data is as reliable as can be found and that although there could be errors, the appraiser is not aware of them.

Effect of Adverse Conditions on Value (14)

Certification 14 is an all-encompassing statement in which the appraiser certifies that important data was not omitted from the report and that environmental problems and their impact on the value of the subject have been considered and reported.

Withholding of Significant Information (15)

Next, the appraiser affirms that no significant data has been left out of the appraisal report and that the data is true and correct. This statement can be used against the appraiser if the report is found to be defective or misleading. If the previous certification was not enough to make the appraiser accept responsibility, then this statement should do the trick.

Assumptions and Limiting Conditions (16)

This next statement is required by USPAP. It serves to prevent appraisers from invoking unknown and undisclosed limiting conditions when it suits them.

Absence of Present or Prospective Interest in the Property (17)

Certification 17 is also required by USPAP Standard 2-3. The appraiser must sign his or her name to this statement for it to have its intended effect.

Predetermination of Specific or Minimum Value (18)

Certification 18 is another attestation required by USPAP. Appraisers must also sign their name to this statement, which removes the excuse for poor appraisal behavior.

Personal Responsibility for the Preparation of the Report (19)

USPAP Standard 2-3 requires the appraiser to certify that he or she performed the work and that no other party participated in the development of the appraisal unless that party is named. Certification 19 removes any defense that the appraiser is not responsible for the report. This certification was needed to stop appraisers from blaming underlings for flawed appraisal reports.

Identification of the User (20)

In this last statement, the appraiser certifies that the client for whom the report was developed is known and identified for the report's delivery.

Uniform Residential Appraisal Report

File #

21. The lender/client may disclose or distribute this appraisal report to: the borrower; another lender at the request of the borrower; the mortgagee or its successors and assigns; mortgage insurers; government sponsored enterprises; other secondary market participants; data collection or reporting services; professional appraisal organizations; any department, agency, or instrumentality of the United States; and any state, the District of Columbia, or other jurisdictions; without having to obtain the appraiser's or supervisory appraiser's (if applicable) consent. Such consent must be obtained before this appraisal report may be disclosed or distributed to any other party (including, but not limited to, the public through advertising, public relations, news, sales, or other media).

22. I am aware that any disclosure or distribution of this appraisal report by me or the lender/client may be subject to certain laws and regulations. Further, I am also subject to the provisions of the Uniform Standards of Professional Appraisal Practice that pertain to disclosure or distribution by me.

23. The borrower, another lender at the request of the borrower, the mortgagee or its successors and assigns, mortgage insurers, government sponsored enterprises, and other secondary market participants may rely on this appraisal report as part of any mortgage finance transaction that involves any one or more of these parties.

24. If this appraisal report was transmitted as an "electronic record" containing my "electronic signature," as those terms are defined in applicable federal and/or state laws (excluding audio and video recordings), or a facsimile transmission of this appraisal report containing a copy or representation of my signature, the appraisal report shall be as effective, enforceable and valid as if a paper version of this appraisal report were delivered containing my original hand written signature.

25. Any intentional or negligent misrepresentation(s) contained in this appraisal report may result in civil liability and/or criminal penalties including, but not limited to, fine or imprisonment or both under the provisions of Title 18, United States Code, Section 1001, et seq., or similar state laws.

SUPERVISORY APPRAISER'S CERTIFICATION: The Supervisory Appraiser certifies and agrees that:

1. I directly supervised the appraiser for this appraisal assignment, have read the appraisal report, and agree with the appraiser's analysis, opinions, statements, conclusions, and the appraiser's certification.

2. I accept full responsibility for the contents of this appraisal report including, but not limited to, the appraiser's analysis, opinions, statements, conclusions, and the appraiser's certification.

3. The appraiser identified in this appraisal report is either a sub-contractor or an employee of the supervisory appraiser (or the appraisal firm), is qualified to perform this appraisal, and is acceptable to perform this appraisal under the applicable state law.

4. This appraisal report complies with the Uniform Standards of Professional Appraisal Practice that were adopted and promulgated by the Appraisal Standards Board of The Appraisal Foundation and that were in place at the time this appraisal report was prepared.

5. If this appraisal report was transmitted as an "electronic record" containing my "electronic signature," as those terms are defined in applicable federal and/or state laws (excluding audio and video recordings), or a facsimile transmission of this appraisal report containing a copy or representation of my signature, the appraisal report shall be as effective, enforceable and valid as if a paper version of this appraisal report were delivered containing my original hand written signature.

APPRAISER

Signature ____________________
Name ____________________
Company Name ____________________
Company Address ____________________
____
Telephone Number ____________________
Email Address ____________________
Date of Signature and Report ____________________
Effective Date of Appraisal ____________________
State Certification # ____________________
or State License # ____________________
or Other (describe) ____________ State # ________
State ____________________
Expiration Date of Certification or License ____________

ADDRESS OF PROPERTY APPRAISED
____
____

APPRAISED VALUE OF SUBJECT PROPERTY $ ____________

LENDER/CLIENT
Name ____________________
Company Name ____________________
Company Address ____________________
____
Email Address ____________________

SUPERVISORY APPRAISER (ONLY IF REQUIRED)

Signature ____________________
Name ____________________
Company Name ____________________
Company Address ____________________
____
Telephone Number ____________________
Email Address ____________________
Date of Signature ____________________
State Certification # ____________________
or State License # ____________________
State ____________________
Expiration Date of Certification or License ____________

SUBJECT PROPERTY

☐ Did not inspect subject property
☐ Did inspect exterior of subject property from street
Date of Inspection ____________________
☐ Did inspect interior and exterior of subject property
Date of Inspection ____________________

COMPARABLE SALES

☐ Did not inspect exterior of comparable sales from street
☐ Did inspect exterior of comparable sales from street
Date of Inspection ____________________

Appraiser's Certification (continued), Supervisory Appraiser's Certification, and Signature Block

Page 6 of the URAR and Form 2055 are the same except for the signature block area, which will be discussed separately for each form.

Appraiser's Certification (continued)

Disclosure and Distribution of the Report (21)

Certification 21 sets forth the individuals and groups to whom the report may be given. This certification does not represent a change in this report or a change in practice; rather, it is–and always has been–a liability issue.

Terms of Disclosure and Distribution (22)

The next certification sets forth the applicable privacy laws. It specifically references USPAP rules that focus on the appraiser's obligations toward the client regarding confidentiality. This statement remains consistent with current appraisal practice.

Use of the Appraisal (23)

Certification 23 is controversial because some appraisers believe it elevates the borrower to the level of an intended user. Appraisers with concerns about this topic should seek the advice of an attorney regarding any increase in liability that may be caused by Certification 23. The Appraisal Foundation and Fannie Mae have both discussed this certification in various publications.

Validity and Enforceability of Electronically Transmitted Appraisals (24)

The next certification states that electronic and facsimile copies of an appraisal report that bear an electronic signature are valid within federal law.

Penalty for Intentional or Negligent Misrepresentations (25)

The last appraiser's certification statement sets forth the penalty according to the U.S. Code for an appraiser who intentionally or negligently misrepresents facts in performing an appraisal. The specific part of the U.S. Code is Title 18, Section 1001, and is available through the U.S. House of Representatives Office of the Law Revision Counsel at *http://uscode.house.gov*. This part of the Code is outlined as follows:

Page 6 of 6

appraisal report containing a copy or represen
valid as if a paper version of this appraisal rep

25. Any intentional or negligent misrepresenta
criminal penalties including, but not limited to,
Code, Section 1001, et seq., or similar state la

SUPERVISORY APPRAISER'S CERTIFIC

1. I directly supervised the appraiser for this ap
analysis, opinions, statements, conclusions, an

2. I accept full responsibility for the contents of th
statements, conclusions, and the appraiser's ce

3. The appraiser identified in this appraisal repo
appraisal firm), is qualified to perform this appra

4. This appraisal report complies with the Unifo
promulgated by the Appraisal Standards Boar
report was prepared.

5. If this appraisal report was transmitted as an
defined in applicable federal and/or state laws
appraisal report containing a copy or represen
valid as if a paper version of this appraisal rep

APPRAISER

Signature
Name
Company Name
Company Address

Telephone Number
Email Address
Date of Signature and Report
Effective Date of Appraisal
State Certification #
or State License #
or Other (describe) State #
State
Expiration Date of Certification or License

ADDRESS OF PROPERTY APPRAISED

APPRAISED VALUE OF SUBJECT PROPERTY $
LENDER/CLIENT
Name
Company Name
Company Address

Email Address

Freddie Mac Form 70 March 2005

(a) Except as otherwise provided in this section, whoever, in any matter within the jurisdiction of the executive, legislative, or judicial branch of the Government of the United States, knowingly and willfully -

1. Falsifies, conceals, or covers up by any trick, scheme, or device a material fact;
2. Makes any materially false, fictitious, or fraudulent statement or representation; or
3. Makes or uses any false writing or document knowing the same to contain any materially false, fictitious, or fraudulent statement or entry;

Shall be fined under this title, imprisoned not more than 5 years or, if the offense involves international or domestic terrorism (as defined in section 2331), imprisoned not more than 8 years, or both. If the matter relates to an offense under chapter 109A, 109B, 110, or 117, or section 1591, then the term of imprisonment imposed under this section shall be not more than 8 years.

(b) Subsection (a) does not apply to a party to a judicial proceeding, or that party's counsel, for statements, representations, writings, or documents submitted by such party or counsel to a judge or magistrate in that proceeding.

(c) With respect to any matter within the jurisdiction of the legislative branch, subsection (a) shall apply only to -

1. Administrative matters, including a claim for payment, a matter related to the procurement of property or services, personnel or employment practices, or support services, or a document required by law, rule, or regulation to be submitted to the Congress or any office or officer within the legislative branch; or
2. Any investigation or review, conducted pursuant to the authority of any committee, subcommittee, commission or office of the Congress, consistent with applicable rules of the House or Senate.[1]

This citation is likely to have a chilling effect on appraisers who are asked to mislead the intended users to a false value conclusion.

Supervisory Appraiser's Certification

The supervisory certifications are similar to the previously discussed appraiser's certifications. They require that the supervisory appraiser confirm the conclusion arrived at in the report. Some appraisers who have licenses to practice in multiple states supervise trainees in each state in which they have a license. They may not effectively supervise each trainee, but they do sign off on the reports. This statement should make them think twice about certifying the work of trainees they do not supervise directly.

This requirement poses a problem for supervisors who sign appraisal reports without reviewing them carefully. Appraisers who have trainees should contact an attorney about the potential personal liability incurred by certifying appraisals without reviewing them.

Signature Block for the URAR

The signature block for the most current version of the URAR form has been revised to include the telephone number and e-mail address for the appraiser and supervisory appraiser.

1. Office of the Law Revision Council, U.S. House of Representatives, *U.S. Code, Title 18, Section 1001* (January 8, 2008). Available at *http://uscode.house.gov*. Direct link: *http://uscode.house.gov/search/criteria.shtml* (Enter "Title 18" and "Section 1001" in the search box.)

Lender/Client

The lender/client section requires appraisers to identify the client who hired them. This part is important because it identifies the individual with whom the appraiser has a contract to perform the work, and it cannot be changed later. A new appraisal report can be prepared for a new client, but this report must be intended for this client only.

Subject Property

☐ **Did not inspect subject property**

☐ **Did inspect exterior of subject property from street**
Date of Inspection

☐ **Did inspect interior and exterior of subject property**
Date of Inspection

Comparable Sales

☐ **Did not inspect exterior of comparable sales from street**

☐ **Did inspect exterior of comparable sales from street**
Date of Inspection

The URAR provides check boxes to certify the inspection of the subject property and the comparable sales, whereas the older version of the form combined this certification with the signature line. By separating the two, the importance of the inspection is given more prominence than before.

Signature Block for Form 2055

The only difference between the signature blocks on the URAR and Form 2055 is that check boxes for Form 2055 are for an exterior-only inspection, whereas those for the URAR are for both interior and exterior inspections of the subject property. With the previous form, some supervisors could certify that they inspected the subject property and not be specific, leading clients to think that an interior inspection was made when it was not. This change eliminates that problem.

Fannie Mae discusses the appraiser's certification in depth in their single-family *Selling Guide*, Section B4-1.2-07, Certifications and Statements of Assumptions and Limiting Conditions, available at *www.efanniemae.com.*

To access the guide, type "Selling Guide" in the search box that appears in the top right corner of the home page. The *Selling Guide* can also be accessed by first clicking on "Appraisers" under the "Industry Specialists" heading. Next, click on "Single-Family Guides for free online" under the heading "AllRegs Online." A list of documents will then appear. If pop-ups are blocked, click on "View Support Tips and AllRegs Contact Info" under the "AllRegs Online" heading to access directions for changing the browser settings to allow pop-ups.

Market Conditions Addendum to the Appraisal Report

File No.

The purpose of this addendum is to provide the lender/client with a clear and accurate understanding of the market trends and conditions prevalent in the subject neighborhood. This is a required addendum for all appraisal reports with an effective date on or after April 1, 2009.

Property Address | City | State | ZIP Code

Borrower

Instructions: The appraiser must use the information required on this form as the basis for his/her conclusions, and must provide support for those conclusions, regarding housing trends and overall market conditions as reported in the Neighborhood section of the appraisal report form. The appraiser must fill in all the information to the extent it is available and reliable and must provide analysis as indicated below. If any required data is unavailable or is considered unreliable, the appraiser must provide an explanation. It is recognized that not all data sources will be able to provide data for the shaded areas below; if it is available, however, the appraiser must include the data in the analysis. If data sources provide the required information as an average instead of the median, the appraiser should report the available figure and identify it as an average. Sales and listings must be properties that compete with the subject property, determined by applying the criteria that would be used by a prospective buyer of the subject property. The appraiser must explain any anomalies in the data, such as seasonal markets, new construction, foreclosures, etc.

MARKET RESEARCH & ANALYSIS

Inventory Analysis	Prior 7–12 Months	Prior 4–6 Months	Current – 3 Months	Overall Trend		
Total # of Comparable Sales (Settled)				☐ Increasing	☐ Stable	☐ Declining
Absorption Rate (Total Sales/Months)				☐ Increasing	☐ Stable	☐ Declining
Total # of Comparable Active Listings				☐ Declining	☐ Stable	☐ Increasing
Months of Housing Supply (Total Listings/Ab.Rate)				☐ Declining	☐ Stable	☐ Increasing
Median Sale & List Price, DOM, Sale/List %	Prior 7–12 Months	Prior 4–6 Months	Current – 3 Months	Overall Trend		
Median Comparable Sale Price				☐ Increasing	☐ Stable	☐ Declining
Median Comparable Sales Days on Market				☐ Declining	☐ Stable	☐ Increasing
Median Comparable List Price				☐ Increasing	☐ Stable	☐ Declining
Median Comparable Listings Days on Market				☐ Declining	☐ Stable	☐ Increasing
Median Sale Price as % of List Price				☐ Increasing	☐ Stable	☐ Declining
Seller-(developer, builder, etc.) paid financial assistance prevalent? ☐ Yes ☐ No				☐ Declining	☐ Stable	☐ Increasing

Explain in detail the seller concessions trends for the past 12 months (e.g., seller contributions increased from 3% to 5%, increasing use of buydowns, closing costs, condo fees, options, etc.).

Are foreclosure sales (REO sales) a factor in the market? ☐ Yes ☐ No If yes, explain (including the trends in listings and sales of foreclosed properties).

Cite data sources for above information.

Summarize the above information as support for your conclusions in the Neighborhood section of the appraisal report form. If you used any additional information, such as an analysis of pending sales and/or expired and withdrawn listings, to formulate your conclusions, provide both an explanation and support for your conclusions.

CONDO/CO-OP PROJECTS

If the subject is a unit in a condominium or cooperative project, complete the following: **Project Name:**

Subject Project Data	Prior 7-12 Months	Prior 4-6 Months	Current – 3 Months	Overall Trend		
Total # of Comparable Sales (Settled)				☐ Increasing	☐ Stable	☐ Declining
Absorption Rate (Total Sales/Months)				☐ Increasing	☐ Stable	☐ Declining
Total # of Active Comparable Listings				☐ Declining	☐ Stable	☐ Increasing
Months of Unit Supply (Total Listings/Ab. Rate)				☐ Declining	☐ Stable	☐ Increasing

Are foreclosure sales (REO sales) a factor in the project? ☐ Yes ☐ No If yes, indicate the number of REO listings and explain the trends in listings and sales of foreclosed properties.

Summarize the above trends and address the impact on the subject unit and project.

APPRAISER

Signature	Signature
Appraiser Name	Supervisory Appraiser Name
Company Name	Company Name
Company Address	Company Address
State License/Certification # State	State License/Certification # State
Email Address	Email Address

Freddie Mac Form 71 March 2009 Page 1 of 1 Fannie Mae Form 1004MC March 2009

The Market Conditions Form (Fannie Mae Form 1004MC/Freddie Mac Form 71)

This last section discusses the newest addition to appraisers' reporting requirements: the Market Conditions Addendum to the Appraisal Report, Fannie Mae Form 1004MC or Freddie Mac Form 71, which will be referred to here as the Market Conditions Form. This new form is not considered to cause a substantial increase in scope of work, since appraisers should have been researching and reporting on market conditions in the subject's neighborhood or market in the past. However, this form does cause an increase in reporting requirements because there was no form like this prior to 2009. Some appraisers would also argue that the scope of work has been increased because lender skepticism has created a need for much additional support beyond the minimums required by the form.

Introduction

The Market Conditions Form was initially released in November of 2008 but revised in March of 2009. It is required for use in all residential appraisals for loans to be sold to Fannie Mae or Freddie Mac with an effective date of April 1, 2009, or later.

Fannie Mae's *Announcement 08-30* on appraisal-related policy changes and clarifications provides instructions for using the new Market Conditions Form as well as other important updates and clarifications, so appraisers should review the entire announcement before preparing the form for the first time.

Announcement 08-30 is posted on Fannie Mae's Web site, *www.efanniemae.com.* To access the announcement, type "Announcement 08-30" in the search box that appears in the top right corner of the home page. The announcement can also be accessed by first clicking on "Appraisers" under the "Industry Specialists" heading. Next, click on "Single-Family Guides for free online" under the heading "AllRegs Online." A list of documents will then appear. If pop-ups are blocked, click on "View Support Tips and AllRegs Contact Info" under the "AllRegs Online" heading to access directions for changing the browser settings to allow pop-ups.

The announcement introduces the new Market Conditions Form and summarizes Fannie Mae policy changes for appraisers.

Freddie Mac has an introduction to the Market Conditions Form in their November 24, 2008 Bulletin, posted on their Web site at *www.freddiemac.com.* Access the bulletin by typing "November 24, 2008 Bulletin" in the search box located at the top right corner of the home page.

One-Unit Housing Trends			
Property Values	☐ Increasing	☐ Stable	☐ Declining
Demand/Supply	☐ Shortage	☐ In Balance	☐ Over Supply
Marketing Time	☐ Under 3 mths	☐ 3-6 mths	☐ Over 6 mths

It is important to keep the goal of this new Market Conditions Form in mind. It is not the goal of Fannie Mae or Freddie Mac to make real estate appraisals more difficult for appraisers to prepare or to make appraisers jump through hoops for no reason. It is, however, a goal of both organizations to ensure that appraisers have support for their neighborhood market trend conclusions.

The market conditions analysis required on the form may sometimes seem meaningless. Other times, it may seem to be too detailed and to provide too much information. Both cases may be true for a few applications, but this analysis should be meaningful and not burdensome in most cases. Keep in mind that most appraisers have already been doing part of this analysis for many years while completing the supply and demand study section above the sales comparison grid on page two of the URAR and Form 2055. Also, appraisers should have some support for their conclusions of supply and demand in the neighborhood section on page 1 of the URAR and Form 2055, which means that they should have been doing something to support their opinions before this form was introduced.

Some appraisers may find completing this new form to be redundant to their current efforts, while others may have never even thought about providing this much support for a conclusion of market trends. The Market Conditions Form is designed to be as local and therefore as specific as possible. Other sources of general data may be considered when reconciling an opinion of market conditions.

Market Research & Analysis Section: Preamble, Address, and Instructions

Market Conditions Addendum to the Appraisal Report **File No.**

The purpose of this addendum is to provide the lender/client with a clear and accurate understanding of the market trends and conditions prevalent in the subject neighborhood. This is a required addendum for all appraisal reports with an effective date on or after April 1, 2009.			
Property Address	City	State	ZIP Code
Borrower			
Instructions: The appraiser must use the information required on this form as the basis for his/her conclusions, and must provide support for those conclusions, regarding housing trends and overall market conditions as reported in the Neighborhood section of the appraisal report form. The appraiser must fill in all the information to the extent it is available and reliable and must provide analysis as indicated below. If any required data is unavailable or is considered unreliable, the appraiser must provide an explanation. It is recognized that not all data sources will be able to provide data for the shaded areas below; if it is available, however, the appraiser must include the data in the analysis. If data sources provide the required information as an average instead of the median, the appraiser should report the available figure and identify it as an average. Sales and listings must be properties that compete with the subject property, determined by applying the criteria that would be used by a prospective buyer of the subject property. The appraiser must explain any anomalies in the data, such as seasonal markets, new construction, foreclosures, etc.			

The preamble to the Market Conditions Form states that "The purpose of this addendum is to provide the lender/client with a clear and accurate understanding of the market trends and conditions prevalent in the subject neighborhood. This is a required addendum for all appraisal reports with an effective date on or after April 1, 2009."

This preamble should not be too difficult to understand. The neighborhood is defined as the market and the conclusions drawn from the analysis presented on this form should correlate to the neighborhood section of all the residential government lending forms.

Next, the address block is very similar to other address sections in most other appraisal report forms. This part should not pose a problem for most appraisers, since the software companies will likely tie this block to the other forms and exhibits in the report.

The instructions for the form state the following:

> The appraiser must use the information required on this form as the basis for his/her conclusions, and must provide support for those conclusions, regarding housing trends and overall market conditions as reported in the Neighborhood section of the appraisal report form. The appraiser must fill in all the information to the extent it is available and reliable and must provide analysis as indicated below. If any required data is unavailable or is considered unreliable, the appraiser must provide an explanation. It is recognized that not all data sources will be able to provide data for the shaded areas below; if it is available, however, the appraiser must include the data in the analysis. If data sources provide the required information as an average instead of the median, the appraiser should report the available figure and identify it as an average. Sales and listings must be properties that compete with the subject property, determined by applying the criteria that would be used by a prospective buyer of the subject property. The appraiser must explain any anomalies in the data, such as seasonal markets, new construction, foreclosures, etc.

The following are some keys points to keep in mind from these instructions:

- The appraiser must provide the information as much as is available and reliable. If the information is not available or reliable, some narrative discussion is needed. It would not be acceptable to put "Not Available" in certain spaces of the form and not provide any further explanation.
- The mean (average) of the data can be presented if the median is not available. The median is the middle point in the sorted data.
- The shaded areas of the form are not expected to be completed in all markets. However, the appraiser should complete these areas as best as possible if the data is available. The shading is meant to lower investor and underwriter expectations.
- The sales and listings must be properties that compete with the subject real estate. This is the same criteria as for the analysis on the top of page 2 of the URAR and Form 2055, as well as other forms.
- The appraiser should explain any irregularities or other information that is not readily apparent to the reader.

Market Research & Analysis Section: Inventory Analysis

Inventory Analysis	Prior 7–12 Months	Prior 4–6 Months	Current – 3 Months	Overall Trend		
Total # of Comparable Sales (Settled)				☐ Increasing	☐ Stable	☐ Declining
Absorption Rate (Total Sales/Months)				☐ Increasing	☐ Stable	☐ Declining
Total # of Comparable Active Listings				☐ Declining	☐ Stable	☐ Increasing
Months of Housing Supply (Total Listings/Ab.Rate)				☐ Declining	☐ Stable	☐ Increasing

The inventory analysis grid is designed to help appraisers correctly analyze current market conditions as well as conditions from the recent past to develop an opinion of property value trends.

The goal of this grid is to provide support for the market trend opinion. The key word here is *trend.* Keep in mind that this new form and the work required to complete it do not have to be the total

Market Conditions Form

in the analysis. If data sources provide the required informatio
average. Sales and listings must be properties that compete wi
subject property. The appraiser must explain any anomalies in t

Inventory Analysis	Prior 7–12
Total # of Comparable Sales (Settled)	
Absorption Rate (Total Sales/Months)	
Total # of Comparable Active Listings	
Months of Housing Supply (Total Listings/Ab.Rate)	
Median Sale & List Price, DOM, Sale/List %	Prior 7–1
Median Comparable Sale Price	
Median Comparable Sales Days on Market	
Median Comparable List Price	

amount of work done by the appraiser to reach this goal. It is quite possible for appraisers to support their conclusions with other data and analysis, such as sales and resales of the same properties or regression analysis. Of course, the appraiser would still be required to submit this other data and analysis.

After the appraiser researchers and reports the required data, he or she is also asked to report his or her opinion on the overall trend for the rates and ratios listed. The check boxes under the "Overall Trend" heading are organized so that the boxes in the left column represent markets with increasing prices and good demand, the boxes on the right represent markets with falling prices and/or oversupply, and the boxes in the middle section represent markets in balance.

The inventory analysis is similar to many other such analyses prepared for many other industries to enable correct decisions on production levels. For example, automobile manufacturers study the inventory levels in the new car lots and rates of sale to see how many new units will be ordered in the near future.

This part of the form is focused on developing an absorption rate of inventory currently in place to show in relative terms how much inventory is for sale and as a result how many months of inventory can be compared to the recent past to develop an opinion of market trends.

Total # of Comparable Sales (Settled)

The time windows listed in the grid headings are "Prior 7-12 Months," "Prior 4-6 Months," and "Current – 3 Months." It is very important to note that six months are represented in the first column, three months in the middle column, and three months in the right column. This difference can be a little confusing to appraisers if they do not automatically work the math in prepared software programs. For example, if the sales rates are 12 units in all three columns, then the absorption rate would be two units per month for the prior seven to 12 months, four units per month for the prior four to six months, and four units per month for the past three months. The appraiser must remember to use the correct time window (6 months, 3 months, and 3 months) if computer software is not being used.

Absorption Rate (Total Sales/Months)

The first and second lines of the grid are essentially tied together. The first line asks for the overall number of sales and the second line is that amount divided by the number of months in each column. For example, if gross sales were 12 for the prior seven to 12 months, 12 for the prior four to six months, and 18 for the past three months, the sales rates would be 2, 4, and 6 per month, respectively, and the trend would be increasing over the entire analysis period.

This part of the grid asks for the number of comparable sales over the time window. This data is probably easy to find in most markets where MLS computers tally the sales. However, this data could be difficult for the appraiser to find if the subject is in a market with no active MLS computer or database. Some markets do not have an MLS system but do have county records that can be used for sales data. The accumulated sales in the time window can be retrieved by asking for sales with closing dates between x and y dates.

Total # of Comparable Active Listings

It is a real problem for some appraisers to obtain the "prior number of listings" in the prior time windows. Many MLS systems are not designed to track the number of listings in a previous time period in a geographic area as defined by the appraiser. In some markets, it is possible for an MLS system to keep a total of the number of listings on any given date, making the number of listings for the time window available to the appraiser. For all three time windows, the appraiser should try to research the number of properties that were listed for sale for comparison with the number of sales in the same time window. The appraiser will need to know which properties were offered for sale on the first day of the time window and then add to that the number of properties that were new listings during the time window. The sum of the properties on the market on the first day of the window and the number of properties added to the "for sale" properties will be the accumulated number of properties for sale in that time window. If the data is not available, the appraiser should state this in the report. The difficulty of obtaining this data is supported by the fact that the directions imply as much and this section is shaded on the form.

Months of Housing Supply (Total Listings/Ab. Rate)

Assuming that the prior months' "accumulated for sale" inventory is not available, most appraisers would think the last column should be used to show the current number of listings versus the sales rate. The mathematics of the columns can be a problem. For example, if the last column (Current - 3 Months) is used for a ratio of the "current" listings versus the number of sales only from the last three months, the mathematical result will be to ignore the ratios calculated for the first two columns. Consider the following table:

Inventory Analysis	Prior 7-12 Months	Prior 4-6 months	Current - 3 Months	Overall Trend		
Total # of Comparable Sales (Settled)	30	15	6	? Increasing	? Stable	Declining
Absorption Rate (Total Sales/Months)	5.00	5.00	2.00	? Increasing	? Stable	Declining
Total # of Comparable Active Listings	Not available	Not available	24	? Declining	? Stable	Increasing
Months of Housing Supply (Total Listings/Ab. Rate)	Not available	Not available	12.00	? Declining	? Stable	Increasing

The number of current listings in the defined market is 24 units. The sales rate for the "7-12 months ago" time window was five units per month and the sales rate for "4-6 months ago" was also five units per month. The sales rate for "current to 3 months ago" was negatively affected by the winter holiday season, resulting in only two units per month. The mathematics of this form takes the sales rate for the last quarter year and divides it into the total "current" listings to get a rate of absorption that may mislead the reader to a false impression. There appears to currently be a 12-month inventory, but the appraiser may want to reconcile the sales rate at 4.5 or 5.0 units per month (giving weight to the prior periods), which would result in a 5.33- or 4.80-month inventory rather than a 12.0-month inventory, as shown using only the last quarter.

Market Research & Analysis Section: Median Sale & List Price, DOM, Sale/List %

Median Sale & List Price, DOM, Sale/List %	Prior 7–12 Months	Prior 4–6 Months	Current – 3 Months	Overall Trend		
Median Comparable Sale Price				☐ Increasing	☐ Stable	☐ Declining
Median Comparable Sales Days on Market				☐ Declining	☐ Stable	☐ Increasing
Median Comparable List Price				☐ Increasing	☐ Stable	☐ Declining
Median Comparable Listings Days on Market				☐ Declining	☐ Stable	☐ Increasing
Median Sale Price as % of List Price				☐ Increasing	☐ Stable	☐ Declining
Seller-(developer, builder, etc.) paid financial assistance prevalent? ☐ Yes ☐ No				☐ Declining	☐ Stable	☐ Increasing

In addition to the inventory analysis, the Market Conditions Form also asks the appraiser to develop the following:

Median Comparable Sale Price

The median comparable sale price data is generally available in most databases and MLS systems and should be generally retrievable. The "median" is the middle point in the data set if it has been sorted by price. The median value is meaningless for unsorted data. If there is no value in the middle (in cases when there is an even number of sales), the median value is the mean of the two values closest to the middle point. If the median sale price is declining, it is assumed to be an indication of declining prices. Conversely, increasing median sale prices are assumed to be an indication of increasing prices.

Search Parameters

This inventory analysis does not necessarily include all sales and listings in the neighborhood. Only those sales and listings that are comparable (i.e., competing properties) should be included. The appraiser should define the search criteria as comparable properties in the neighborhood so that it will be similar to the market analysis section on page 2 of the appraisal forms. Since the neighborhood can include many different market segments, search criteria other than geographic boundaries may also be needed. Keep in mind that a neighborhood can also include diverse but compatible properties, such as apartments or commercial buildings. This analysis should be done with properties that would compete for the same buyers if the subject and comparable were both on the market as of the effective date of appraisal.

The median price analysis can be flawed if the search parameters include the sale price of the properties in the market, such as a search for homes priced from $400,000 to $450,000, which will usually force-fit the median price to a value near $425,000. The fact that real estate prices are nearly random numbers will allow that to vary, but the overall analysis is flawed.

For example, consider the following comparable sales from a neighborhood with 30 sales in the first year of a five-year study. The properties went down in price by 3.0% each year, and the appraiser asked for sales between $300,000 and $350,000. As the property values went down, the median and mean prices went down and then up. The median and mean prices are listed on the bottom of Exhibit 23. The graph in Exhibit 24 shows the change from year to year. Even though the property values fell by 3%, the median did not. When searching for comparable sales to use in this analysis, including the price of the sales or listings is not advisable.

Exhibit 23. Sales Data

Note: Sales between $300,000 and $350,000 are highlighted.

Sale	Year 1	Year 2	Year 3	Year 4	Year 5
	Year	- 3% growth	- 3% growth	- 3% growth	- 3% growth
1	$301,200	$292,164	$283,399	$274,897	$266,650
2	$312,600	$303,222	$294,125	$285,302	$276,743
3	$316,700	$307,199	$297,983	$289,044	$280,372
4	$323,200	$313,504	$304,099	$294,976	$286,127
5	$324,200	$314,474	$305,040	$295,889	$287,012
6	$326,300	$316,511	$307,016	$297,805	$288,871
7	$326,800	$316,996	$307,486	$298,262	$289,314
8	$331,600	$321,652	$312,002	$302,642	$293,563
9	$332,200	$322,234	$312,567	$303,190	$294,094
10	$336,700	$326,599	$316,801	$307,297	$298,078
11	$342,600	$332,322	$322,352	$312,682	$303,301
12	$348,100	$337,657	$327,527	$317,701	$308,170
13	$354,200	$343,574	$333,267	$323,269	$313,571
14	$355,800	$345,126	$334,772	$324,729	$314,987
15	$361,500	$350,655	$340,135	$329,931	$320,033
16	$362,000	$351,140	$340,606	$330,388	$320,476
17	$364,300	$353,371	$342,770	$332,487	$322,512
18	$364,900	$353,953	$343,334	$333,034	$323,043
19	$365,900	$354,923	$344,275	$333,947	$323,929
20	$365,900	$354,923	$344,275	$333,947	$323,929
21	$366,900	$355,893	$345,216	$334,860	$324,814
22	$367,600	$356,572	$345,875	$335,499	$325,434
23	$369,200	$358,124	$347,380	$336,959	$326,850
24	$371,300	$360,161	$349,356	$338,875	$328,709
25	$374,400	$363,168	$352,273	$341,705	$331,454
26	$376,300	$365,011	$354,061	$343,439	$333,136
27	$377,300	$365,981	$355,002	$344,352	$334,021
28	$384,500	$372,965	$361,776	$350,923	$340,395
29	$397,700	$385,769	$374,196	$362,970	$352,081
30	$398,200	$386,254	$374,666	$363,426	$352,524
Year	**1**	**2**	**3**	**4**	**5**
Median	$326,550	$321,652	$334,772	$332,761	$323,929
Change		-1.50%	4.08%	-0.60%	-2.65%
Mean	$326,850	$323,159	$329,817	$328,047	$323,265
Change		-1.13%	2.06%	-0.54%	-1.46%

Market Conditions Form

Absorption Rate (Total Sales/Months)	
Total # of Comparable Active Listings	
Months of Housing Supply (Total Listings/Ab.Rate)	
Median Sale & List Price, DOM, Sale/List %	Prior 7
Median Comparable Sale Price	
Median Comparable Sales Days on Market	
Median Comparable List Price	
Median Comparable Listings Days on Market	
Median Sale Price as % of List Price	
Seller-(developer, builder, etc.) paid financial assistance pr	
Explain in detail the seller concessions trends for the past 1 fees, options, etc.).	

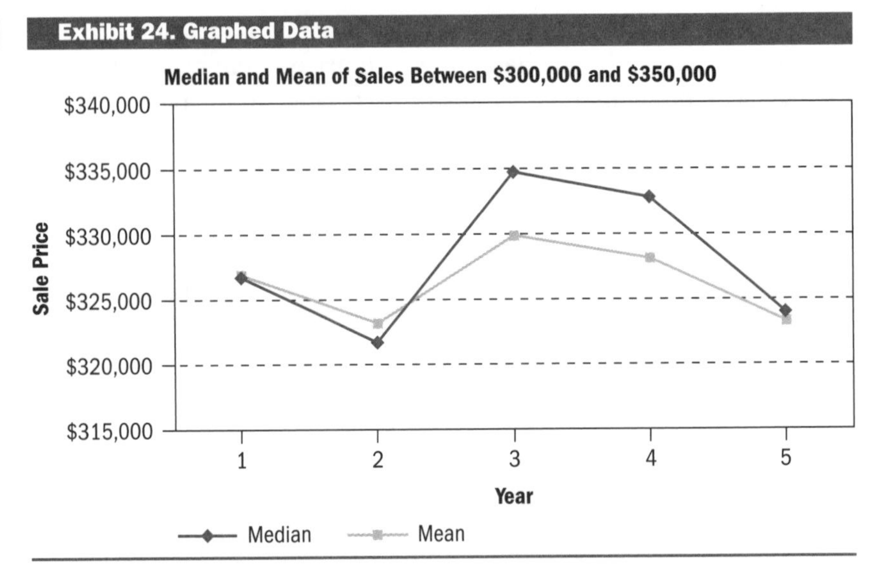

Exhibit 24. Graphed Data

The data shown in Exhibits 23 and 24 implies that the best analysis would be devoid of a sale or list price as a parameter and would focus instead on the assets of the property such as site size, gross living area, age of improvement, and so forth.

Median Comparable Sales Days on Market

The median number of days on the market for comparable sales is also available in most MLS systems with standard searches or is retrievable in a custom search with additional analysis. The appraiser can download the sales data, convert it to a spreadsheet program, and then develop several meaningful analyses including the number of days on the market. Some databases automatically calculate the median amount for the user. It is assumed that this median information is a reflection of market trends because a longer amount of time on the market would indicate more difficulty encountered in selling a property. Exhibit 25 provides an example of this type of analysis. The data in the graph was downloaded from an MLS system into a spreadsheet program. This graph shows a trend toward a larger amount of days on the market for sold properties.

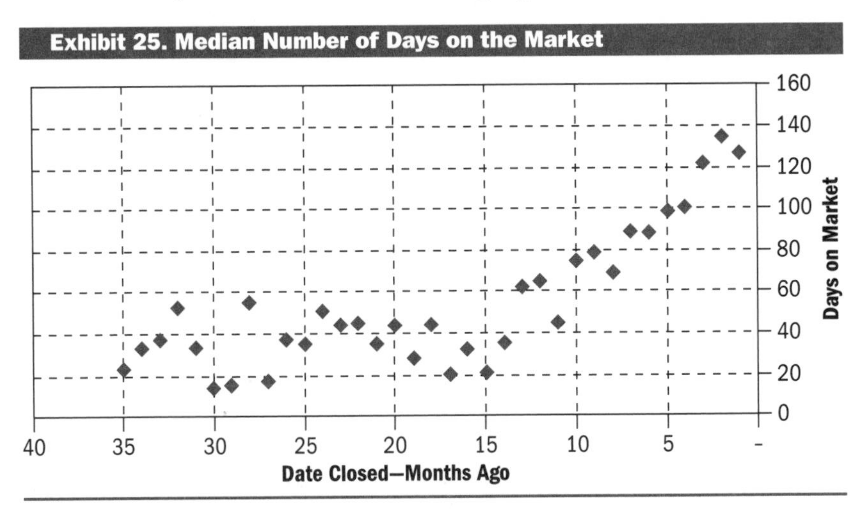

Exhibit 25. Median Number of Days on the Market

Median Comparable List Price

The median comparable list price is an easy number to obtain for current listings but may be difficult to obtain for prior dates in many databases. If this data is available, the appraiser should report the number of listings that were on the market on the first day of the time window and then include any new listings added to that market during the time window. In most cases, some of the same listings will appear in each of the time windows. The resulting double-counting of the same data may compromise the analysis. If the data is not available, the appraiser should indicate this in the report. As stated in the directions, it is anticipated that this data will often be unavailable. This area of the grid is shaded to reflect that. If this data was not available for the inventory analysis, it will probably not be available now.

Median Comparable Listings Days on Market

The median number of days on the market for comparable listings is usually not available in most MLS systems, which is why this area of the grid is also shaded. If the median comparable list price is not available, the median number of days on the market for comparable listings will probably not be available either.

Median Sale Price as % of List Price

The next line of the grid asks the appraiser to research, calculate, and report the ratio of the sale price to the list price for *comparable sales* within the specified time windows. This rate can be calculated directly from the comparable sales downloaded and used in the prior parts of this analysis. This number is easy to obtain in most databases; it is *not* the ratio of the median list prices for current offerings versus the median sale prices for sold units but *is* the ratio of sale prices to list prices for the comparable sales only.

Seller-(developer, builder, etc.) paid financial assistance prevalent? ☐ Yes ☐ No

The last line of the grid asks the appraiser to report if seller-paid actual assistance is common in this market. An upward trend in seller-paid concessions is commonly construed as evidence of a weak market.

Market Research & Analysis Section: Overall Trend

The overall trend section on the right side of the grids is designed to show readers and intended users the direction in which market trends are going. If some of the data is not available in a particular market, it will be impossible to complete this part of the form and indicate whether the trend is increasing, stable, or declining.

Interpretations

The overall trend portion of the grids is designed to be interpreted quickly because left column responses all support an appreciating

Market Conditions Form

red unreliable, the appraiser must provide an
able, however, the appraiser must include the data
ıld report the available figure and identify it as an
a that would be used by a prospective buyer of the
reclosures, etc.

Overall Trend		
☐ Increasing	☐ Stable	☐ Declining
☐ Increasing	☐ Stable	☐ Declining
☐ Declining	☐ Stable	☐ Increasing
☐ Declining	☐ Stable	☐ Increasing
Overall Trend		
☐ Increasing	☐ Stable	☐ Declining
☐ Declining	☐ Stable	☐ Increasing
☐ Increasing	☐ Stable	☐ Declining
☐ Declining	☐ Stable	☐ Increasing
☐ Increasing	☐ Stable	☐ Declining
☐ Declining	☐ Stable	☐ Increasing

ı, increasing use of buydowns, closing costs, condo

market while right column responses indicate a weaker market. Center column responses indicate a stable market.

Databases in some markets do not provide necessary information such as the median or mean of prior list prices. In markets where some of the required data is not available, appraisers must still support their conclusions as reported on the appraisal report forms. It would be improper for appraisers to use lack of data as an excuse to not support the conclusions on the appraisal forms. It is acceptable to say that the lack of data invalidates the analysis listed on the Market Conditions Form, but not acceptable to provide no support at all.

Goals

The Market Conditions Form is not intended to be a stand-alone form independent of the URAR, 2055, and other appraisal forms. The conclusions from this analysis should be incorporated into the conclusions in the appraisal report. A significant problem for many appraisers occurs when one conclusion is reached in one section of the report and then a different conclusion is reported in another section of the report. It would be inconsistent to say that prices are going up or down on this form and in the neighborhood section of the report, but then not make market conditions adjustments in the sales comparison approach or at least provide an explanation for why this adjustment was not made.

Scope of Work and Reporting Requirements

The market conditions analysis provides support for the conclusions reported in the neighborhood section of the report. Notice the use of the word *trend* on the Market Conditions Form and the URAR neighborhood section. If the absorption rate is the same each period, would the trend be increasing, stable, or declining? The Market Conditions Form is designed to lead the appraiser to support his or her conclusions regarding neighborhood price trends. This form is not designed to make the appraiser do research and analysis that was not called for in the past but is designed to ensure that the appraiser has done the necessary analysis and shows the results.

Page 2 of the URAR and Other Forms

Looking at the Market Conditions Form, think about the parameters that define the market. The goal is to find out if prices in the subject's market are increasing or decreasing. This analysis is not new but is slightly different from the corresponding section of the URAR and Form 2055 because the time windows are segregated into months on the Market Conditions Form. The first two lines of page 2 of the URAR and Form 2055 should correlate to the results of the Market Conditions Form. Both forms are asking for "comparable properties in the neighborhood."

Uniform Residential Appraisal Report File #

There are	comparable properties currently offered for sale in the subject neighborhood ranging in price from $	to $
There are	comparable sales in the subject neighborhood within the past twelve months ranging in sale price from $	to $

These first two lines of page 2 of the URAR and Form 2055 are also included on the Small Residential Income Property Appraisal Report (Fannie Mae Form 1025/Freddie Mac Form 72) and the Individual Condominium Unit Appraisal Report (Fannie Mae Form 1073/Freddie Mac Form 465). If the appraiser does not use price as a search parameter, then the ranges listed on the two lines would be the result of the search rather than the parameter of the search. If the price is used as a search criterion, the range lines would match up but the analysis may be flawed because of the previously presented problem.

Market Research & Analysis Section: Additional Information

RESEARCH & ANALYSIS

Explain in detail the seller concessions trends for the past 12 months (e.g., seller contributions increased from 3% to 5%, increasing use of buydowns, closing costs, condo fees, options, etc.).

Are foreclosure sales (REO sales) a factor in the market? ☐ Yes ☐ No If yes, explain (including the trends in listings and sales of foreclosed properties).

Cite data sources for above information.

Summarize the above information as support for your conclusions in the Neighborhood section of the appraisal report form. If you used any additional information, such as an analysis of pending sales and/or expired and withdrawn listings, to formulate your conclusions, provide both an explanation and support for your conclusions.

Explain in detail the seller concessions trends for the past 12 months (e.g., seller contributions increased from 3% to 5%, increasing use of buydowns, closing costs, condo fees, options, etc.)

The next section of the Market Conditions Form has to do with concessions. This section asks for a discussion of the direction (increase or decline) of seller concessions, which is an indication of the seller's motivations or the buyer's ability to purchase. Support may be provided with statistics on seller-paid concessions, but in most markets this observation will be subjective. This section may also be used to talk about unusual incentive programs and methods to promote home ownership.

It may be quite the project for the appraiser to research the "concession du jour." There seems to be a new type of popular concession each year. Because of these rapid changes, appraisers should ask about such terms and conditions when sales data is confirmed. Financing concessions in the comparable sales can lead to overvaluing the subject property.

Market Conditions Form

Median Comparable Listings Days on Market

Median Sale Price as % of List Price

Seller-(developer, builder, etc.) paid financial assistance

Explain in detail the seller concessions trends for the past 12 fees, options, etc.).

RESEARCH & ANALYSIS

Are foreclosure sales (REO sales) a factor in the market?

Cite data sources for above information.

Summarize the above information as support for your conclu an analysis of pending sales and/or expired and withdrawn

If the subject is a unit in a condominium or cooperative proje

Subject Project Data

Total # of Comparable Sales (Settled)

Are foreclosure sales (REO sales) a factor in the market?

The next section of the Market Conditions Form deals with foreclosure properties, which are commonly called *real estate owned* (REO). In banking circles, these properties may be known as *other real estate owned* (OREO).

This section asks the appraiser about foreclosures and the subsequent impact on value of the additional competition. Competition from REO properties is significant in some markets and has a devastating effect on property values.

Cite data sources for above information.

The next section also asks the appraiser to cite the sources of data used. These sources should presumably be cited for the data in all the previous sections of the form, including the supply and demand analysis. This section provides protection for the appraiser who may get different answers than a review appraiser reviewing the document.

Summarize the above information as support for your conclusions in the Neighborhood section of the appraisal report form.

The next section asks for a summary of the supporting information. Support may include a discussion of listings, pending sales, or expired and withdrawn listings. It can be any logical analysis that an appraiser would develop. Some appraisers may be forced to use a variety of other tools to accomplish the goal of supporting a conclusion of the "trend" of property values in competing properties if data is lacking in the market; this is especially true in rural areas where lack of data is a chronic problem.

Condo/Co-Op Projects Section

CONDO/CO-OP PROJECTS

If the subject is a unit in a condominium or cooperative project, complete the following:				Project Name:		
Subject Project Data	Prior 7-12 Months	Prior 4-6 Months	Current – 3 Months	Overall Trend		
Total # of Comparable Sales (Settled)				☐ Increasing	☐ Stable	☐ Declining
Absorption Rate (Total Sales/Months)				☐ Increasing	☐ Stable	☐ Declining
Total # of Active Comparable Listings				☐ Declining	☐ Stable	☐ Increasing
Months of Unit Supply (Total Listings/Ab. Rate)				☐ Declining	☐ Stable	☐ Increasing

Are foreclosure sales (REO sales) a factor in the project? ☐ Yes ☐ No If yes, indicate the number of REO listings and explain the trends in listings and sales of foreclosed properties.

Summarize the above trends and address the impact on the subject unit and project.

The next section of the Market Conditions Form is dedicated to condominium and cooperative properties. If the subject is a condominium or cooperative unit, the grid in this section must be completed **in addition to** the previously discussed grid at the top of the form.

Condominium is a legal term, not a design or lifestyle term. The term the word was derived from, *co-dominion*, refers to more than one person owning a parcel of real estate. Since this is a legal issue rather than a design or lifestyle issue, an appraiser cannot determine if a property is a condominium by just looking at it. Research is required. Determination of condominium ownership may involve contacting the title insurance company and its attorney. Do not classify a property as a condominium based on design or lifestyle.

Cooperative is also a legal term rather than a design or lifestyle term. It refers to real property that is usually held in fee simple by a corporation, and each unit owner holds one share in the corporation. The unit owners usually also hold a proprietary lease, which entitles them to occupancy rights. Many fees are associated with this type of ownership, and the corporation usually has a master mortgage that will be paid out of the common fees.

This analysis is very similar to the first section of the form and would be used to describe the market in the subject project. Notice that the first column heading in the grid is for subject project data. Data from outside the project is not to be included. Subject project data may not be obtainable in the MLS or other databases but could be found by simply calling the project manager.

Condo/Co-Op Projects Grid

Total # of Comparable Sales (Settled)

The total number of settled comparable sales should not be difficult for most appraisers to obtain from the common databases. To obtain this information from most databases, a data search with only the

Market Conditions Form

If the subject is a unit in a condominium or cooperative proje

Subject Project Data	Prior 7-1
Total # of Comparable Sales (Settled)	
Absorption Rate (Total Sales/Months)	
Total # of Active Comparable Listings	
Months of Unit Supply (Total Listings/Ab. Rate)	

CONDO/CO-OP PROJECTS

Are foreclosure sales (REO sales) a factor in the project?
foreclosed properties.

Summarize the above trends and address the impact on the s

APPRAISER

Signature
Appraiser Name
Company Name
Company Address
State License/Certification # Stat
Email Address

Freddie Mac Form 71 March 2009

subject's legal description will work. Searching with specific dates is also required.

Absorption Rate (Total Sales/Months)

The absorption rate data required here is similar to that required in the prior section of the form and also includes the same time windows as in the first grid. Data for the first two lines of this analysis should be obtainable in most databases. Data for lines three and four may be difficult to obtain for the prior seven- to twelve-month or four- to six-month windows. It is the appraiser's responsibility to do the necessary research and reporting when the data is available and provide necessary explanation when the data is not available.

Total # of Active Comparable Listings

The next line asks for the total number of active comparable listings as in the previous grid, but this time for the project only. This data is also difficult to obtain in most markets. The appraiser should obtain the data if it is available, but it is expected to not be available in most cases. This line has been shaded to reflect the anticipated difficulty of obtaining this information.

Months of Unit Supply (Total Listings/Ab. Rate)

The next line asks for the number of months of unit supply as in the previous grid, but also for the project only. If the total number of active comparable listings for the project was not available, the number of months of unit supply is not going to be available either. This line is also shaded to reflect the expected difficulty in obtaining this information.

Are foreclosure sales (REO sales) a factor in the project?

The next part of the condo/co-op project section of the Market Conditions Form asks about foreclosure property sales in the project. For condominiums and cooperatives, the data requested in this section may be more obtainable because of the similarity of units and the availability of other sources such as homeowners associations, brokers that focus on one type of project, or management companies. The number of REO listings can be a significant factor in these projects because of the similarity of the units and because the exterior maintenance is often taken care of by the association. The "yes" or "no" check boxes in this section make it impossible for appraisers to avoid the issue. For most projects, the appraiser should comment on the ensuing impact if more than 5% of the units have foreclosed. In some projects, this percentage amount could be more or less. For example, a single REO property in a condominium project with only 10 units would make 10% of the total properties and would not inhibit the sales of other units beyond the time it takes to sell that unit. Alternatively, 50 REO units in a project of 1,000 units make up 5% of the total units and could inhibit the sales of non-REO properties for years. A discussion of the absorption rates and the number of REO properties would be appropriate here.

Summarize the above trends and address the impact on the subject unit and project.

The last part of the condo/co-op project section is an area reserved for explanation of the previously discussed issues in this section. An appraiser can use this area to explain the lack of data, the health of the project, or any difficulty in selling units. This would also be the place to talk about oversupply or undersupply of competitive units in the project.

Appraiser Section (Signature Block)

APPRAISER				
Signature		Signature	
Appraiser Name		Supervisory Appraiser Name	
Company Name		Company Name	
Company Address		Company Address	
State License/Certification #	State	State License/Certification #	State
Email Address		Email Address	

Freddie Mac Form 71 March 2009 Page 1 of 1 Fannie Mae Form 1004MC March 2009

The signature block on the Market Conditions Form is standard. It includes lines for both the appraiser and the supervisory appraiser.

Other Methods of Measuring Change in a Market

The Market Conditions Form is required on appraisals for loans sold to Fannie Mae and Freddie Mac with an effective date on or after April 1, 2009. This form includes a few methods for measuring a market, but there are also other methods that are not included on this form. Appraisers may also support conclusions through the analysis of prior sales of the same comparable property (known as "sale and resale analysis") as well as the analysis of national databases, sales and resales of the subject, and comparable listings.

Analyzing Comparable Listings

The analysis of comparable listings is usually the easiest and most applicable method in markets with minimal statistical data, such as rural markets. If values are declining, appraisers should consider adding comparable listings to the analysis. Many relocation companies, mortgage investors, and other buyers of real estate emphasize the use of comparable listings as the best data available in a downturn market. If a market has falling prices, the comparable listings are driving it that way and also best illustrate the trend. Buyers cannot buy comparable sales, but they can buy comparable listings. If the listings are going down in price, so will the value of the subject. Comparable listings are an appraiser's best friend in a downturn market. If comparable sales are not definitive because the market may have changed since they sold, the comparable listings will put a cap on the value and keep the value opinion grounded. Listings may not show what a property is worth but they will often support what it is *not* worth. This analysis can be done by merely adding one, two, or three active listings to the sales comparison grids in addition to the comparable sales. Of course, pending sales can be analyzed, even if the sale price is unknown. The list price is probably more valid as an indicator of value if the sale is pending because in most cases it would indicate that the list price was not too far off base.

Tracking the Median Price from Month to Month

In many databases, the provider will show a median price for a township, school district, taxing district, or other predetermined delineation. Tracking the median price of a whole township can be used for data if the neighborhood data is not conclusive.

The following is an example of an analysis done by a local residential database that reports the month-by-month **median** sale price for all properties. This median sale price is not the same as the median price analysis on the Market Conditions Form because it includes all properties in the area rather than just the comparable ones and assumes that similar amounts of property are sold in all price ranges each month. The following example shows the median sale prices for Johnson Township in Washington County. This data can easily be graphed using a spreadsheet program if it is not already done in the database.

Exhibit 26. Median Sale Prices for Johnson Township in Washington County

Sale Date—Months Ago	Median Price
-36	162,500
-35	176,500
-34	167,500
-33	168,500
-32	172,800
-31	183,000
-30	194,500
-29	187,778
-28	199,500
-27	212,945
-26	222,278
-25	209,500
-24	205,500
-23	228,290
-22	237,900
-21	244,750
-20	250,000
-19	262,500
-18	277,827
-17	257,727
-16	289,900
-15	277,722
-14	294,850
-13	292,828
-12	282,778
-11	257,628
-10	262,828
-9	250,000
-8	237,950
-7	250,775
-6	262,500
-5	237,900
-4	228,278
-3	222,000
-2	212,900
-1	205,794
0	200,629

Exhibit 27. Graphed Data of Johnson Township Median Sale Prices

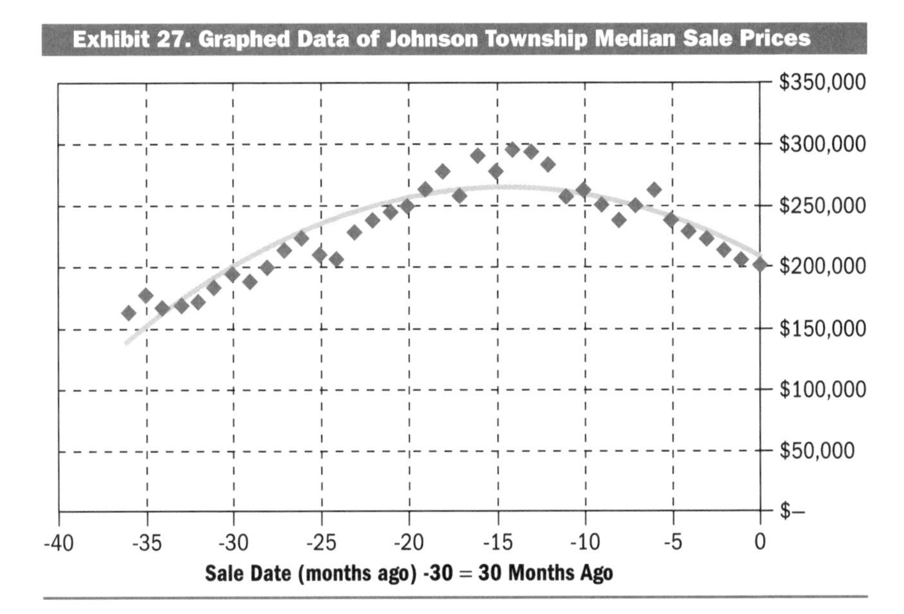

The changes in the median price are not the same each month. The median price first increases and then decreases slightly. In Exhibit 27, a trend line added by a spreadsheet program more or less shows the overall trend in the median price. Envision what the sale and resale of the same property would look like in this market. The sale of a median-priced property 30 months ago and its resale today would show almost no change over the period, even though this did not actually happen. Trending the market is seldom simple.

Analyzing Sales and Resales

Extracting trends from a market via sales and resales of the same property has been a favorite method of many analysts and appraisers. This method assumes that a property that sold 24 months ago and then sold again could provide an indication of what is happening in a market. When reviewing this type of analysis, keep in mind the previously presented graph that shows that results could be much different on a sale-to-sale basis as compared to the overall trend. Exhibit 28 shows three sales that have prior sales in the recent past. This analysis compensates for financing concessions, changes in the property, and even deferred maintenance.

Exhibit 28. Extraction of Value Changes in the Market

Appreciation Analysis	Sale 1	Date	Sale 2	Date	Sale 3	Date
Initial sale price & date	$325,000	9 mos. ago	$311,000	16 mos. ago	$335,000	29 mos. ago
Less seller concessions	$-		$-		$-	
Adjusted initial sale price	$325,000		$311,000		$335,000	
Second sale price & date	$325,000	1 mo. ago	$335,600	2 mos. ago	$365,000	9 mos. ago
Less seller concessions	$(5,500)		$(9,500)		$-	
Adjusted second sale price	$319,500		$326,100		$365,000	
Difference (price and months)	$(5,500)	8	$15,100	14	$30,000	20
Less improvements after 1st sale	$(3,000)		$(15,000)		$(13,000)	
Deferred maintenance needed	-		$-		$-	
Net difference in sale prices	$(8,500)		$100		$17,000	
% increase or decrease overall	-2.62%	8	0.03%	14	5.07%	20
Amt. of apprec. or deprec./year (%)	-3.92%		0.03%		3.04%	

This example shows the methodology of how to extract a rate of change from sales and resales of the same property. It would be nice if all property values increased, decreased, or did not change over time. In reality, prices usually increase or decrease from one month to the next, or the rate of change varies. Consider the graph showing market trends. Does this sale and resale activity show a similar trend with the older sale and resale showing positive movement but the newer sale showing a negative trend?

Using National Databases

Various companies and organizations keep statistics on property values on a national, regional, or local basis. The problem with most of these statistics is the lack of analysis on the neighborhood level. It is quite possible for a regional market to be suffering from undersupply or oversupply but a smaller area such as a suburban city or even a neighborhood to have a much different market condition at the same time. The national databases are used by the national media, national lenders, and even policy makers to see what the trends are. This information should be used only with accompanying explanation of what the data represents or in this case what it does *not* represent.

National Association of Realtors

The National Association of Realtors (NAR) Web site, found at *www.realtor.org*, offers many features, but the most important features for appraisers are the "Research" and "Housing Statistics" areas. To find housing statistics, first click on "Research" under the "Site by Topic" heading on the left-hand side of the home page and then click on "Housing Statistics."

On the housing statistics page, the user can click on several data compilations. The most relevant and local data compilation is the "Metropolitan Area Prices" located under "The Statistics" heading. After clicking on this option, click on "Current Report: Single-family."

National Association of REALTORS®

Median Sale Prices for Existing Single-Family Homes for Metropolitan Areas

CBSA Code	Metropolitan Area	2006	2007	2008	2008.II	2008.III	2008.IV	2009.I r	2009.II p	%Chya
						(Not Seasonally Adjusted, 000s)				
	U.S.	221.9	217.9	196.6	206.4	200.4	180.2	167.3	174.1	-15.6%
	NE	280.3	288.1	271.5	272.3	269.9	248.8	235.2	246.0	-9.7%
	MW	164.8	161.4	150.5	160.7	158.9	139.5	131.6	146.8	-8.6%
	SO	183.7	178.8	169.4	176.9	173.8	156.7	146.6	158.6	-10.3%
	WE	350.5	342.5	276.1	289.7	268.0	249.3	229.2	212.6	-26.6%
10420	Akron, OH	114.6	119.3	100.5	106.5	108.1	86.1	50.1	88.0	-17.4%
10580	Albany-Schenectady-Troy, NY	195.4	198.9	197.9	198.4	205.5	193.1	184.5	189.4	-4.5%
10740	Albuquerque, NM	184.2	198.5	192.6	199.4	193.4	183.7	182.6	182.2	-8.6%
10900	Allentown-Bethlehem-Easton, PA-NJ	248.1	260.8	243.6	251.5	245.4	238.0	218.0	225.6	-10.3%
11100	Amarillo, TX	114.9	118.4	124.7	124.6	128.3	122.6	122.0	127.3	2.2%
31100	Anaheim-Santa Ana, CA (Orange Co.)	709.0	709.5	533.2	578.0	516.0	464.8	435.8	468.1	-19.0%
11540	Appleton, WI	129.2	130.0	127.4	134.9	127.5	127.6	110.3	113.9	-15.6%
12060	Atlanta-Sandy Springs-Marietta, GA	171.8	172.0	149.5	158.3	151.3	129.2	115.6	121.4	-23.3%
12100	Atlantic City, NJ	254.8	269.7	253.3	255.9	248.9	229.1	219.1	218.7	-14.5%
12420	Austin-Round Rock, TX	173.7	183.7	188.6	194.2	190.9	184.8	182.3	194.0	-0.1%
12580	Baltimore-Towson, MD	279.9	286.1	274.1	280.5	279.2	260.1	245.8	253.0	-9.8%
12700	Bamstable Town, MA	389.5	384.7	341.9	350.2	337.9	325.5	276.7	325.6	-7.0%
12940	Baton Rouge, LA	169.5	174.4	165.0	165.7	170.9	156.4	159.4	168.5	1.7%
13140	Beaumont-Port Arthur, TX	112.7	123.0	127.4	124.9	129.6	132.6	129.1	138.6	11.0%
13780	Binghamton, NY	96.9	111.2	113.7	120.9	115.5	105.8	110.3	117.7	-2.6%
13820	Birmingham-Hoover, AL	165.1	161.3	153.9	163.5	156.1	135.4	130.4	152.3	-6.9%
13900	Bismarck, ND	134.9	152.9	155.2	152.5	146.3	164.5	153.3	157.8	3.5%
14060	Bloomington-Normal, IL	152.2	154.0	159.8	152.8	168.4	159.3	153.8	153.0	0.1%
14260	Boise City-Nampa, ID	N/A	206.0	188.7	191.0	187.3	168.8	157.1	160.4	-16.0%
14460	Boston-Cambridge-Quincy, MA-NH**	402.2	395.6	361.1	366.7	374.1	336.0	290.7	336.1	-8.3%
14500	Boulder, CO	366.4	376.2	359.6	375.8	361.5	324.7	328.4	373.3	-0.7%
14860	Bridgeport-Stamford-Norwalk, CT	473.7	486.6	437.9	449.9	471.6	380.6	347.4	442.9	-1.6%
15380	Buffalo-Niagara Falls, NY	97.9	104.0	105.4	108.2	114.2	106.2	99.2	115.4	6.7%
15940	Canton-Massillon, OH	109.3	110.3	92.5	102.8	98.5	80.4	66.2	101.5	-1.3%

Source: National Association of Realtors Web site (*www.realtor.org/research/research/metroprice*).

The report shows median sale prices for various metropolitan areas. This information is to the regional level but not to the local or neighborhood level. It may be wrong to assume that this data is indicative of all markets.

Federal Housing Finance Agency

The Office of the Federal Housing Enterprise Oversight (OFEO) has been folded into the new agency known as the Federal Housing Finance Agency (FHFA). This new agency's Web site, *www.fhfa.gov*, is very similar to the original OFEO site and features much of the same data sources.

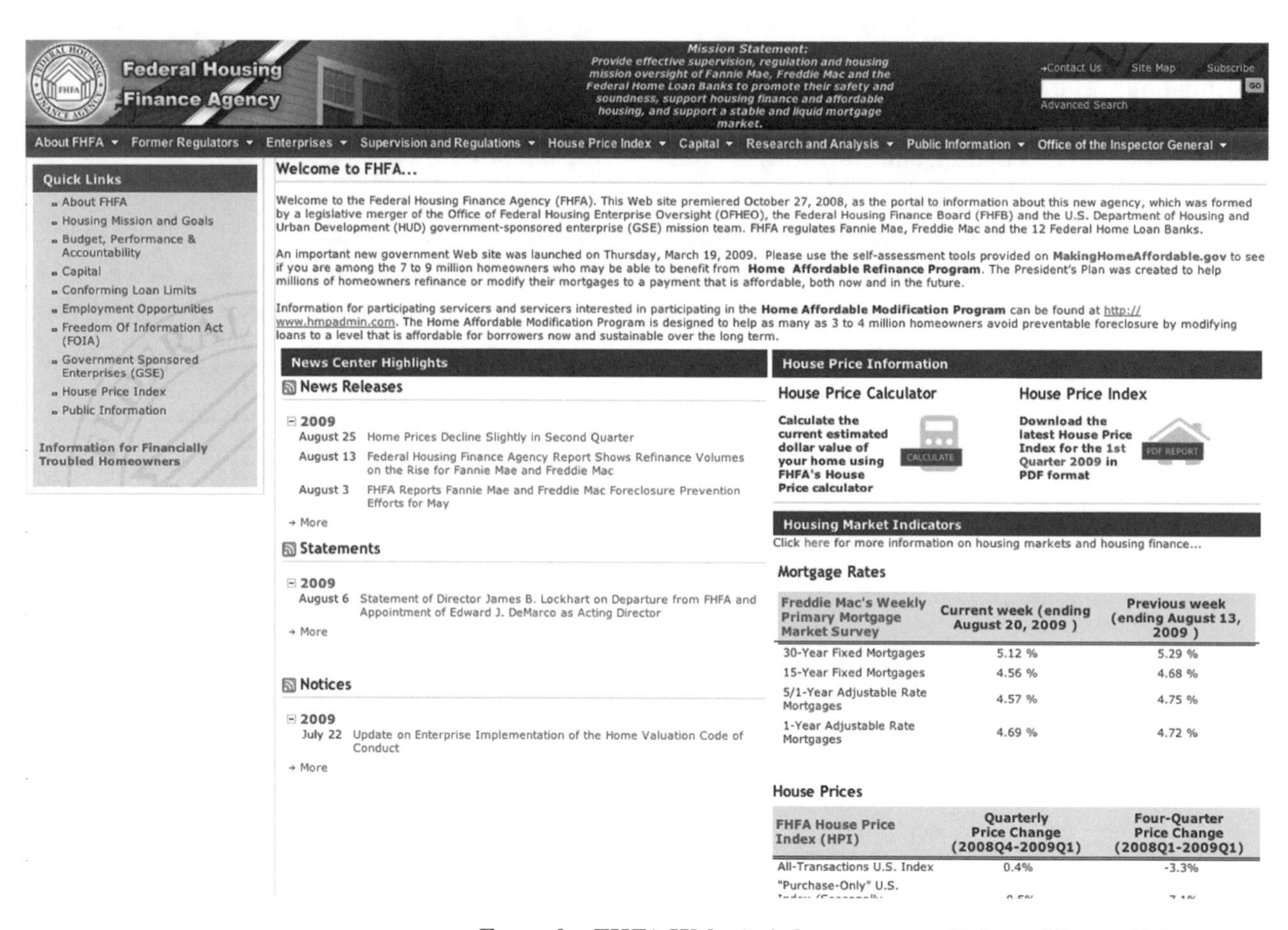

From the FHFA Web site's home page, click on "House Price Index" under the "Quick Links" heading on the left-hand side of the page to access statistics and links to other areas.

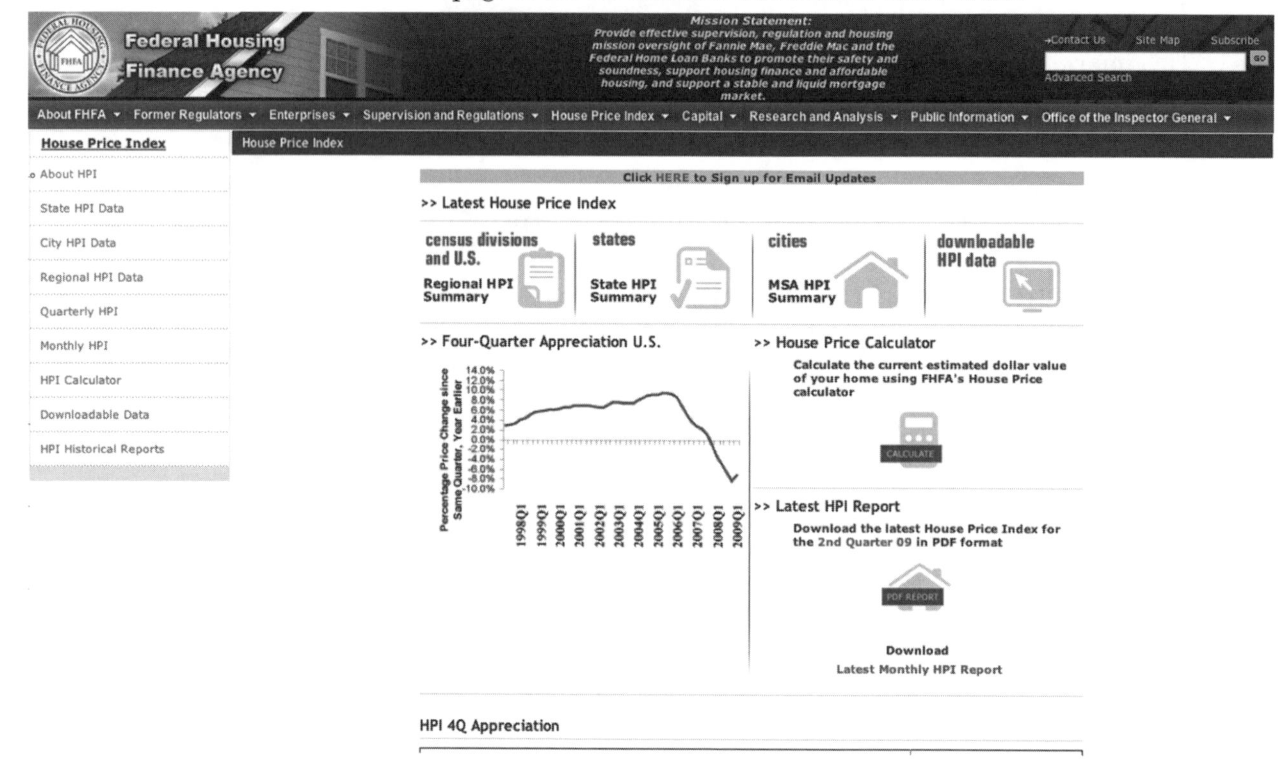

Next, click on "Downloadable Data" under the "House Price Index" heading on the left-hand side of the page.

Several relevant databases are available here. The Metropolitan Statistical Areas and Divisions (Excel format) database is the most local and its information can be downloaded. This Excel file has about 52,000 lines, and many cities are included. The following data sample shows Los Angeles from the second quarter of 2001 to the fourth quarter of 2008.

Los Angeles-Long Beach-Glendale, CA (MSAD)	31084	2001	2	140.25
Los Angeles-Long Beach-Glendale, CA (MSAD)	31084	2001	3	143.4
Los Angeles-Long Beach-Glendale, CA (MSAD)	31084	2001	4	146.75
Los Angeles-Long Beach-Glendale, CA (MSAD)	31084	2002	1	151.63
Los Angeles-Long Beach-Glendale, CA (MSAD)	31084	2002	2	157.61
Los Angeles-Long Beach-Glendale, CA (MSAD)	31084	2002	3	163.69
Los Angeles-Long Beach-Glendale, CA (MSAD)	31084	2002	4	168.94
Los Angeles-Long Beach-Glendale, CA (MSAD)	31084	2003	1	173.54
Los Angeles-Long Beach-Glendale, CA (MSAD)	31084	2003	2	177.78
Los Angeles-Long Beach-Glendale, CA (MSAD)	31084	2003	3	185.07
Los Angeles-Long Beach-Glendale, CA (MSAD)	31084	2003	4	198.94
Los Angeles-Long Beach-Glendale, CA (MSAD)	31084	2004	1	207.17
Los Angeles-Long Beach-Glendale, CA (MSAD)	31084	2004	2	220.66
Los Angeles-Long Beach-Glendale, CA (MSAD)	31084	2004	3	243.61
Los Angeles-Long Beach-Glendale, CA (MSAD)	31084	2004	4	252.35
Los Angeles-Long Beach-Glendale, CA (MSAD)	31084	2005	1	262.75
Los Angeles-Long Beach-Glendale, CA (MSAD)	31084	2005	2	277.65
Los Angeles-Long Beach-Glendale, CA (MSAD)	31084	2005	3	292.68
Los Angeles-Long Beach-Glendale, CA (MSAD)	31084	2005	4	311.35
Los Angeles-Long Beach-Glendale, CA (MSAD)	31084	2006	1	323.7
Los Angeles-Long Beach-Glendale, CA (MSAD)	31084	2006	2	331.77
Los Angeles-Long Beach-Glendale, CA (MSAD)	31084	2006	3	337.57
Los Angeles-Long Beach-Glendale, CA (MSAD)	31084	2006	4	338.94
Los Angeles-Long Beach-Glendale, CA (MSAD)	31084	2007	1	338.04
Los Angeles-Long Beach-Glendale, CA (MSAD)	31084	2007	2	336.64
Los Angeles-Long Beach-Glendale, CA (MSAD)	31084	2007	3	330.86
Los Angeles-Long Beach-Glendale, CA (MSAD)	31084	2007	4	322.38
Los Angeles-Long Beach-Glendale, CA (MSAD)	31084	2008	1	307.64
Los Angeles-Long Beach-Glendale, CA (MSAD)	31084	2008	2	286.3
Los Angeles-Long Beach-Glendale, CA (MSAD)	31084	2008	3	267.97
Los Angeles-Long Beach-Glendale, CA (MSAD)	31084	2008	4	258.65

Source: Federal Housing Finance Agency Web site (*www.fhfa.gov/webfiles/14797/2q09hpi_cbsa.txt*).

The following shows a graph of this data created in Excel.

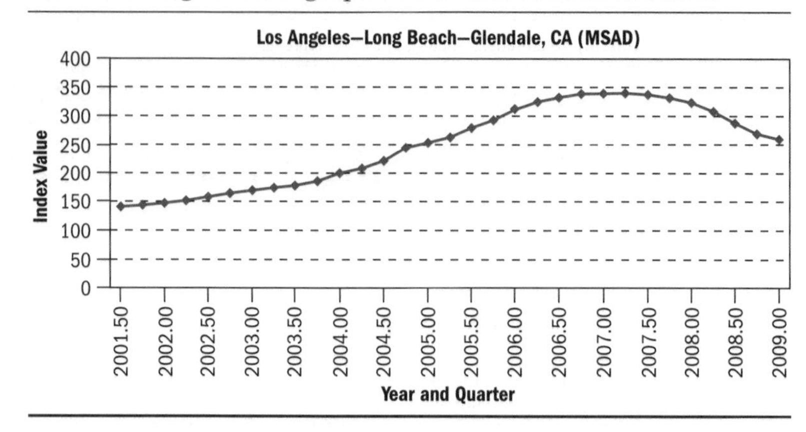

Underlying assumptions are important in the analysis of any database. While the data from this source does not reflect all home sales, it does include capital values (market values) of homes that were refinanced and the loans sold to Fannie Mae or Freddie Mac. Because this resource is an index, the values are not mean or median sale prices.

Case-Shiller Home Price Index

The Case-Shiller home price index, available at the Standard & Poor's Web site at *www2.standardandpoors.com*, tracks sales and resales of the same properties located in the 20 largest cities in the United States. Since most cities and states are not included in this index, it would be very difficult to apply data found here to most appraisal reports. The logic of presenting sales and resales of the same properties is sound, but the applicability of this data is weak due to its geographic limits.

To access the Case-Shiller Home Price Index, enter "Case Shiller" in the search box of *Google.com* or *Bing.com*. The direct link to the index on Standard & Poor's Web site will be the top search result.

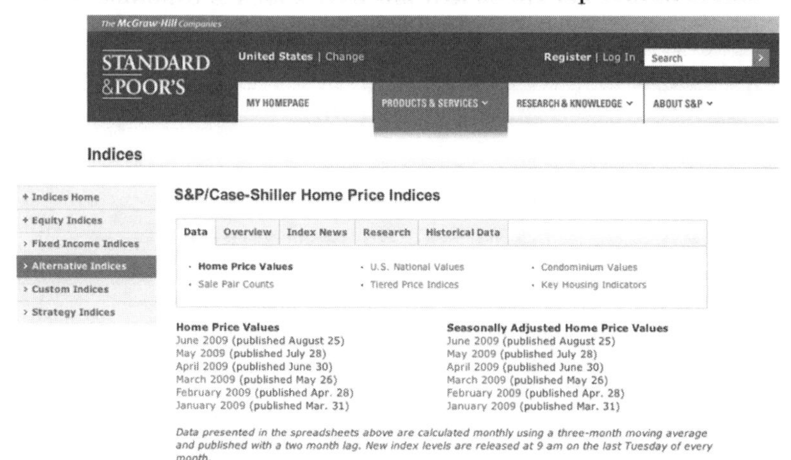

From the main Case-Shiller page, click on the most recent month listed under "Home Price Values" to access the most recent monthly amounts.

Row	Date	AZ-Phoenix PHXR	CA-Los Angeles LXXR	CA-San Diego SDXR	CA-San Francisco SFXR	CO-Denver DNXR	DC-Washington WDXR
231	January 2006	221.81	265.92	247.46	214.78	137.42	247.70
232	February 2006	222.65	267.75	247.89	215.50	137.12	248.39
233	March 2006	223.53	268.23	248.09	216.04	136.93	248.86
234	April 2006	225.12	270.44	249.35	217.52	137.28	250.17
235	May 2006	226.51	272.12	249.14	218.37	138.31	251.07
236	June 2006	227.42	273.22	249.60	218.12	139.46	250.99
237	July 2006	227.38	273.85	249.05	217.63	140.26	249.92
238	August 2006	227.01	273.80	247.30	217.22	140.28	247.94
239	September 2006	226.20	273.94	246.60	216.37	139.65	244.78
240	October 2006	224.50	273.66	244.03	215.42	138.62	243.73
241	November 2006	223.13	273.05	242.11	213.84	137.65	242.28
242	December 2006	221.50	270.03	238.08	212.13	137.11	240.45
243	January 2007	220.20	268.68	237.15	211.78	135.86	238.85
244	February 2007	218.07	266.63	235.53	210.78	134.86	237.98
245	March 2007	216.86	264.58	233.27	211.09	134.20	237.14
246	April 2007	215.04	263.37	232.66	211.47	134.86	236.17
247	May 2007	213.94	263.19	231.78	210.89	136.32	235.41
248	June 2007	212.52	262.12	231.36	209.48	138.09	234.02
249	July 2007	210.78	260.84	229.66	208.64	139.24	232.17
250	August 2007	208.86	258.07	226.73	208.15	139.72	230.21
251	September 2007	205.28	254.79	222.82	206.46	138.44	229.25
252	October 2007	200.72	249.50	217.02	202.03	136.09	227.56
253	November 2007	194.45	240.43	209.60	195.49	133.36	223.85
254	December 2007	187.67	233.03	202.45	189.23	130.98	218.35
255	January 2008	180.06	224.41	197.45	183.81	128.96	213.20
256	February 2008	172.72	214.83	190.34	174.54	127.47	207.95
257	March 2008	166.97	207.11	185.42	168.38	127.40	203.39
258	April 2008	161.33	202.45	180.56	164.63	128.49	201.32
259	May 2008	157.32	198.54	178.03	162.70	129.73	199.27
260	June 2008	153.19	195.70	175.37	159.83	131.66	197.61
261	July 2008	149.09	192.55	172.20	156.88	132.67	195.44
262	August 2008	144.83	189.18	168.23	151.42	132.64	194.16
263	September 2008	139.79	184.54	164.12	145.53	130.96	190.01
264	October 2008	135.18	179.82	159.12	139.44	129.05	184.82
265	November 2008	130.54	175.85	155.47	135.28	127.65	180.27
266	December 2008	123.93	171.40	152.16	130.12	125.74	175.55
267	January 2009	117.11	166.54	148.25	124.33	122.33	171.97

Row	Date	FL-Miami MIXR	FL-Tampa TPXR	GA-Atlanta ATXR	IL-Chicago CHXR	MA-Boston BOXR	MI-Detroit DEXR	MN-Minneapolis MNXR	NC-Charlotte CRXR
231	January 2006	268.25	228.98	130.59	163.98	178.17	126.66	169.56	119.96
232	February 2006	271.68	230.91	130.61	164.67	176.28	126.39	169.32	120.51
233	March 2006	274.02	233.57	130.62	164.89	177.12	126.12	168.71	121.41
234	April 2006	276.37	235.85	131.51	165.58	177.62	124.30	169.69	123.38
235	May 2006	278.68	237.92	132.72	166.61	178.61	123.78	170.38	124.70
236	June 2006	278.22	237.68	134.01	167.10	177.90	123.12	170.90	126.48
237	July 2006	278.33	238.09	134.90	167.57	177.79	123.24	170.74	127.96
238	August 2006	276.80	236.82	135.27	167.99	177.28	123.00	170.97	128.72
239	September 2006	277.23	236.42	135.10	168.60	176.34	122.54	171.12	129.04
240	October 2006	278.91	234.02	134.73	168.59	175.72	121.79	170.64	128.51
241	November 2006	280.30	232.86	134.18	168.18	172.59	120.94	169.85	128.94
242	December 2006	280.87	230.91	134.01	167.65	170.31	119.51	168.82	128.88
243	January 2007	279.42	228.86	133.45	167.52	168.29	117.96	167.95	129.43
244	February 2007	279.43	228.46	133.30	167.49	168.04	116.85	166.83	129.31
245	March 2007	276.89	226.58	133.22	167.04	168.52	116.44	165.56	130.44
246	April 2007	273.53	224.13	134.27	165.87	169.61	114.38	164.78	131.98
247	May 2007	269.52	221.96	135.03	165.68	170.96	112.16	164.40	133.42
248	June 2007	264.89	219.28	136.11	165.94	171.29	110.72	164.29	135.05
249	July 2007	260.39	217.14	136.47	166.13	171.77	111.86	164.97	135.60
250	August 2007	255.29	212.92	136.44	165.77	170.84	111.59	164.67	135.88
251	September 2007	249.61	210.14	135.55	164.42	170.73	110.83	164.20	135.13
252	October 2007	244.35	206.38	133.86	163.12	169.33	108.15	162.12	133.98
253	November 2007	237.99	203.45	131.34	161.61	167.39	105.24	159.09	132.68
254	December 2007	231.71	200.13	129.61	160.03	164.58	103.30	155.72	131.90
255	January 2008	225.40	194.64	127.76	156.42	162.59	100.17	151.06	131.70
256	February 2008	218.74	188.59	125.98	153.29	160.31	97.61	146.02	131.22
257	March 2008	208.88	182.26	124.46	150.33	158.52	95.57	142.35	131.52
258	April 2008	200.42	178.50	123.62	150.43	158.68	93.76	139.45	131.81
259	May 2008	193.19	177.14	124.29	149.94	160.34	92.76	140.26	133.16
260	June 2008	189.87	175.11	124.61	150.11	162.30	92.68	141.54	133.45
261	July 2008	186.84	175.07	124.73	149.55	162.57	93.21	143.47	133.20
262	August 2008	183.48	174.30	124.32	149.46	162.74	92.44	142.18	132.10
263	September 2008	178.72	171.24	122.71	147.83	160.98	90.17	140.79	130.40
264	October 2008	173.42	165.44	119.79	145.48	159.17	86.10	136.03	128.02
265	November 2008	169.62	160.86	116.46	141.39	155.03	83.42	132.99	125.61
266	December 2008	165.01	156.04	113.00	137.16	153.05	80.93	126.17	122.40
267	January 2009	159.04	149.21	109.44	130.80	150.73	77.56	120.18	120.91

Source: Standard & Poor's Web site (*www2.standardandpoors.com*).

This data can also be graphed easily in Excel, as shown below. This type of graphic analysis can be flawed, but overall it presents a fairly consistent trend. The graph shows that homes in Dallas and Detroit are generally priced lower but are not falling as much as prices in Phoenix and Los Angeles.

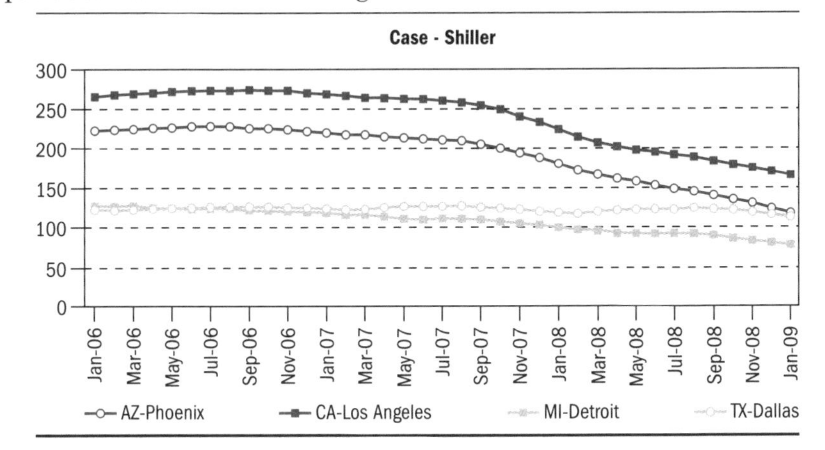

Other Tools

The other methods of developing market trend opinions that have been mentioned here are by no means all of the existing possibilities. Appraisers often develop other tools to read the market, including talking to real estate brokers, watching advertisements for clues to market changes, and even observing buyer attitudes.

Summary and Conclusion

The goal of residential appraisal reports and the new Market Conditions Form is to support the market value of the property and the value trends in that market. Clearly, an appraiser needs to develop opinions of trends and values and complete the forms. However, the forms should not be the limit. The scope of work should include whatever is necessary to make as convincing a case for the opinion as possible. The tools available to appraisers are many and varied but more or less applicable depending on the situation. The previously presented material was designed to be a representation of possible methods but should not be considered comprehensive. There are many ways to support conclusions and appraisers should try to find and use the best tools available in their specific market or markets.